CAMBRIDGE TEXTS IN THE
HISTORY OF POLITICAL THOUGHT

———

HERBERT SPENCER
Political Writings

CAMBRIDGE TEXTS IN THE
HISTORY OF POLITICAL THOUGHT

Series editors
RAYMOND GEUSS
Reader in Philosophy, University of Cambridge

QUENTIN SKINNER
Regius Professor of Modern History in the University of Cambridge

Cambridge Texts in the History of Political Thought is now firmly established as the major student textbook series in political theory. It aims to make available to students all the most important texts in the history of western political thought, from ancient Greece to the early twentieth century. All the familiar classic texts will be included, but the series seeks at the same time to enlarge the conventional canon by incorporating an extensive range of less well-known works, many of them never before available in a modern English edition. Wherever possible, texts are published in complete and unabridged form, and translations are specially commissioned for the series. Each volume contains a critical introduction together with chronologies, biographical sketches, a guide to further reading and any necessary glossaries and textual apparatus. When completed the series will aim to offer an outline of the entire evolution of western political thought.

For a list of titles published in the series, please see end of book

HERBERT SPENCER

Political Writings

EDITED BY

JOHN OFFER

Senior Lecturer in the Department of Social Administration and Policy,
University of Ulster at Coleraine

CAMBRIDGE
UNIVERSITY PRESS

CAMBRIDGE UNIVERSITY PRESS
Cambridge, New York, Melbourne, Madrid, Cape Town, Singapore, São Paulo

Cambridge University Press
The Edinburgh Building, Cambridge CB2 8RU, UK

Published in the United States of America by Cambridge University Press, New York

www.cambridge.org
Information on this title: www.cambridge.org/9780521431422

First published 1994
Reprinted 2001

A catalogue record for this publication is available from the British Library

Library of Congress Cataloguing in Publication data
Spencer, Herbert, 1829–1903.
Political writings / Herbert Spencer: edited by John Offer.
p.   ca. – (Cambridge texts in the history of political
thought)
Contents: The Proper Sphere of Government – The Man *versus* The State
ISBN 0 521 43142 5 (hc). – ISBN 0 521 43740 7 (pb)
1. State, The.   2. Individualism.   I. Offer, John, 1949–   ·
II. Spencer, Herbert, 1820–1903.   Proper Sphere of Government.
1994.   III. Spencer, Herbert, 1820–1903. Man *versus* The State.
1994.   IV. Title.   V. Series.
JC571.S764   1993
320.5′ 12–dc20   92–35996   CIP

ISBN 978-0-521-43142-2 hardback
ISBN 978-0-521-43740-0 paperback

Transferred to digital printing 2007

Contents

Introduction

The Proper Sphere of Government was Spencer's first attempt to determine what relationships there should be between government and the individual, while *The Man versus The State* was the more famous sequel. In the intervening years his publications ranged far beyond the boundaries of political theory. The *Manchester Guardian* judged Spencer on his death England's one contemporary philosopher of world-wide reputation and ranked him 'among the two or three most influential writers of the last half-century'. Arnold Bennett conjures up a magnificent picture of what Spencer's unorthodox thoughts could unleash when the young Carlotta discovers *The Study of Sociology* in *Sacred and Profane Love*:

I went to bed early, and I began to read. I read all night, thirteen hours ... Again and again I exclaimed: 'But this is marvellous!' I had not guessed that anything so honest, and so courageous, and so simple, and so convincing had ever been written.

It was imperative that a book so exhilarating, toppling conventional wisdom on every page, had to be concealed from her hidebound aunt: Carlotta tore from their binding the pages of *The Old Helmet*, 'probably the silliest novel in the world', and inserted her treasure in their place. Spencer's impact survived subsequent reflection undiminished: 'he taught me intellectual courage; he taught me that nothing is sacred that will not bear inspection; and I adore his memory'.

Herbert Spencer was born at his parents' house in Derby on 27 April 1820. His father was the dominant figure in the household although illness which was apparently related to anxiety restricted his activities. His income came from teaching and the ownership of some small houses, although teaching was deserted for three years from 1824 when he moved the family to Nottingham to try his luck in the manufacture of lace. The enterprise failed and, money lost and lessons learned, he moved the family back to Derby and resumed teaching. At about this time he also abandoned his adherence to the Wesleyan church, taking nonconformity to extremes and becoming opposed to all forms of priesthood. In contrast, Spencer's mother retained her Wesleyanism throughout her life. She is portrayed by Spencer as placid and unquestioning and the victim of gruff and callous treatment from his father.

In such an atmosphere it can be no surprise that the boy sought sanctuary in reveries: imagining adventures, or 'castle-building' as he described it, remained a habit into youth and beyond. Although his mother gave birth to eight more children, only one survived for more than a few days, a sister named Louisa, who died before Spencer was four years old. In effect he was to grow up as an only child. He took to solitary rambles in the countryside and alongside the nearby river. Out of his rambles came an interest in entomology, in the study of which he was helped by his father. This early interest in nature was buttressed by two other important paternal contributions. Spencer's father was honorary secretary to the Derby Philosophical Society, a connection which gave Spencer access to a scientific library and contact with the scientific developments of the day. His father also trained him to look for the causes of things and to question authority, religious or otherwise. This training thus emphasised self-help rather than book learning in the acquisition of scientific expertise.

The emphasis on an unorthodox mental discipline dominated his boyhood education, parts of which were conducted in a notably haphazard manner. By his own account at the age of thirteen his knowledge of Greek and Latin was minimal and he was uninstructed in English grammar, history and mathematics.

There followed an abrupt change in his life. It had been arranged that he should leave home and reside with his uncle Thomas Spencer, at Hinton Charterhouse about five miles south of Bath, who was to continue his schooling. He endured the unfamiliar discipline for some days but then rebelled in fine spirit and set off back to Derby, walking about 120 miles. However, he was soon sent to Hinton again and settled in reasonably well, completing his schooling by June 1836. But his learning was eclectic rather than comprehensive. Some additional Greek and Latin was acquired, and French was begun, but history, poetry and fiction were excluded. Trigonometry, mechanics and chemistry, however, were included. Thomas believed that Herbert's disregard of authority and self-will had been checked, although not to a sufficient degree or lasting extent: to Spencer's father he wrote that the boy 'must part with some of his confidence in his own judgment' (Duncan, Life and Letters, p. xvi).

More important than Spencer's formal education at Hinton was the model provided by his uncle's life. Having taken above average honours at Cambridge in 1820 he was then ordained; a period as Fellow of St John's College ended on his marriage, and he subsequently assumed the perpetual curacy of Hinton. An evangelical by conviction, he was by no means comfortable in the established church. On settling at Hinton he strove to reinvigorate the presence of the church in what had been a neglected appendage to a larger parish. His unflagging enthusiasm was not always popular. Whilst Spencer was his pupil the uncle's unremitting energy found a new outlet in the preparation of what became a large family of pamphlets: the first, published in 1836, was in response to the report on the poor laws of 1834 and discussed the ideas in relation to relief reforms which he was effecting in Hinton; later ones treated a range of poor law, social and evangelical Christian concerns. Thomas accepted the argument that unless relief was administered strictly it encouraged pauperism, eagerly opening his arms to the principle of less eligibility. He soon became the first chairman of the new Bath Poor Law Union Board of Guardians. Spencer was an interested participant in daily discussions on the poor law and corrected his uncle's proofs. An early and portentous consequence was the publication of a short article of his own in 1836 on the poor laws in a local magazine launched that year, and it is republished here for the first time (see Appendix). The article was not, in fact, quite his first publication since the same magazine had also published a piece by him on crystals. However, it is the first in a long line of publications which display a dominant or at least substantial concern with 'welfare'. Thomas' example was the inspiration.

The article is a reply to a communication antagonistic to poor law reform (as enacted in 1834) which had already appeared in the

magazine. Spencer commends the new measures in ebullient and pug-
nacious fashion. Two prominent features display the stamp of uncle on
nephew. He follows Thomas in using 'human nature' as an explanatory
concept, in a way that he never abandoned. Thus lax poor relief is
adjudged harmful because of the 'natural tendency in human nature to
lean upon any support that may be afforded' (p. 179). He also follows
his uncle in lauding political economy (pp. 180–1):

Is that science to be despised, upon which are founded all the principles
of good government? which teaches the philanthropist, and the statesman
the best methods of following their several pursuits? On the contrary,
political economy is a subject which ought to be admired, and more
studied, than it has hitherto been.

His patchy formal education at an end, Spencer needed employment. Undoubtedly an intelligent young man, and very much science-
minded, he also possessed the potentially unattractive cocksure confidence and iconoclastic and nonconformist predilections of father
and uncle. A brief period as a teacher, a 'false start' he called it, was
terminated when a family friend offered him employment in railway
construction. Charles Fox, who had been a pupil of his father, had
substantial engineering responsibilities in connection with the
London and Birmingham line. Early in November 1837, Spencer
moved to London to commence work in Fox's office. With its rapid
advances over a succession of technological frontiers and its immense
economic and social repercussions, the railway 'industry' of 1837
offered to a young participant of Spencer's character the most stimu-
lating and challenging set of experiences available.

His work involved making surveys in association with the contractors for the line. Serious-minded to a fault, he neither read novels
nor attended any of the capital's places of amusement. In September
1838 he moved on to a new post in Worcester. His didactic tendencies were not conducive to friendship or to easy relations with his
superiors, although both eventually were established. His engineer-
in-chief at Worcester, Captain W. S. Moorsom, in fact 'promoted'
him to be his secretary in April 1840 and he moved to Powick, three
miles from Worcester, to be close to Moorsom's home. By now his
engineering responsibilities had spurred him on to write some articles
for the *Civil Engineer and Architect's Journal,* and to make some related
inventions. He was also expressing a wish to make public some ideas

upon the state of the world and religion, together with a few remarks on education.

Rambles along the raw cuttings of the line led Spencer to an interest in palaeontology and geology and to the purchase of a copy of Lyell's *Principles of Geology*. Whilst Lyell criticised Lamarck's opinions on the origin of species, Spencer responded by leaning towards them, thus accepting that 'organic forms' had 'arisen by progressive modifications, physically caused and inherited'. The congruity of this view 'with the course of procedure throughout things at large, gave it an irresistible attraction; and my belief in it never afterwards wavered' (*Autobiography*, Vol. 1, pp. 176–7). Indeed, it was to be pivotal in all his subsequent work.

A temporary break from railway work began in April 1841. He returned to Derby to work on an invention with his father, a venture soon abandoned. To plug the gap Spencer learnt to read music, took to glee singing, and developed an interest in phrenological psychology. After a year he returned to Hinton. Back in an environment where political ideas were discussed daily, and impressed by his uncle's devotion to his own pamphlets, Spencer immediately resumed writing on social matters, the first result being a series of twelve 'letters' published serially in the *Nonconformist* and given the general title *The Proper Sphere of Government*. Acceptance for publication was expedited by a letter of introduction sent by Thomas to the editor, his friend and fellow supporter of such radical reforms as complete suffrage, Edward Miall. Spencer saw his return to Hinton and the preparation of *The Proper Sphere of Government* as of crucial importance to his own subsequent achievements:

Had it not been for this visit to Hinton – had it not been for these political conversations with my uncle – possibly had it not been for his letter of introduction to Mr Miall, the first of these letters would not have seen the light, and the rest of them would never have been written. Had they never been written, *Social Statics*, which originated from them, would not even have been thought of. Had there been no *Social Statics*, those lines of enquiry which led to *The Principles of Psychology* would have remained unexplored. And without that study of life in general initiated by the writing of these works, leading, presently, to the study of the relations between its phenomena and those of the inorganic world, there would have been no *System of Synthetic Philosophy*.

(*Autobiography*, Vol. 1, p. 211)

Spencer was reluctant to consign the letters to the obscurity of the back numbers of a newspaper and early in 1843 arranged for them to be reprinted as a pamphlet, which duly appeared later the same year. This work secured for him neither the fame nor the fortune for which he had hoped, although he did receive some encouraging words from Carlyle, who had been sent a copy.

To a friend Spencer described the contents as 'political pills', adding that they are 'very good remedies for Tyranny and Toryism, and when duly digested are calculated to drive away crude notions and brace the system' (*Life and Letters*, p. 41). The series of letters opens with Spencer seeking to set a limit to the intervention of the state in social life. After presenting a version of the 'social contract' theory of the origin of civil government, Spencer declares that the role of government is (p. 7)

to defend the natural rights of man – to protect person and property – to prevent the aggressions of the powerful upon the weak – in a word, to administer justice. This is the natural, the original, office of a government. It was not intended to do less: it ought not to be allowed to do more.

The role of government thus defined allows 'the laws of society' full scope. Just as there are physical laws there are also psychical laws and social laws; in each case transgression, he says, produces its own punishment. To interfere is to transgress (p. 6):

there is in society, as in every other part of creation, that beautiful self-adjusting principle, which will keep all its elements in equilibrium; . . . so the attempt to regulate all the actions of a community by legislation, will entail little else but misery and confusion.

Spencer proceeds to condemn the utilitarian modes of thought that attempt to justify intervention by arguing that the 'general good' is thereby promoted. This thinking lies behind the restrictions placed on the import of corn, the establishment of a state church and the existence of the poor law, but in each case injustice and harm rather than good has ensued. In the third and fourth letters the case of the poor law is explored in detail. Poor law legislation was a highly controversial matter in both England and Ireland at the time Spencer was writing, with new statutes emphasising that relief was best granted only on condition that an applicant entered the workhouse of the poor law union concerned. Yet even a poor law set against wage subsidies and outdoor relief is unacceptable to Spencer. Poor relief does not remove but rather prolongs the improvidence which causes distress and discourages the exercise of real benevolence. In a style which exemplifies the tenor of contemporary evangelical *laissez-faire* social thought – soteriological rather than incarnational – Spencer tells us that (pp. 21–2):

by allowing the wicked to take advantage of the right held out by the poor law, we not only annul the just punishment awarded to them, but we also take away the most effectual prompter to repentance and improvement.

Letters V and VI deal with possible challenges to his position arising from the view that war and colonisation are duties of government. He points out the deleterious consequences of colonisation on the mother country, the emigrants and the indigenous peoples. For Spencer neither colonisation nor treaties, but rather free trade with other countries, which is what justice demands, is vindicated. Wars of aggression are harmful and unnecessary, although defensive wars may be necessary. This concession, he says, does not indicate an imperfection in his definition of the duties of the state, but rather that the definition needs to be applied in all states. He later described his views on war as 'utterly untenable', although in a way which implies he had forgotten his point on wars fought for reasons of defence (*Autobiography*, Vol. i, pp. 209–10).

There is now a change of purpose. In the next three letters Spencer argues against the necessity for new legislative supervision demanded of government in the fields of education and health. Uniformity of instruction, which he believes would accompany a system of national education, is judged to be undesirable because it will reduce the diversity of minds and opinion: progress and truth have 'ever originated from the conflict of mind with mind' (p. 35). In education as in everything else competition is the only principle which can 'hold out promise of future perfection' (p. 37).

The campaign for public health legislation which led to the establishment of a General Board of Health in 1848 was already under way as Spencer wrote. Edwin Chadwick's *Report on the Sanitary Conditions of the Labouring Population* of 1842 was a rigorous analysis of the consequences of non-intervention and a decisive propaganda tool. Spencer's chief argument owes something to his understanding of Lamarck. An interruption to the exercise of a species' faculties weakens them and 'an ultimate degeneracy of the race will inevitably ensue' (p. 49). Thus state measures to protect health, in doing for people 'what they are naturally fitted to do for themselves', are 'one of the most efficient means of lowering the standard of national character' (p. 50).

Letter X looks at some of the consequences of the neglect of which he alleges government is guilty in its proper sphere of activity, the administration of justice. The next letter relates his views about the duties of the state to the nature of the electorate; he finds no objection to the enfranchisement of 'the working classes'. The final letter of the series is for the most part a summary of what has gone before.

As political philosophy the essays are not perhaps particularly distinctive and Spencer is slapdash over what precise meaning is to be given to the 'aggressions' which justice is supposed to prevent. However, they do display well the distinctive mixture of evangelical and social and economic thought which characterised much early nineteenth-century political writing, and which Spencer never discarded entirely. They also show the kind of opposition faced by proponents of new legislation on social matters in the 1840s.

Spencer returned to Derby before he had completed *The Proper Sphere*. For the next few years until December 1848 his life was unsettled. He had intermittent employment on a range of railway projects which entailed considerable travel around England and Wales. On occasion he attended the parliamentary committees which scrutinised bills on new railways. Sometimes he based himself in London, sometimes in Derby. He continued to write articles for the *Nonconformist* and other journals, and also served in 1842 as the honorary secretary of the Derby branch of the Complete Suffrage Movement (less militant than the Chartists) and worked as sub-editor on a new Birmingham-based Complete Suffrage newspaper the *Pilot* in 1844. However, in the summer of 1848 another of his uncle's letters of introduction worked its magic; the end of the year saw him installed as a sub-editor on *The Economist*, at first resident on the premises. This was to give his life a new pattern.

His duties were not arduous and permitted him to complete a book subsequently published as *Social Statics*. The preparation of it had begun in 1846, prompted by thoughts 'which had made me dissatisfied with the letters on *The Proper Sphere of Government* – dissatisfied not so much with the conclusions set forth, as with the foundations on which they stood' (*Autobiography*, Vol. 1, p. 305). The main new point is that there is a moral principle, from which the right role of the state can be derived: 'Every man has freedom to do all that he wills; provided he infringes not the equal freedom of any other man' (*Social Statics*, p. 103). However, this principle was foreshadowed in the earlier work, especially in the discussions of health and education. The principle guarantees that men's faculties will adapt to their circumstances in the optimum manner and hence guarantees progress; progressive modifications which mankind is undergoing as a result of adaptation are, moreover, the result of 'a law underlying the whole organic creation' (p. 65). It should also be noted that *Social Statics* proclaims that women should have the same freedom as men, although he substantially recanted on this position in later life.

Through his post with *The Economist*, residence in London and the publication of his book, new friendships were being made and intellectual and cultural horizons expanding. He first formed friendships with Marian Evans (later known as George Eliot) and G. H. Lewes in 1850. There were rumours that Evans and Spencer were to marry, which Spencer denied. Spencer never married. T. H. Huxley, the biologist, was another friend made in these years.

Early in 1853, Thomas died. The money which Spencer inherited allowed him to relinquish his sub-editing work and devote himself to his own writing. From now until 1860 he produced an impressive number of substantial essays for the top journals of the day: 'Over-legislation'; 'The Universal Postulate'; 'The Genesis of Science'; 'Railway Morals and Railway Policy'; 'Progress: its Law and Cause'; 'The Origin and Function of Music'; 'Representative Government: What Is It Good For?'; 'State Tamperings with Money and Banks'; 'The Morals of Trade'; 'The Social Organism'; 'Parliamentary Reform: the Danger and the Safeguards'; and 'Prison Ethics'. All of these essays were subsequently reprinted in his *Essays: Scientific, Political and Speculative* (three volumes). From this time also came four essays on education (which developed ideas first expressed in *The Proper Sphere*); issued as a book they became of considerable importance as a source of criticism of rote learning in schools. The summer of 1854 saw him resolved upon a further project: a book on psychology, which, he decided, could be commenced abroad; he embarked first for Le Tréport on the north coast of France and then went on to Paris.

For some time his health had been of concern to him. Although he often described himself as idle, he was working very hard indeed. A crash came in July 1855 on a visit to North Wales:

> One morning soon after beginning work, there commenced a sensation in my head – not pain, nor heat, nor fullness, nor tension, but simply a sensation, bearable enough but abnormal. The seriousness of the symptom was at once manifest to me. I put away my manuscript and sallied out, fishing-rod in hand, to a mountain tarn in the hills behind the hotel, in pursuance of a resolve to give myself a week's rest; thinking that would suffice.
>
> (*Autobiography*, Vol. 1, p. 467)

Sleeplessness and a diminished ability to concentrate for long periods on writing were from now on to be fixed features of his life of which he often complained. However, his physical health remained in general good, and, indeed, there was no relaxing of his authorial ambitions. Nor was travel abandoned.

The Principles of Psychology duly appeared later in 1855. This book grafted his developmentalism on to associationist psychology, and thus attempted to remedy a defect of associationism by offering an explanation of the differences between the learning abilities of species. Among those impressed by the book was John Stuart Mill, though not without significant criticism of it. It also sought to answer epistemological questions about the nature of certainty in psychological terms. Once the book was out he travelled once more. First he went back to Le Tréport, and then to Devon to try a rural life on the advice of a physician. In 1856 he was on a yachting excursion to the Channel Islands and France, and followed this up with a stay in Scotland at Ardtornish, overlooking Mull, to visit a friend, Octavius Smith. (Ardtornish, which accommodated Spencer's fondness for salmon fishing, became a favourite resort.) In the autumn he was in Paris and met Comte (with whom he was in disagreement over the classification of the sciences). Early in 1857 Mill was added to his list of acquaintances.

Spencer's work in the 1850s led to an outcome destined to dominate the rest of his life. By 1858 a 'complete concept of evolution' had occurred to him, and he drew up a draft scheme of the volumes to elucidate this on 6 January. During the 1850s the idea of progressive development in the organic world had been worked out in the essays. 'A Theory of Population' of 1852 argued that among human beings the survival of those who are the select of their generation (in other words those most adapted to circumstances) is a cause of development. This 'survival of the fittest', Spencer's own but later coinage, was now perceived, however, as only the organic world's version of a process which also applied to the inorganic. In 1851, says Spencer, he had become 'acquainted with von Baer's statement that the development of every organism is a change from homogeneity to heterogeneity. The substance of the thought was not new to me, though its form was' (*Autobiography*, Vol. 2, pp. 8–9). Spencer, however, saw this as a description of change 'not necessarily limited to the organic world' (p. 9), and indeed he went on to generalise from the distinguished European embryologist's cautious claim. Spencer's belief that the homogeneous was intrinsically unstable and his acceptance of the monistic principle from physical science of the conservation of energy (or, as he called it, the 'persistence of force') – that energy in its various manifestations can be transformed but not destroyed or created – completed the heady cocktail. Spencer believed he had discovered a master key. His definition of evolution was modified over the years, but this is its final form in *First Principles*:

Evolution is an integration of matter and concomitant dissipation of motion; during which the matter passes from a relatively indefinite, incoherent homogeneity to a relatively definite, coherent heterogeneity; and during which the retained motion undergoes a parallel transformation.

Spencer named the ten volumes which were to introduce and apply his theory 'A System of Synthetic Philosophy'. The initial volume, *First Principles*, came out in book form in 1862. (Divisions of this book, and some subsequent ones in the series, were issued to subscribers ahead of publication in the completed volume.) *The Principles of Biology* (two volumes) was completed in 1867, the recast *Principles of Psychology* (two volumes) in 1872, *The Principles of Ethics* (two volumes) in 1893 and *The Principles of Sociology* (three volumes) in 1896. A panic about his health had led him to break from the logical sequence and complete the *Ethics* (designed as the culmination to the whole 'System') ahead of the *Sociology*. Sundry modifications to the original scheme had been made *en route*.

Something more must be said here about Spencer's theory of evolution since it is an important part of the context in which *The Man versus The State* was written. The theory was formulated before

Darwin's *Origin of Species* was published, in 1859, and is very different from Darwin's work. Darwin had a hesitant interest in grand evolutionary theory and the *Origin* did not articulate a theory of evolution in that sense at all (indeed the word itself scarcely occurs). Rather, it propounded the mechanism whereby species change occurs. Whereas Spencer was wedded to the Lamarckian mechanism of inheritance of acquired characteristics, Darwin argued for a mechanism which involved spontaneous variations being thrown up and subjected to a struggle for existence from which not all survived – natural selection. They are the 'fittest' only in the neutral sense that they have survived. Spencer tends to give 'fittest' an evaluative meaning. This indeed is one reason why some of the ideas referred to by the imprecise label 'social Darwinism' are better described as Spencerian. Spencer's mechanism appears to guarantee directional indeed progressive change, whereas Darwin's does not. In the *Biology* Spencer admitted a role in organic evolution for Darwin's mechanism but emphasised his own as well. The subsequent late-century vindication of natural selection by genetics dealt Spencer's theory a mortal blow. An elegant recognition of this came from A. J. Balfour in his *A Fragment on Progress* of 1892 whilst pondering the inheritance of acquired characteristics (p. 13):

> there is one systematic philosopher of our own day who has applied this principle so persistently in every department of his theory of Man, that were it to be upset, it is scarcely too much to say that his Ethics, his Psychology and his Anthropology would all tumble to the ground with it.

Spencer's 'System' and *First Principles* in particular brought him attention world-wide. His friend in America, Youmans, secured publication of Spencer's books there, and there were translations into French, German and other languages besides. It is hard for us to see what caused the fuss. It may be that progressive evolution was a compensatory secular simulacrum of Providence for Victorians who were sliding into unbelief – Beatrice Potter (to become Beatrice Webb) to whom Spencer, a friend of her parents, was a mentor, certainly experienced *First Principles* in this manner. Indeed, the very vocabulary through which the theory was unfolded, long words, magisterially sonorous and recondite, heightened the impression of a superior and scientific authority. To those simply perplexed by pell-mell social, political and economic change there was revealed the reassurance of an underlying explanation. The eager response of Jack London, exemplified in *Martin Eden*, and Arnold Bennett in his *Journals* was of this nature.

The case of Sir Hubert Parry is interesting. In the 1870s, as a young man, the composer read and discussed Spencer with enthusiasm. In 1874 they met at a festival in Gloucester:

> Herbert Spencer attended some of the performances, and moved the horror of the orthodox by not standing up in the ... choruses in which the public adopted that posture. I had a few words with him on casual subjects and felt quite overwhelmed by the honour, so that I could hardly speak without trembling.
> (C. L. Graves, *Hubert Parry*, Vol. 1, London, Macmillan, 1926, p. 146)

By the 1890s Parry was a leading figure in music, Director of the Royal College of Music and Professor of Music at Oxford. His book of 1896 *The Evolution of the Art of Music* (first issued in 1893 as *The Art of Music*) proved to be very influential well into the present century. For Parry, music historiography was the study not of a few 'great names' but of the gradual organic development of music, with the movement from homogeneity to heterogeneity given pride of place.

Probably the biggest impact of Spencer's theory of evolution, certainly the longest lived, was on sociology and anthropology. In the late 1880s, early in their careers as major figures in sociology, Durkheim in France and Tönnies in Germany felt it necessary to engage at length with Spencer's ideas, and their own sociological analyses were in some debt to his work. In both cases two topics were paramount: his claims that a society should be considered as an organism and that there were two types (he hinted at a third to come in the future) of social relations – militant and industrial. The 'social organism' idea had first appeared in a substantial form in *Social Statics* and figured prominently in *The Principles of Sociology*. It emphasised the need to study social life in terms of a society's component 'structures' and 'functions'. This part of Spencer's thought also had an impact on Malinowski and Radcliffe-Brown in anthropology. What the logical relationship of the social organism perspective was to his political individualism remains a matter of controversy. The militant–industrial contrast was first put forward in *First Principles* and developed later in the *Sociology*. It is introduced when Spencer considers the possibility of cases which might be alleged to contradict his teaching that (social) evolution produces an increase in definiteness, and in the 1867 edition of *First Principles* runs thus (p. 374):

Should it be objected that among civilized nations there are examples of decreasing definiteness, (instance the breaking down of limits between ranks), the reply is, that such apparent exceptions are the accompaniment of a social metamorphosis – a change from the military or predatory type of social structure, to the industrial or mercantile type, during which the old lines of organization are disappearing and the new ones becoming more marked.

The classification appears to originate as a rather desperate device to fit a range of threatening, recalcitrant facts into his theory. Spencer was no stranger to the art of Procrustes.

And this points to what appear to be fundamental problems in Spencer's use of evidence in constructing his theory of evolution. In a letter to Alexander Bain of 1863 John Stuart Mill wrote of Spencer (*Collected Works of John Stuart Mill*, Vol. 15, p. 901):

He is a considerable thinker though anything but a safe one ... The conservation of force has hardly yet got to be believed, & already its negation is declared inconceivable. But this is Spencer all over; he throws himself with a certain deliberate impetuosity into the last new theory that chimes with his general way of thinking & treats it as proved as soon as he is able to found a connected exposition of phenomena upon it.

Darwin was not convinced by Spencer's conclusions and considered them definitions rather than laws of nature, and Huxley chided Spencer that his idea of a tragedy was a deduction killed by a fact.

Facts which failed to corroborate Spencer's theory thus tended to be ignored by him, or 'absorbed' in some way. The only real 'public' difference between a case of 'differentiation' and a case of 'disintegration' could be that in the case of the second it was something disliked or unexpected by Spencer. Social occurrences of which he disapproved would indicate a move to 'militant' rather than 'industrial' social relations. Alternatively, a 'problem' might be 'solved' by pointing to the fluctuations which occurred because of 'rhythm'; or even by declaring that a period of 'dissolution' had appeared. Endemic conceptual slipperiness meant that Spencer's theory became irrefutable in principle: he produced not the intended bang of a theory of everything but the whimper of what was at best a cumbrous and unreliable *redescription* of everything. Spencer's 'logic of scientific discovery' puts one in mind of Swift:

> All philosophers, who find
> Some favourite system to their mind,
> In every point to make it fit,
> Will force all nature to submit.

A further point needs noting. There is an inconsistency in his work over what would seem the easy question for Spencer of whether or not the phenomenon of harmony in music had 'evolved'. In *First Principles* an approximate date is suggested when 'music in parts evolved' (p. 357), but in an essay in *Mind* for 1891 he says that 'the new kind of effect suddenly achieved cannot be considered as *evolved*, without stretching somewhat unduly the meaning of the word' ('On the Origin of Music', Vol. 16, p. 537). This is an amazing admission from Spencer. It is fascinating that on this one topic he was prepared to be baulked. He seems worried that it had not gradually developed but been *invented*. Was Spencer here glimpsing the need for a much more adequate conception of human agency and the meaningful nature of action than his evolutionary sociology permitted?

Spencer's life had become preoccupied with the writing of the 'System' and anxieties over his health. Nevertheless travel continued: the summer and autumn of 1862 saw him in North Wales, Scotland and Paris. In 1868 there was a Spring tour of Italy, where he witnessed an eruption of Vesuvius. Through the 1870s numerous visits to Scotland and visits to Ireland, France, Switzerland and the Isle of Wight, offered opportunities for him to 'recruit'. At the end of 1879 a winter holiday was arranged, to Egypt and 'up the Nile' with a return through Venice. In early 1882 he was at Antwerp, Amsterdam and Cologne, an overture to sailing to America in August for a stay lasting until November, through part of which he was 'minded' by his friend Youmans. He mostly managed to avoid admiring interviewers and crowds which he dreaded, but he did deliver a speech at a dinner in his honour a few days before departure. He disembarked at Liverpool convinced that his health had suffered, taking him closer to invalid life.

In 1866 Spencer had found 'permanent' lodgings in London, close to Kensington Gardens. The money inherited on his father's death (in the same year) gave both his life and the 'System' financial stability. Two 'institutions' dominated his social life. In 1864 the 'X Club' was inaugurated. Spencer and Huxley were founding members of this select group of 'men of science'. There were regular dinners, with Spencer 'synthesising' menus. Early in 1868 he was elected into the Athenaeum Club; this became a second home where routinely he read, dined and played billiards. He also served on the committee of the Club and of the London Library.

It is indeed remarkable that Spencer found time away from the heavy demands of his 'System' and his travels for two additional books. During 1872 and 1873 he prepared his *The Study of Sociology*. This book sold well, and its writing prepared him for *The Principles of Sociology*. *The Man versus The State* followed in 1884.

How this book originated emerges from a letter written by Spencer to Youmans on 13 November 1883 (Duncan, *Life and Letters*, p. 238):

I shall probably commit myself to a series of four political articles. For some time past I have been getting more and more exasperated at the way in which things are drifting towards Communism with increasing velocity; and though I fear little is to be done I am prompted to make a vehement protest, and am intending to say some very strong things. Oddly enough, yesterday while exciting myself over it, as I have been doing lately, the editor of the *Contemporary Review* called on me, wanting me to take up the question, which has just been raised in a very startling way by an article of Lord Salisbury's on the dwellings of the industrial classes. Though I have not yet committed myself I shall probably do so. Of course, I do not like to suspend other work, but the matter is pressing and important, and, in a sense, permanent; for, these four articles I contemplate, dealing with the questions not after a temporary, but after a permanent manner, will have their future value.

Part of the work was done in singular circumstances with Spencer going out to Kensal Green in the mornings and playing quoits, dictating between games. The articles appeared in issues of the *Contemporary Review* in 1884 entitled 'The New Toryism', 'The Coming Slavery', 'The Sins of Legislators' and 'The Great Political Superstition'. They appeared in book form under the title *The Man versus The State* in the same year, accompanied by a Postscript designed to deal with possible objections.

Spencer was on breakfasting terms with Gladstone, and Gladstone wrote of Spencer's 'signal abilities' when congratulating him on completion of the 'System' and joining in a request for permission to have painted a portrait of him. But it was Gladstonian Liberalism which was the prime target of *The Man versus The State*. The main theme of the first essay is that Liberals have come to confuse the rectification of evils – reducing the range of governmental authority – which was their original contribution with the positive achievement of 'good': 'popular good has come to be sought by Liberals, not as an end to be indirectly gained by relaxations of restraints, but as the end to be indirectly gained' (p. 69). Liberalism is becoming coercive, or 'militant' in the language of the typology which Spencer here uses again. Spencer gives many illustrations of the trend from the record of legislation, and adds that legislation now being advocated will be even more interventionist in character. One example refers to an issue then much discussed (p. 75):

> plausible proposals are made that there should be organized a system of compulsory insurance, by which men during their early lives shall be forced to provide for the time when they will be incapacitated.

Spencer has in mind the scheme put forward by William Lewery Blackley in an article in the November 1878 issue of the *Nineteenth Century* called 'National Insurance: a Cheap, Practical, and Popular Means of Abolishing Poor Rates'. Blackley, an Irishman, was at this time rector of North Waltham in Hampshire. His scheme would have given a pension to elderly people and a benefit in times of sickness in return for compulsory contributions. There was a great deal of debate about it in the reviews of the day; and the National Providence League was formed in 1880 to promote the idea with Blackley as prominent campaigner. A Select Committee of the House of Commons investigated Blackley's scheme from 1885 to 1887, but was not enthusiastic. It was not until 1908 that pensions for the elderly were legislated, the Act introducing a means-tested *non*-contributory pension. Compulsory insurance for times of sickness and unemployment was introduced in the Insurance Act of 1911. The hegemony of the poor law was comprehensively broken by these Liberal reforms.

Blackley's scheme may have been influenced by discussions about insurance in Germany in the 1870s. Bismarck introduced legislation on contributory pensions and sickness benefit in the 1880s, but not along Blackley's lines. To Spencer, Blackley's scheme was an accursed thing and he rounded on it again when developing his argument in 'The Coming Slavery' (p. 90):

Habits of improvidence having for generations been cultivated by the Poor Law, and the improvident enabled to multiply, the evils produced by compulsory charity are now proposed to be met by compulsory insurance.

The cumulative effect and the unintended consequences of the legislation promulgated by politicians are ignored by them: the question of questions is not asked – 'What type of social structure am I tending to produce?' (p. 88). The result is a drift towards bureaucracy and socialism with labouring for one's own benefit curtailed and coercion into labouring for the benefit of others, and the emergence of an army of civil officials giving despotic power to its head. This outcome is inevitable because 'the welfare of a society and the justice of its arrangements are at bottom dependent on the characters of its members' (p. 105). The socialists, and the so-called liberals treading the same path, believe that 'an ill-working humanity may be framed into well-working institutions. It is a delusion.' The peroration culminates in a flourish which, rare enough for Spencer, alludes to Plato's *Republic* (p. 105):

The defective natures of citizens will show themselves in the bad acting of whatever social structure they are arranged into. There is no political alchemy by which you can get golden conduct out of leaden instincts.

The third essay is concerned with the ignorance of legislators, principally ignorance of the laws of evolution as identified by Spencer and the mischief which ensues. A letter to Youmans dated 13 May 1884 indicates one objective of the essay (*Life and Letters*, p. 243): 'showing that legislation was to blame for the immense evils that have, during the last six months, been a current topic – the evils set forth in the Bitter Cry of the Outcasts of London'. Spencer is referring to Andrew Mearns' *The Bitter Cry of Outcast London* of 1883. For Spencer, the point to emphasise is that the natural processes of adaptation and Darwinian natural selection must not be interfered with (p. 131):

And yet, strange to say, now that this truth is recognized by most cultivated people – now that the beneficent working of the survival of the fittest has been so impressed on them that, much more than people in past times, they might be expected to hesitate before neutralizing its action –

now more than ever before in the history of the world are they doing all they can to further survival of the unfittest!

One interesting part of the essay is the sequence in which Spencer draws a distinction between 'family-ethics' and 'state-ethics' in respect of the principles of distribution. In immaturity 'benefits received must be inversely as the power or ability of the receiver', but in adult life each person gets 'benefit in proportion to merit – reward in proportion to desert' (p. 127). Failure to observe this distinction engenders unfitness.

The essay also contains criticisms of Henry George and H. M. Hyndman. George and Spencer were already at loggerheads. In *Social Statics* Spencer had sought to justify in connection with the equal freedom principle some version of land nationalisation and George cited Spencer's views on this with approval in his *Poverty and Progress* of 1885. By then Spencer felt embarrassed by the implications of this commitment and thus attempted to put an interpretation on the words in question which was quite at variance with that fairly enough assumed by George. A squabble developed, culminating in George's *A Perplexed Philosopher* of 1893, the subtitle of which ran 'an examination of Mr Herbert Spencer's various utterances on the land question, with some incidental reference to his synthetic philosophy'. George's tart comments were not too unreasonable: Spencer had argued for consistency in his views where acknowledging that he had changed them would have been more honest. Henry Mayers Hyndman, a lapsed Tory, was a leading late Victorian socialist who played an important part in organising the Democratic Federation in 1881, to which Spencer refers. For a while William Morris was a prominent member. Hyndman was indebted to Marx and a supporter of nationalisation – the attack from Spencer is not surprising.

'The Great Political Superstition', wrote Spencer in a letter to Youmans (*Life and Letters*, p. 243), 'is altogether revolutionary in its view, and will greatly astound people, perhaps even more in America than in England, since its essential principle is the denial of the right of the majority save within certain definable limits.' Once again, the theme is the legitimate sphere of government action, and, once again, an appeal is made to 'natural rights', a concept which he enjoyably but not satisfactorily defends in the essay against Bentham. It is somewhat unusual to see the doctrine of natural rights 'becoming the cornerstone of alarmed Conservatism' (Barker, *Political Thought in England*, p. 127) since it had most often been used as a weapon to injure it. One problem in these essays, and elsewhere in Spencer, is his use of 'nature'. Reformist legislation, socialism, trade unions, strikes and so forth, are not 'natural' and to be condemned. Yet, as Mill pointed out in his essay 'Nature' (published in 1874, but written in 1854) there are no compelling reasons why we ought to follow 'nature' – so contrasted with social life – and indeed moral reasons why we ought not. Huxley and Ritchie argued against Spencer on similar lines. Spencer would point to the survival of the fittest and the theory of evolution generally as laws which it would be singularly beneficial to follow. But this is unhelpful: the moral supremacy of this way of living is simply not demonstrated. Moreover, the contrast between things 'natural' and 'artificial' (or whatever) which Spencer is trying to draw is arbitrary and unsatisfactory. However, Mill also identified an emphatically different, all-encompassing definition of 'nature' – all that there is, including all social life. Such a definition of 'nature' makes impossible Spencer's contrast, and renders illogical the claim that certain activities are breaches of laws of nature. The activities in question must either show, by their very existence, that the alleged law of nature is not a *law* at all, or that the law is not being broken. But although an all-encompassing definition of 'nature' thus wrecks Spencer's arguments to 'administrative nihilism' it is precisely the meaning given to the word when we talk of 'laws of nature'.

To those self-styled 'individualists' anxious to roll back the state Spencer now became a mentor, with *The Man versus The State* their manifesto. One important body with this aim was the Liberty and Property Defence League, formed in 1882 as a federation of various associations committed to propaganda and lobbying on behalf of extreme *laissez-faire*. The Earl of Wemyss was the architect, spearheading with some success parliamentary opposition to proposed legislation, particularly bills proposed by the London County Council. W. H. Mallock and Thomas Mackay were just two League men who wrote extensively in a Spencerian manner. Spencer himself contributed financially and wrote an introduction – 'From freedom to bondage' – to a League book, *A Plea for Liberty* of 1891, edited by Mackay. Mackay was the chief exponent of Spencerism in the Charity Organisation Society, founded in 1869 to encourage charities to foster a sense of individual responsibility amongst those helped and to co-operate with rather than wastefully duplicate the poor law. An alliance between the League and the Society seems to have obtained a place for C. S. Loch, the society's secretary, on the Royal Commission on the Poor Laws of 1905, alongside Beatrice Webb.

Indeed, by 1891, Spencer had become nearly as worried by charitable activity to alleviate poverty as he was by the state's efforts. In his opinion the work of the Society for the Prevention of Cruelty to Children would bring objectionable intrusions into the domestic circle, and lead to some interference with the survival of the fittest, although he did concede that some philanthropic feeling mitigating the rigour of natural law was defensible. The second volume of *The Principles of Ethics* confirmed the trend. Spencer pioneers a tripartite classification of the ways of meeting 'needs':

We have the law-established relief for the poor by distribution of money compulsorily exacted; with which may fitly be joined the alms derived from endowments. We have relief of the poor carried on by spontaneously organized societies, to which funds are voluntarily contributed. And then, lastly, we have the help privately given now to those who stand in some relation of dependence, now to those concerning whose claims partial knowledge has been obtained, and now haphazard to beggars.

(*The Principles of Ethics*, vol. 2, p. 376)

Today, modified to refer to more than money, these would be called statutory, voluntary and informal care: the 'rediscovery' of informal care and the need for the other two sectors to take it into account has been a strong theme in contemporary social policy. Spencer, however, is concerned to condemn voluntary as well as state action because social machinery, whether compulsory or non-compulsory, 'wastes power' and works other effects than those intended – it cannot discriminate between the deserving and undeserving poor. Even privately given assistance, although it will involve personal knowledge of the recipients, runs the risk of transforming a recipient into a cunning trickster. Spencer follows his logic to its bitter end and would prefer to see the principle of the survival of the fittest left to operate in all its sternness in order to clear away the great and threatening mass of degraded people produced by interventionists, although he ruefully recognises that 'our present sentiments' do not allow this.

After *The Man versus The State* Spencer continued to work, and completed the 'System' when he finished the third volume of the

Sociology in 1896. He also resumed writing his *Autobiography*. Essays from his later years together with some lightweight 'salon' pieces appeared in *Various Fragments* of 1897 and his last book *Facts and Comments* of 1902. There were also revisions to make to earlier work. An abridged and revised edition of *Social Statics* was issued in 1892. To the end he maintained his policy of declining the honorary degrees and awards which were offered to him.

Outside 'individualist' circles Spencer's reputation, at least in Britain, began to plummet in the 1880s. Biological evidence told against his evolution theory. New thinking in political philosophy, emphasising 'positive freedom' rather than 'negative freedom' and a less limited role for the state – in which T. H. Green and other 'idealist' philosophers at Oxford played a part – was an explicit and attractive alternative to Spencer's quintessential 'do nothingness'. Spencer's pessimism about the future took hold in these years as his theory and his politics required protection against repeated criticism. Some writers, notably Benjamin Kidd, 'modified' Spencer to the extent that struggles between nations were of overriding importance, with 'internal' co-operation, not competition, required. Even friends deserted his teaching for socialism: the case of Beatrice Webb who eventually joined the Fabian Society, founded as the *Contemporary Review* began to issue *The Man versus The State*, was the most poignant.

His health remained a cause for anxiety throughout his later years. In 1889 he had belatedly set up his own household in London, but he abandoned the arrangement in 1897 and moved to 5 Percival Terrace, Brighton. Beatrice Webb visited and tried to lighten his pessimism. He died at 4.40 on the morning of Tuesday, 8 December 1903. His body was taken by train to London for cremation at Golders Green and the remains were deposited in Highgate Cemetery. The Dean of Westminster refused permission for a memorial in Westminster Abbey, after a request from Spencer's admirers, for the reason that his achievements in philosophy and science, once highly regarded, seemed unlikely to command recognition in the future.

It is Spencer's unflagging espousal of political individualism which has done most to keep his name alive to the present day. H. G. Wells' *parti pris* sentiments in his article 'The Labour Unrest' resonate uncannily in the early 1990s:

We do but emerge now from a period of deliberate happy-go-lucky and the influence of Herbert Spencer who came near raising public shiftlessness to the dignity of a national philosophy. Everything would adjust itself – if only it was left alone.

(*An Englishman Looks at the World*, Cassell, London, 1914, p. 69)

So too, however, do the more measured words of Spencer's obituarist in the *Manchester Guardian*: 'when socialism begins to produce reaction Spencer's political writings will be a mine of arguments for the critics of paternal government'.

Principal events in Spencer's life

1820   Born 27 April, Derby
1833   June: begins period of education from his uncle Thomas Spencer, at Hinton Charterhouse, near Bath
1836   March: first article on social matters (the poor law) published in *Bath and West of England Magazine*
1837   Summer: undertakes teaching in Derby
     November: commences work on the London and Birmingham Railway under Charles Fox as a civil engineer, based in London
1838   September: moves to Worcester to continue railway work
1842   May: visits Thomas at Hinton. Begins writing the letters forming *The Proper Sphere of Government* for publication in the *Nonconformist*
     Autumn: involved in the Complete Suffrage Movement and for a time secretary of the Derby branch
1843   August: *The Proper Sphere of Government* issued as pamphlet
1844   August to October: living temporarily in Birmingham, sub-editor of the *Pilot*
     October: resumes railway work
1848   December: moves to London to commence employment as sub-editor with *The Economist*
1851   January (or possibly December, 1850): publication of *Social Statics*. The book is dated 1851, but Spencer claimed in his preface to the 1892 edition that it was published in December 1850
1852   March: 'The Development Hypothesis' published
     April: 'A Theory of Population' published

1853   January: Thomas Spencer dies. His bequest to Herbert allows
        him to relinquish his post at *The Economist* by beginning of
        July
        July: 'Over-legislation' published
        October: 'The Universal Postulate' published
1854   July: 'The Genesis of Science' published
        August and September: first visit abroad, to France
        October: 'Railway Morals and Railway Policy' published
1855   July: complains of serious nervous symptoms whilst working
        on *The Principles of Psychology* in Wales
        August: publication of *The Principles of Psychology*
1857   April: 'Progress: its Law and Cause' published
        October: 'The Ultimate Laws of Physiology', 'The Origin
        and Function of Music' and 'Representative Government:
        What Is It Good For?' published
1858   January: first draft prepared of his complete conception of
        evolution (the basis of 'A System of Synthetic Philosophy')
1859   November: Darwin's *Origin of Species* published
1860   January: 'The Social Organism' published
        March: issues detailed programme of 'A System of Philo-
        sophy' (later rechristened 'A System of Synthetic Philosophy')
        April: 'Parliamentary Reform: the Dangers and the Safe-
        guards' published
        July: 'Prison Ethics' published
1861   June: makes ready for publication *Education: Intellectual, Moral
        and Physical* (a collection of four articles, previously published
        by Spencer in the 1850s)
1862   June: publication of *First Principles*[1]
1864   October: first volume of *The Principles of Biology* published
1866   April: father dies
1867   March: second volume of *Biology* completed
        May: mother dies
1870   December: publication of first volume of *The Principles of Psy-
        chology* (a revision of the book of 1855)
1872   October: second volume of *Psychology* completed

---

[1] Dates of the earlier publication of parts of *First Principles, The Principles of Biology,
The Principles of Psychology, The Principles of Sociology* and *The Principles of Ethics* not
given here.

July: publication of the first book in the *Descriptive Sociology* series, a series designed to collect and classify facts from various races which illustrate social evolution

1873 November: publication of *The Study of Sociology* (constituent chapters previously issued in periodicals in Britain and America)

1875 May: begins preparation of *An Autobiography*

1876 December: publication of the first edition of the first volume of *The Principles of Sociology*

1882 March: second volume of *The Principles of Sociology* completed

1884 February to July: publication of the essays constituting *The Man versus The State* in the *Contemporary Review*, followed by publication of the book

1892 June: first volume of *The Principles of Ethics* completed

1893 Second volume of *The Principles of Ethics* issued

1896 August: completion of third and final volume of *The Principles of Sociology*, and of the 'System of Synthetic Philosophy' as a whole.

1897 *Various Fragments* published (a collection of short essays)

1902 *Facts and Comments* published (another collection of short essays)

1903 8 December: dies in Brighton. 14 December: cremated in London and ashes placed in Highgate Cemetery

1904 Publication of *An Autobiography* (two volumes)

Bibliographical note

This note includes full details of references made in the Introduction.

Life and background

On Spencer's life and work in general his *An Autobiography* (two volumes), London, Williams and Norgate, 1904 and David Duncan, *Life and Letters of Herbert Spencer*, London, Williams and Norgate, 1911 (first issued in 1908 by Methuen) are indispensable sources. Duncan contains a full list of Spencer's publications. See also Beatrice Webb, *My Apprenticeship*, London, Longmans Green, 1926 and John Fiske, *Life and Letters of Edward Livingston Youmans*, London, Chapman and Hall, 1894. Spencer's papers are at the University of London Library.

Good general studies of Spencer are J. D. Y. Peel, *Herbert Spencer: The Evolution of a Sociologist*, London, Heinemann, 1971 and D. Wiltshire, *The Social and Political Thought of Herbert Spencer*, Oxford, Oxford University Press, 1978. The evangelical context of Spencer's thought is considered in Boyd Hilton's *The Age of Atonement*, Oxford, Clarendon Press, 1988. Crane Brinton's brief essay on Spencer in his *English Political Thought in the Nineteenth Century*, New York and Evanston, Harper and Row, 1962, is entertaining and shrewd. An important critical appraisal of Spencer in his own lifetime is A. J. Balfour, *A Fragment on Progress*, Edinburgh, David Douglas, 1892.

xxxiii

Evolutionary theory

A helpful discussion of the phrenological context of Spencer's evolutionary psychology is available in R. M. Young, *Mind, Brain and Adaptation in the Nineteenth Century*, Oxford, Clarendon Press, 1970. Antony Flew's *Evolutionary Ethics*, London, Macmillan, 1967 is an excellent, rigorous analysis of attempts to derive ethics from evolutionary theory, and is good too on the differences between Darwin and Spencer, as is D. Freeman, 'The Evolutionary Theories of Charles Darwin and Herbert Spencer', *Current Anthropology*, Vol. 15, No. 3, 1974, pp. 211–37.

A useful study of the development of evolutionary thought in the nineteenth century is D. R. Oldroyd, *Darwinian Impacts*, Milton Keynes, Open University Press, 1980. R. M. Young, *Darwin's Metaphor*, Cambridge, Cambridge University Press, 1985, is an advanced trreatment of some of the key issues. See also P. J. Bowler, 'The Changing Meaning of "Evolution"', *Journal of the History of Ideas*, Vol. 36, No. 1, 1975, pp. 95–114. Also of value is J. W. Burrow, *Evolution and Society*, Cambridge, Cambridge University Press, 1966 although it is somewhat cryptic on the differences between Spencer and Darwin over natural selection.

The nature and logical status of Spencer's theory of evolution is given particular attention in R. M. Young, 'The Development of Herbert Spencer's Concept of Evolution', *Actes du XIᵉ Congrès International d'Histoire des Sciences*, Vol. 2, pp. 273–8, Warsaw, Ossolineum, 1967; Ellen Frankel Paul, 'Herbert Spencer: the Historicist as a Failed Prophet', *Journal of the History of Ideas*, Vol. 64, 1983, pp. 619–38, and John Offer, 'Interpreting Spencer', *Sociology*, Vol. 14, No. 1, 1980, pp. 131–40.

Mill's views on Spencer are recorded in *The Later Letters of John Stuart Mill 1849–1873*, edited by F. E. Mineka and D. N. Lindley, Toronto and Buffalo, University of Toronto Press, and London, Routledge and Kegan Paul, 1972, which form Vols. 14 to 17 of *The Collected Works of John Stuart Mill* from the same publishers.

Political aspects and influences

In addition to Wiltshire's book, there are helpful overviews in W. H. Greenleaf, *The British Political Tradition*, Vol. 2, London, Routledge,

1988, especially pp. 48–88, and E. Barker, *Political Thought in England*, London, Williams and Norgate, 1915, ch. 4.

The nineteenth-century poor law in relation to Spencer is discussed in R. Pinker, *Social Theory and Social Policy*, London, Heinemann, 1971. Late nineteenth-century debates about charity and social policy are well treated in A. M. McBriar, *An Edwardian Mixed Doubles: The Bosanquets versus The Webbs*, Oxford, Clarendon Press, 1987. On ideas of national insurance see E. P. Hennock, *British Social Reform and German Precedents*, Oxford, Clarendon Press, 1987. On Canon Blackley in particular see M. J. J. Blackley, *Thrift and National Insurance as a Security Against Pauperism*, London, Kegan Paul, Trench Trubner, 1906.

On the land nationalisation question see W. L. Miller, 'Herbert Spencer's Drift to Conservatism', *History of Political Thought*, Vol. 3, No. 3, 1982, pp. 483–97; J. Paul, 'The Socialism of Herbert Spencer', *History of Political Thought*, Vol. 3, No. 3, 1982, pp. 499–514; and H. Steiner, 'Land, Liberty and the Early Herbert Spencer', *History of Political Thought*, Vol. 3, No. 3, 1982, pp. 516–33. On H. M. Hyndman see M. Bevin, 'H. M. Hyndman: a Rereading and a Reassessment', *History of Political Thought*, Vol. 12, No. 1, 1991, pp. 125–45.

Spencer's conception of justice is discussed in D. Miller, *Social Justice*, Oxford, Clarendon Press, 1976. Miller's interpretation is strongly challenged by T. S. Gray in 'Herbert Spencer's Theory of Social Justice – Desert or Entitlement', *History of Political Thought*, Vol. 2, No. 1, 1981, pp. 161–86. See also J. N. Gray, 'Spencer on the Ethics of Liberty and the Limits of State Duty', *History of Political Thought*, Vol. 3, No. 3, 1982, pp. 465–89.

Two articles dealing with the Liberty and Property Defence League and Spencer are E. Bristow, 'The Liberty and Property Defence League and Individualism', *Historical Journal*, Vol. 18, No. 4, 1975, pp. 761–89, and N. Soldon, '*Laissez-Faire* as Dogma: the Liberty and Property Defence League', ch. 9 of K. D. Brown (ed.), *Essays in Anti-Labour History*, London, Macmillan, 1974. See also M. Taylor, *Man Versus The State*, Oxford, Clarendon Press, 1992. T. Mackay (ed.), *A Plea for Liberty*, London, John Murray, 1891, sets out some League priorities.

Sociological aspects and influences

Peel's book remains a good place to begin an assessment of Spencer as a sociologist. J. H. Turner, *Herbert Spencer: A Renewed Appreciation*, Beverly Hills, Sage, 1985, bravely argues the case for the revival of Spencer's sociology. See too the wide-ranging article by R. L. Carneiro, 'Herbert Spencer as an Anthropologist', *Journal of Libertarian Studies*, Vol. 5, 1981, pp. 153–210.

The impact of Spencer's sociology on Durkheim is considered in P. A. Corning, 'Durkheim and Spencer', *British Journal of Sociology*, Vol. 33, No. 3, 1982, pp. 359–82, and S. Lukes, *Emile Durkheim*, Harmondsworth, Penguin, 1975. On Tönnies and Spencer see J. Offer, 'Tönnies and Spencer', in L. Clausen and C. Schlüter (eds.), *Ausdauer, Geduld und Ruhe: Aspekte und Quellen der Tönnies-Forschung*, Hamburg, Rolf Fechner Verlag, 1991, pp. 271–90.

Spencer's idea of the 'social organism' is reviewed in W. M. Simon, 'Herbert Spencer and the Social Organism', *Journal of the History of Ideas*, Vol. 21, 1960, pp. 294–9. Concentrating on political rather than epistemological individualism T. S. Gray has argued that Spencer's individualism and organicism are not necessarily in conflict in 'Herbert Spencer: Individualist or Organicist?', *Political Studies*, Vol. 33, 1985, pp. 236–53.

Spencer's treatment of welfare matters is discussed in J. Offer, 'Spencer's Sociology of Welfare', *Sociological Review*, Vol. 31, No. 4, 1983, pp. 719–52. The influence of Spencer and evolutionary thought on music historiography is reviewed in W. D. Allen, *Philosophies of Music History*, New York, Dover, 1962 (first published in 1939). See also J. Offer, 'Dissonance over Harmony: a Spencer Oddity', *Sociology*, Vol. 17, No. 2, 1983, pp. 274–7; C. H. H. Parry, *The Evolution of the Art of Music*, London, Kegan Paul, Trench Trubner, 1931 (tenth edition), which first appeared in 1893 as *The Art of Music*.

Spencer and social Darwinism in the USA is reviewed in S. Fine, *Laissez-Faire and the General Welfare State*, Ann Arbor, University of Michigan Press, 1956, and R. Hofstadter, *Social Darwinism in American Thought*, New York, Braziller, 1959. See also R. C. Bannister, ' "Survival of the Fittest": Histrionics?', *Journal of the History of Ideas*, Vol. 31, 1970, pp. 3277–98. Social Darwinism in England is indeed the topic of G. Jones, *Social Darwinism and English Thought*, Brighton,

Harvester, 1980. Further reflections are available in R. J. Halliday, 'Social Darwinism: a Definition', *Victorian Studies*, Vol. 14, No. 4, 1971, pp. 389–405, and J. A. Rogers, 'Darwinism and Social Darwinism', *Journal of the History of Ideas*, Vol. 33, 1972, pp. 265–80.

Two contrasting examples of sympathetic but critical response to Spencer's thought are W. H. Mallock, *Aristocracy and Evolution*, London, Adam and Charles Black, 1898 and B. Kidd, *Social Evolution*, London, Macmillan, 1895.

Editor's note

The version of *The Proper Sphere of Government* used here is that of the reprint of the letters originally published in the *Nonconformist* issued by W. Brittain of Paternoster Row, London in 1843. Similarly the version of *The Man versus The State* is that issued by Williams and Norgate in London after the original appearance of the component chapters in the *Contemporary Review*, for which Spencer added a postscript, also reproduced here.

Spencer's original punctuation and spelling have been retained, with a few corrections of apparent errors. Expanded and corrected or otherwise annotated references appear after the original footnotes in square brackets.

In the preparation of this book I have no doubt tested the patience of many individuals: two deserve special thanks – Pamela Compton, sub-librarian at the University of Ulster, Coleraine, and Valerie Canny who prepared the typescript. I also wish to thank the London Library, and in particular Michael Higgins, Deputy Librarian, for help regarding Spencer's original references. Work was in part assisted by a small personal research grant awarded by the British Academy, for which I am grateful.

THE
PROPER
SPHERE OF GOVERNMENT

A
REPRINT OF A SERIES OF LETTERS,
ORIGINALLY PUBLISHED IN

"THE NONCONFORMIST"

BY
HERBERT SPENCER

The Proper Sphere of Government

Letter I.

Things of the first importance – principles influencing all the transactions of a country – principles involving the weal or woe of nations, are very generally taken for granted by society. When a certain line of conduct, however questionable may be its policy – however momentous may be its good or evil results, has been followed by our ancestors, it usually happens that the great masses of mankind continue the same course of action, without ever putting to themselves the question – Is it right? Custom has the enviable power, of coming to conclusions upon most debatable points, without a moment's consideration – of propositions of a very doubtful character into axioms – and of setting aside almost self-evident truths as unworthy of consideration.

Of all subjects thus cavalierly treated, the fundamental principles of legislation, are perhaps the most important. Politicians – all members of the community who have the welfare of their fellow-men at heart, have their hopes, opinions, and wishes, centred in the actions of government. It therefore behoves them fully to understand the nature, the intention, the proper sphere of action of a government. Before forming opinions upon the best measures to be adopted by a legislative body, it is necessary that well defined views of the power of that body should be formed; that it be understood how far it can go consistently with its constitution; that it be decided what it may do and what it may not do. And yet, how few men have ever given the matter any serious consideration; how few, even of those who are

3

interested in the affairs of society, ever put to themselves the question – Is there any boundary to the interference of government? and, if so, what is that boundary?

We hear one man proclaiming the advantages that would accrue, if all the turnpike roads in the kingdom were kept in repair by the state; another would saddle the nation with a medical establishment, and preserve the popular health by legislation; and a third party maintains that government should make railways for Ireland, at the public expense. The possibility of there being any impropriety in meddling with these things never suggests itself. Government always *has* exercised the liberty of universal interference, and nobody ever questioned its right to do so. Our ancestors, good people, thought it quite reasonable that the executive should have unlimited power (or probably they never troubled themselves to think about it at all); and as they made no objection, we, in our wise veneration for the "good old times," suppose that all is as it should be. Some few, however, imbued with the more healthy spirit of investigation, are not content with this simple mode of settling such questions, and would rather ground their convictions upon reason, than upon custom. To such are addressed the following considerations.

Everything in nature has its laws. Inorganic matter has its dynamical properties, its chemical affinities; organic matter, more complex, more easily destroyed, has also its governing principles. As with matter in its integral form, so with matter in its aggregate; animate beings have their laws, as well as the material, from which they are derived. Man, as an animate being, has functions to perform, and has organs for performing those functions; he has instincts to be obeyed, and the means of obeying those instincts; and, so long as he performs those functions, as he obeys those instincts, as he bends to the laws of his nature, so long does he remain in health. All disobedience to these dictates, all transgression, produces its own punishment. Nature will be obeyed.

As with man physically, so with man spiritually. Mind has its laws as well as matter. The mental faculties have their individual spheres of action in the great business of life; and upon their proper development, and the due performance of their duties, depend the moral integrity, and the intellectual health, of the individual. Psychical laws must be obeyed as well as physical ones; and disobedience as surely brings its punishment in the one case, as in the other.

4

As with man individually, so with man socially. Society as certainly has its governing principles as man has. They may not be so easily traced, so readily defined. Their action may be more complicated, and it may be more difficult to obey them; but, nevertheless, analogy shows us that they must exist. We see nothing created but what is subject to invariable regulations given by the Almighty, and why should society be an exception? We see, moreover, that beings having volition, are healthy and happy, so long only as they act in accordance with those regulations; and why should not the same thing be true of man in his collective capacity?

This point conceded, it follows that the well being of a community, depends upon a thorough knowledge of social principles, and an entire obedience to them. It becomes of vital importance to know, what institutions are necessary to the prosperity of nations; to discover what are the duties of those institutions; to trace the boundaries of their action; to take care that they perform their functions properly; and especially to see, that they aim not at duties for which they were not intended, and for which they are not fitted.

The legislature is the most important of all national institutions, and as such, it claims our first attention in the investigation of social laws. An attempt to arrive at its principles, from the analysis of existing governments, with all their complex and unnatural arrangements, would be a work of endless perplexity, and one from which it would be extremely difficult, if not impossible, to educe any satisfactory result. To obtain clear ideas, we must consider the question abstractly; we must suppose society in its primitive condition; we must view circumstances and requirements as they would naturally arise; and we shall then be in a position to judge properly, of the relation which should exist, between a people and a government.

Let us, then, imagine a number of men living together without any recognised laws – without any checks upon their actions, save those imposed by their own fears of consequences – obeying nothing but the impulses of their own passions – what is the result? The weak – those who have the least strength, or the least influence – are oppressed by the more powerful: these, in their turn, experience the tyranny of men still higher in the scale; and even the most influential, are subject to the combined vengeance of those whom they have injured. Every man, therefore, soon comes to the conclusion, that his individual interest, as well as that of the community at large, will best be served by entering into some common bond of protection: all agree to become amenable to the decisions of their fellows, and to obey certain general arrangements. Gradually the population increases, their disputes become more numerous, and they find that it will be more convenient to depute this arbitrative power, to one or more individuals, who shall be maintained by the rest, in consideration of their time being devoted to the business of the public. Here we have a government springing naturally out of the requirements of the community. But what are those requirements? Is the government instituted for the purpose of regulating trade – of dictating to each man where he shall buy and where he shall sell? Do the people wish to be told what religion they must believe, what forms and ceremonies they must practise, or how many times they must attend church on a Sunday?[1] Is education the object contemplated? Do they ask instruction in the administration of their charity – to be told to whom they shall give, and how much, and in what manner they shall give it? Do they require their means of communication – their roads and railways – designed and constructed for them? Do they create a supreme power to direct their conduct in domestic affairs – to tell them at what part of the year they shall kill their oxen, and how many servings of meat they shall have at a meal?[2] In short, do they want a government because they see that the Almighty has been so negligent in designing social mechanisms, that everything will go wrong unless they are continually interfering? No; they know, or they ought to know, that the laws of society are of such a character, that natural evils will rectify themselves; that there is in society, as in every other part of creation, that beautiful self-adjusting principle, which will keep all its elements in equilibrium; and, moreover, that as the interference of man in external nature often destroys the just balance, and produces greater evils than those to be remedied, so the attempt to regulate all the actions of a community by legislation, will entail little else but misery and confusion.

What, then, do they want a government for? Not to regulate commerce; not to educate the people; not to teach religion; not to admin-

---

[1] "We remember a religious society which, in its laws, declared that it was instituted to promote the goodness of God; and truly it may be said that enactments against atheism are passed upon the pretence of endeavouring to promote his existence." – Sidney Smith's *Phrenology*, p. 8 [Edinburgh, 1838].

[2] It is said that the statute book still contains enactments on these points.

6

ister charity; not to make roads and railways; but simply to defend the natural rights of man – to protect person and property – to prevent the aggressions of the powerful upon the weak – in a word, to administer justice. This is the natural, the original, office of a government. It was not intended to do less: it ought not to be allowed to do more.

Letter II.

Philosophical politicians usually define government, as a body whose province it is, to provide for the "general good." But this practically amounts to no definition at all, if by a definition is meant a description, in which the limits of the thing described are pointed out. It is necessary to the very nature of a definition, that the words in which it is expressed should have some determinate meaning; but the expression "general good," is of such uncertain character, a thing so entirely a matter of opinion, that there is not an action that a government could perform, which might not be contended to be a fulfilment of its duties. Have not all our laws, whether really enacted for the public benefit or for party aggrandisement, been passed under the plea of promoting the "general good?" And is it probable that any government, however selfish, however tyrannical, would be so barefaced as to pass laws avowedly for any other purpose? If, then, the very term "definition," implies a something intended to mark out the boundaries of the thing defined, that cannot be a definition of the duty of a government, which will allow it to do anything and everything.

It was contended in the preceding letter, that "the administration of justice" was the sole duty of the state. Probably it will be immediately objected, that this definition is no more stringent than the other – that the word "justice" is nearly as uncertain in its signification as the expression "general good" – that one man thinks it but "justice" towards the landowner, that he should be protected from the competition of the foreign corn grower; another maintains that "justice" demands that the labourer's wages should be fixed by legislation, and that since such varied interpretations may be given to the term, the definition falls to the ground. The reply is very simple. The word is not used in its legitimate sense. "Justice" comprehends only the preservation of man's natural rights. Injustice implies a violation of those rights. No man ever thinks of demanding "justice" unless he is prepared to prove that violation; and no body of men can pretend that "justice" requires the enactment of any law, unless they can show that their natural rights would otherwise be infringed. If it be conceded that this is the proper meaning of the word, the objection is invalid, seeing that in the cases above cited, and in all similar ones, it is not applicable in this sense.

Having thus examined the exact meaning of the new definition, and having observed its harmony with the original wants of society, we may at once proceed to consider its practical applications; and, in the first few cases, it may be well, for the sake of showing the different effects of the two principles, to note, at the same time, the results of the doctrine of "general good." First, the great question of the day – the corn laws. Our legislators tell us that we have an enormous national debt; that we have to pay the interest of it; and that a free trade would so change the value of money, that we should not be able to raise the taxes; moreover, that were we to allow a competition, between foreign and home-grown produce, the land must be thrown out of cultivation – our agricultural population would be deprived of employment – and that great distress must be the result. These and sundry other plausible reasons, they bring forward, to show that restrictions upon the importation of corn, are necessary to the "general good." On the other hand, suppose we had free trade. Could our farmer complain that it was an infringement of his natural rights, to allow the consumers to purchase their food from any other parties whose prices were lower? Could he urge that the state was not acting justly towards him, unless it forced the manufacturer to give him a high price for that, which he could get on more advantageous terms elsewhere? No. "Justice" would demand no such interference. It is clear, therefore, that if the "administration of justice" had been recognised as the only duty of government, we should never have had any corn laws; and, as the test may be applied to all other cases of restrictions upon commerce with a similar result, it is equally evident, that upon the same assumption, we should always have had free trade.

Again, our clergy and aristocracy maintain, that it is eminently necessary for the "general good" that we should have an established church. They would have us believe that the Christian religion is of itself powerless – that it will never spread unless nurtured by the *pure* and *virtuous* hand of the state – that the truth is too weak to make

8

its way without the assistance of acts of parliament – and that mankind are still so universally selfish and worldly, that there is no chance of the gospel being taught, unless comfortable salaries are provided for its teachers – practically admitting, that were it not for the emoluments their own ministry would cease, and thus inadvertently confessing, that their interest, in the spiritual welfare of their fellow-creatures, is co-extensive with their pecuniary expectations. But, what says the other definition? Can it be contended, that it is unjust to the community to allow each individual to put what construction he sees best upon the scriptures? Can the man who disputes the authority of learned divines, and dares to think for himself, be charged with oppression? Can it even be maintained, that he who goes so far as to disbelieve the Christian religion altogether, is infringing the privileges of his fellow-man? No. Then it follows, that an established church is not only unnecessary to the preservation of the natural rights of man, but that inasmuch as it denies the subject the "rights of conscience," and compels him to contribute towards the spread of doctrines of which he does not approve, it is absolutely inimical to them. So that a state, in setting up a national religion, stands in the anomalous position of a transgressor of those very rights, that it was instituted to defend. It is evident, therefore, that the restrictive principle, would never have permitted the establishment of a state church.

And now, let us apply the test to that much disputed question – the Poor law. Can any individual, whose wickedness or improvidence has brought him to want, claim relief of his fellow-men as an act of justice? Can even the industrious labourer, whose distresses have not resulted from his own misconduct, complain that his natural rights are infringed, unless the legislature compels his neighbours to subscribe for his relief? Certainly not. Injustice implies a positive act of oppression, and no man or men can be charged with it, when merely maintaining a negative position. To get a clearer view of this, let us again refer to a primitive condition of society, where all start with equal advantages. One part of the community is industrious and prudent, and accumulates property; the other, idle and improvident, or in some cases, perhaps, unfortunate. Can any of the one class fairly demand relief from the other? Can even those, whose poverty is solely the result of misfortune, claim part of the produce of the industry of the others as a right? No. They may seek their commiseration; they may hope for their assistance; but they cannot take their stand upon the ground of justice. What is true of these parties, is true of their descendants; the children of the one class stand in the same relation to those of the other that existed between their parents, and there is no more claim in the fiftieth or sixtieth generation than in the first. Possibly it may be objected to the assumption that the different classes started upon equal terms, that it is not only entirely gratuitous, but that it is contrary to fact; as we all know, that the property was seized by the few, while the many were left in poverty without any fault of their own, and, that in this circumstance, originates the right in question. I reply, that when it can be shown that the two classes of the present day, are the direct descendants of those alluded to; when it can be shown that our poor are the children of the oppressed, and that those who have to pay poor rates are the children of the oppressors, then, the validity of the objection will be admitted; but that until this is shown to be the truth, or an approach to the truth, the objection may be disregarded. It appears, then, that the proposed definition of the duty of the state, would never have allowed the existence of a poor law.

Letter III.

From preceding arguments it was inferred, that if the administration of justice had been recognised as the only duty of the state, a national church would not have existed, that restrictions upon commerce could never have been enacted, and that a poor law would be inadmissible. As the last conclusion will not meet with such general approbation as its predecessors, it is deemed requisite to enter more fully into the evidence that may be adduced in support of it: and the *Nonconformist* being the organ of a political body, who profess to act upon principle and not upon expediency, and who avow their intention to follow up sound doctrine, whether it may lead to odium or popularity, it is hoped that the arguments brought forward, will meet with a candid consideration, apart from all personal or political bias.

The fund provided by the poor law is usually considered as a contribution from the richer orders of the community, for the support of the destitute; and, coming from the pockets of those in easy circumstances, it is supposed to be a great boon to their poorer neighbours. But this is not a correct mode of viewing the case. A political economist would reason thus. Here is an institution which practically divides the community into two great classes – labourers and paupers, the one doing nothing towards the production of the general stock of food and clothing, and the other having to provide for the consumption of both. Hence it is evident, that each member of the producing class, is injured by the appropriation of a portion of the general stock by the non-producing class. But who form the great bulk of the producing class? The working population. Their labour is the chief ingredient in the wealth of the nation; without them land and capital would be useless. It follows, then, that this provision, set apart for the poor, is mainly provided by the labours of the people, and hence that the burden falls chiefly upon them.

Lest this generalizing style of argument should be unsatisfactory, it may be well to adopt another mode of proof. We know that the average cost of any article is determined by the expenses attendant upon its production; that the price at which the manufacturer sells his calico, is dependent upon the amount of labour expended upon it, the cost of his machinery, the value of the raw material, and so forth; and that the price at which the farmer can afford to sell his corn, is governed by the amount of his rent, the cost of cultivation, &c.; and we also know, that if any one of these expenses is increased, a rise in the price of the produce must follow; that if the landlords double their rents, the farmers must charge more for their grain. Now the poor rates, in some of the unions under the present law, are 40 per cent. upon the rental, and under the old law they were in some cases 75 and 100 per cent. What does this amount to but a doubling of the rent? It matters not whether both portions are paid to the landlord, or whether one half goes to him, and the other to the parish, the effect upon the cost of the produce is the same, and the consumers of that produce, have to pay a higher price for it, than they would have to do, were no such demand made. But *who* form the great mass of consumers? – The working population. *They* then are the parties from whom the greater part of this additional tax comes. Thus we arrive at the same conclusion as before; that not only do the industrious classes contribute a considerable portion of the poor rates directly, but that the greater part of what apparently comes from the upper ranks, is originally derived from them.

Many poor law advocates build their arguments upon the existence of a corn law. They say that were there no bar to the importation of foreign produce, and no consequent check to the demand for our manufactures, they would not object to the working man being dependent upon his own resources; but that so long as the price of food is unnaturally raised, and the call for labour so uncertain, they must maintain the necessity of a public charity. To this there are two replies.

First, That the argument rests upon a wrong hypothesis, originating as it does in the assumption, that public charity proceeds from the stores of the rich, when, as has been shown, the greater portion of it comes from the toils of the labouring classes. The very parties for whose benefit the fund is raised, are, in virtue of their productive industry, chiefly instrumental in raising it. The fact, therefore, that the industrious population are already suffering from a corn law, affords no reason why one part of them should be still further burdened, by having to provide food and clothing for the other.

Secondly, That the new definition of the duty of a government is not in the least affected by the argument, seeing that free trade is a necessary consequence of the same principle that excludes a poor law; and if so, it follows that those objections which are founded upon the existence of commercial restrictions, are not applicable.

But even admitting that a poor law ameliorates the condition of the labouring classes in times of national distress; still it does not follow that it is either a wise, or, ultimately, a benevolent law. So long as the earth continues to produce, and mankind are willing to labour, an extensive distress must indicate something unnatural in the social arrangements. Such is the present condition of England. Europe and America produce more food than they can consume – our artizans are anxious to work, and yet they are bordering upon starvation, consequently there must be something radically wrong, in our political institutions. Is it better to palliate, or to cure the evil? Is it better to mitigate the distress by the distribution of public charity, or to allow it so to manifest itself, as to demand the discovery and removal of its cause? Which do we consider the kindest physician, the one who alleviates the pain of a disease by continually administering anodynes, or the one who allows his patient to experience a little suffering in the exhibition of the symptoms, that he may discover the seat of the malady, and then provide a speedy remedy? The alternative requires no consideration.

It is surprising that writers who have of late been animadverting upon the national collection scheme, and who have pointed out the mockery of recommending charity, in answer to a call for justice, should not perceive that the case is but a type of the poor law. Both are attempts to mitigate an evil, not to remove it; both are means of quieting the complaints of the nation, and both will tend to retard the attainment of those rights which the people demand. The *Times*, in an article upon the national petition, made an observation to the effect, that the contents of the document were not worthy of notice, but that the fact of its presentation, clearly proved the necessity for a "more generous poor law," to satisfy the complainants. Here is a clear exposition of the policy: we must stop the mouths of the people by charity: we need not enter into the question of their rights, but we must give them more parish pay!

A poor law, however, is not only inexpedient in practice, but it is defective in principle. The chief arguments that are urged against an established religion, may be used with equal force against an established charity. The dissenter submits, that no party has a right to compel him to contribute to the support of doctrines, which do not meet his approbation. The rate-payer may as reasonably argue, that no one is justified in forcing him to subscribe towards the maintenance of persons, whom he does not consider deserving of relief. The advocate of religious freedom, does not acknowledge the right of any council, or bishop, to choose for him what he shall believe, or what he shall reject. So the opponent of a poor law, does not acknowledge the right of any government, or commissioner, to choose for him who are worthy of his charity, and who are not. The dissenter from an established church, maintains that religion will always be more general, and more sincere, when the support of its ministry is not compulsory. The dissenter from a poor law, maintains that charity will always be more extensive, and more beneficial, when it is voluntary. The dissenter from an established church can demonstrate that the intended benefit of a state religion, will always be frustrated by the corruption which the system invariably produces. So the dissenter from a poor law, can show that the proposed advantages of state charity, will always be neutralized by the evils of pauperism, which necessarily follow in its train. The dissenter from an established church, objects that no man has a right to step in between him and his religion. So the dissenter from established charity, objects that no man has a right to step in between him and the *exercise* of his religion.

How is it, that those who are so determined in their endeavours to rid themselves of the domination of a national church – who declare that they do not need the instruction of the state in the proper explanation of the gospel – how is it that these same men, are tamely allowing and even advocating, the interference of the state, in the exercise of one of the most important precepts of that gospel? They deny the right of the legislature to explain the theory, and yet argue the necessity of its direction in the practice. Truly it indicates but little consistency on the part of dissenters, that whilst they defend their independence in the article of *faith*, they have so little confidence in their own principles, that they look for extraneous aid in the department of *works*. The man who sees the inhabitants of a country deficient in spiritual instruction, and hence maintains the necessity of a national religion, is doing no more than the one who finds part of the population wanting in food and clothing, and thence infers the necessity of a national charity.

Again, the moral effect of a poor law upon the rate-paying portion of the community is little considered, although one of its most important features. Here, also, there is an evident analogy between established religion and established charity. It is said, that in a system like that of our national church, in which the visible duties of a communicant, consist chiefly, in attendance upon public worship, reception of the sacraments, payment of tithes, church rates, &c., the form will always be substituted for the reality; that the periodical ceremonies will take the place of the daily practice; that the physical will take the place of the spiritual. It may be said, with equal truth, that a similar effect will follow the establishment of a poor law; the same principles in human nature are acted upon; the payment of poor rates will supplant the exercise of real benevolence, and a fulfilment of the legal form, will supersede the exercise of the moral duty. Forced contributions rarely appeal to the kindly feelings. The man who is called upon for a rate, does not put his hand into his pocket out of pure sympathy for the poor; he looks upon the demand as another tax, and feels annoyance rather than pleasure, in paying it. Nor does the effect end here. The poor labourer or artizan, who is struggling hard with the world to maintain his independence, excites no pity. So long as there is a poor law he cannot starve, and it will be time enough to consider his case when he applies for relief. The beggar who knocks at his door, or the way-worn traveler who accosts him in his walk, is told to go to his parish; there is no need to inquire into his history, and to give him private assistance if found deserving, for there is already a public provision for him. Such is the state of mind encouraged by national charity. When the legal demand is paid, the conscience is satisfied; the party is absolved from all exercise of generosity; charity is administered by proxy; the nobler feelings are never required to gain the victory over the selfish propensities; a dormant condition of those feelings necessarily follows, and a depreciation of the national character is the final result. The payment of poor rates bears the same relation to real charity, that the attention to forms and ceremonies bears to real religion.

But, it may be asked, how are we to know that voluntary benevolence would suffice for the relief of the ordinary distresses of the poor, were there no national provision? A somewhat analogous question is put as an objection to the extension of the suffrage – how are we to know that those who are not fitted for the exercise of the franchise, will become so when it is given to them? and a similar reply to that so ably employed by the editor of the *Nonconformist* in that case, will apply here. Men are not in the habit of preparing for duties they are never called upon to perform; they are not in the habit of exhibiting virtues which are never needed; moral vigour cannot co-exist with moral inactivity; and the higher feelings will ever remain inactive, until circumstances prompt them to exercise. Hence, while there is a public provision for poverty, there will be no incentive to the exercise of benevolence on the part of the rich, and no stimulus to prudence and economy on the part of the poor. So long as the one class can point to the pay table, they will not give; and so long as the other have an inexhaustible fund to apply to, they will not save. It may reasonably be concluded, therefore, that were there no poor law, the rich would be more charitable, and the poor more provident. The one would give more, and the other would ask less.

A general view of the arguments shows –

1. That the burden of the poor law falls chiefly upon the industrious classes.
2. That the existence of commercial restrictions, is, therefore, no argument for retaining it.

3. That even assuming a poor law to be directly beneficial, it is indirectly injurious, inasmuch as it prolongs the causes of distress.

4. That established charity is open to many of the strongest objections that can be urged against established religion.

5. That a poor law discourages the exercise of real benevolence, and lowers the standard of national character.

6. That were there no poor law, the increase of voluntary charity, and the decrease of improvidence, would render one unnecessary.

From these reasons it is concluded, that the proposed definition of the duty of a government, in excluding a poor law, is only excluding what is intrinsically bad.

Letter IV.

My last letter, entering as it did rather deeply into the poor law question, might almost be considered by some of your readers, as a digression from the ostensible object of this essay, although a very necessary one to the establishment of the principle advocated. I must now, however, still further trespass upon their patience, in the endeavour to answer the query proposed to me – "Has not every man a right to a maintenance out of the soil?" for this, after all, is the pith of the question submitted.[3] Before proceeding, it may be observed, that the burden of proof falls rather on the party who assert the right, than on those who deny it. The originator of a proposition is usually required to demonstrate its truth; not his opponent to show its fallacy.

Man *has* a claim to a subsistence derived from the soil. It is his natural birth-right – the charter given to him at his creation; and whoever, by iniquitous laws, oppressive taxation, or any other means, puts difficulties in the way of his obtaining that subsistence, is infringing that right. But, the right is conditional – the produce is only promised to him in return for the labour he bestows upon the soil; and if the condition is not fulfilled, the right has no existence. Now the poor law principle recognises this right, as independent of that

---

[3] This refers to some remarks which appeared in the *Nonconformist* upon the previous letter.

condition; it acknowledges the claim to a share in the produce, but demands no equivalent labour. "Yes," it will be replied, "and for a very good reason; because there is no direction in which that labour can be profitably employed." Be it so; it cannot be denied that this is to a certain extent true. But what then? Is this a natural state of things? Is this great evil irremediable? Is this want of a field for labour the inevitable result of the constitution of the world? No, no! It is one of the evil consequences of human selfishness – it is one of the many curses flowing from class legislation. We know that were we righteously governed, we should hear no cry for employment. Every man would find something for his hand to do, and the promised sustenance would flow abundantly from his labour. What, then, is our duty? Ought we, because some of our fellow men, have, in the wantonness of their power, made arrangements whereby a great part of the people are prevented from earning their bread by the sweat of their brow – ought we, I ask, calmly to submit, and give the subsistence without the labour? Ought we not rather to destroy the laws that have induced this disordered state; and by restoring the healthy action of society, allow that natural fulfilment of the promise, which a submission to its accompanying commandment would ensure? The Almighty has given to man a privilege to be enjoyed after obeying a certain condition: a human power steps in, and to a certain extent renders obedience to that condition impossible: shall we grant the privilege without any attention to the condition? or shall we take away the obstacles which prevent our fellow men from satisfying it? The answer is self-evident. We come, then, to the conclusion that the *unconditional* right to a maintenance out of the soil, is inconsistent with one of the fundamental principles of our religion.

It may be objected that though employment be ever so abundant, and society in its most prosperous state, there will still be numerous cases of distress and destitution. Granted; but what then? It must not be inferred that there needs any public provision for them. In nine cases out of ten, such miseries result from the transgressions of the individual or his parents: and are we to take away the just punishment of those transgressions? We are told that the sins of the wicked shall be visited upon the children to the third and fourth generation. That visitation may either exhibit itself in mental derangement, bodily disease, or temporal want. The parent may either transmit to the child bad moral tendencies, a constitutional taint, or may leave it in circumstances of great misery. The visitation may comprehend any or all of these. But the poor law steps in and says, "As far as I can, I will annul this law. However great may have been your misconduct, or that of your parents – notwithstanding your destitution may have resulted solely from that misconduct, now that you are in distress you have a just claim upon the property of your fellow-creatures, and I will relieve you."[4] In doing this it not only takes away the punishment, but it also destroys the most powerful incentive to reformation. Adversity, is, in many cases, the only efficient school for the transgressor. Perhaps it may be asked, where is the justice, or the advantage, of allowing the child to endure the temporal want resulting from the sins of its parents? There is an advantage, and a great one: the same tendency to immorality which characterised the parent is bequeathed to the offspring – the moral disease requires a cure – under a *healthy social condition* that cure will be found in the poverty which has followed in its train. The malady provides its own remedy – the poor-law right prevents that remedy from being administered.

Let not this be misunderstood: it has no reference to the present distresses of the people; it only applies to the few cases of individual destitution, which would occur in a well-governed country.

A natural right, may, usually, be easily defined. Its boundaries are self-existent. But it is not so with the poor law principle. It says that every man has a right to a maintenance out of the soil. But what is a maintenance? One party says that a bare subsistence is all that is implied. Another, that the applicant can demand all the comforts usually enjoyed by those in his station. Another, that he may as fairly claim the luxuries of life as those above him. And the extreme party will be content with nothing short of the socialist principle, of community of property. Who is to say which of these is the true expression of the right? The gradations are infinite, and how can it be decided where the claim begins and where it ends? Who can tell the rate-payer

---

[4] This must not be construed into a reflection upon voluntary benevolence. If, for the sake of ameliorating, to a certain extent, the miseries of the wicked, the Almighty has seen well to implant in their fellow-creatures, sympathies, which shall induce them to pity and assist, it must be at once concluded that the exercise of those sympathies, is conducive to the general happiness. But, this admission in no way involves the approval of a systematic arrangement, set up by fallible men, for the purpose of doing by wholesale, what the Almighty has only seen fit to do partially. Meanwhile, it is greatly to be wished that the charitable, would use a more judicious discrimination, in the distribution of their gifts, and extend their assistance rather to unfortunate industry, than to suffering wickedness.

how much of his property can be justly demanded by his fellow creature? Who can tell the pauper when he asks for more pay, that he receives just as much as he is entitled to? or can explain to him why he has a right to what he already receives, but no right to anything more? And yet, if this were really a right, ought it not to be capable of such a definition?

It is said that property is a conventionalism – that its accumulation by the few, is injurious to the interests of the many – that its very existence is detrimental to those excluded from its enjoyment – and that they have consequently a claim on those possessing it. But is property a conventionalism? Let us investigate this question.

Paley says, "Whatever is expedient is right." This is a startling assertion; but it must be remembered, that the word "expedient" is not used in its ordinary sense. It does not here mean that which will best serve present purposes, but that whose effects, both present and future, direct and collateral, will be most beneficial. He does not defend that expediency which would sacrifice the future welfare of a nation to the interests of the present hour; but, he calls that expedient, the total sum of whose good results, immediate and expectant, is greater than that of its bad ones. When the expression is interpreted in this extended sense, when the evils and benefits that may arise in distant ages meet with the same consideration as the effects of today, the assertion no longer appears extraordinary. Some moralists have, on the strength of this, accused Paley of setting up a standard of right and wrong, independent of that afforded by the Christian religion. They say that he has first acknowledged that the precepts of the gospel form our only safe guide, and then brings forward a principle in opposition to them. They mistake his position. He brings forward a principle not in opposition to, but in accordance with, those precepts. He holds up to view the grand fundamental law, upon which all the commands of our religion are based. He enunciates the great proposition from which the doctrines of Christianity are so many corollaries. God wills the happiness of man. That happiness depends upon the fulfilment of certain conditions. He gives him laws, by obeying which he satisfies those conditions. He says, "Thou shalt not steal;" and why? Because, although the thief may experience a temporary gratification in the acquisition of stolen property, not only is this counterbalanced by the corresponding annoyance on the part of the loser, but the thief himself, as well as every other member of the community, is in constant fear of similar losses. So that the sorrow of losing, added to the general fear of robbery, far outweighs the individual pleasure of acquirement. It follows, then, that obedience to the command, "Thou shalt not steal," is eminently conducive to the general happiness: that is, it is "expedient." Again, man is told to love his neighbour as himself; and why? Because by so doing, he not only increases the comfort of his fellow-creatures, but he also himself reaps a rich reward, in the pleasure that flows from the exercise of genuine benevolence. And similarly in the analysis of every other case, we find that the general happiness is the great end in view; that the commands of the Almighty are such as will best secure that happiness, and hence, that "expediency" is the primitive law of human governance. If, having admitted the truth of this conclusion, we have certain cases presented to us, on which we have no direct expression of the divine will, our proper course is to appeal to the principle which we discover to be in accordance with the spirit of that will. Let us then apply the test to the question in hand.

First – Is the institution of private property expedient? It is. Man's happiness greatly depends upon the satisfaction of his temporal wants. The fruits of the earth are a necessary means of satisfying those wants. Those fruits can never be produced in abundance without cultivation. That cultivation will never prevail without the stimulus of certain possession. No man will sow when others may reap. We have abundant proof of this, in the history of every savage nation. Moreover, we see that so long as their bodily cravings are unsatisfied, men will make no social progress. Without ample provision of food and clothing, they have no time for becoming civilised. And not becoming civilised, is the same thing as making no moral or intellectual advances. And remaining in mental darkness, involves entire insensibility to the highest pleasures, of which the Creator has made human nature capable. Hence, property greatly promotes the mental and bodily happiness of mankind; that is, it is expedient. It must also be borne in mind, that although the test of expediency has been appealed to, in default of any direct command from the Almighty; the scriptures contain abundance of indirect evidence of his will in this matter. Not only in numerous instances does the bible inculcate duties, in which the institution of private property is virtually recognised, but it has one precept, which is clearly decisive. The single command, "Thou shalt not steal," carries with it a complete charter of the rights of possession. Lastly – if these arguments were inconclusive, the simple fact, that there is implanted in every man, a desire to possess, which desire, by the accumulation of property, may be gratified *without injury to his fellow-creatures*, this fact is in itself ample proof, that individual possession is in accordance with the will of the Creator. It follows, therefore, from the law of expediency directly, from the constitution of man directly, and from the revealed will of God by implication, that property is not a *conventional*, but a *natural*, institution.

Now we must either admit the right of possession entirely, or deny it altogether. We cannot say to a man, "So much of the substance you have acquired by your labour is your own, and so much belongs to your fellow-creatures." We cannot divide the right. Either it is a right, or it is not. There is no medium. We must say yes or no. If then, after a review of the arguments, we allow that property is an institution natural to civilised man: if we admit also, what necessarily follows from this – the right of individual possession – and admit that too, as we must, to its full extent; if we do this, the poor-law right vanishes entirely. The two are totally inconsistent, and cannot co-exist.

To return to the test of expediency. The poor law has already been measured by this principle, and found wanting. It was shown that many and great are the evils, that have flowed, and must flow, from its acknowledgement; that those evils have far more than counterbalanced the benefits; and that all the good results, and none of the bad ones, would follow from the substitution of voluntary charity. If the reasoning was conclusive, the right is rejected, without the necessity of an appeal to any of the preceding arguments.

It is submitted, therefore –

1. That under circumstances like ours, in which the poor man is prevented from earning his subsistence by his labour, it is not our duty to give the subsistence without the labour, but to break down those barriers to productive industry, which selfish legislators have set up, and to place the labourer in his proper position, by restoring society to its natural state.
2. That by allowing the wicked to take advantage of the right held

out by the poor law, we not only annul the just punishment awarded to them, but we also take away the most effectual prompter to repentance and improvement.

3. That a real right usually admits of a clear definition, but that the supposed poor-law right does not.

4. That the institution of property, is sanctioned by the law of expediency, by the implied will of God, and by the constitution of man; and that if we acknowledge its rights, we must deny those sought to be established by the poor law.

5. That the admission of a claim to a maintenance out of the soil, is not only inconsistent with the rights of property, but that it is in itself productive of more evil than good; that is, it is inexpedient: and if it is inexpedient it cannot be a right.

Letter V.

It will probably be objected to the proposed theory of government, that if the administration of justice were the only duty of the state, it would evidently be out of its power to regulate our relations with other countries, to make treaties with foreign powers, to enter into any kind of international arrangement whatever, or to levy wars that might be absolutely necessary.

So much of the objection as relates to the absence of power to make treaties, may be disregarded. Commerce, or war, are nearly always, directly or indirectly, the subjects of negotiation between governments, and as free trade is presupposed by the definition, it is clear that commercial treaties would never be called for. The whole of the objection is therefore comprised in its last clause – viz., the want of power to make war. Instead of viewing such a result as an evil, we should rather hail it as one of the greatest benefits that could arise from the recognition of this principle. War has been the source of the greatest of England's burdens. Our landowners would probably never have dared to enact the corn laws, had not the people been intoxicated by the seeming prosperity arising from war. The national debt, with all its direful consequences, would not have been in existence, had our rulers been deprived of the power of going to war. Our country would never have been drained of the hard earnings of her industrious sons, had not the uncurbed ambition of the aristocracy involved us in war. Capital that would have constructed all our railways many times over – that would have given every facility to commerce – that would have set it upon a real instead of a nominal foundation – property, the accumulated labour of generations, the grand national store in time of need, is gone for ever. Not only does England suffer from the yearly draught upon its resources demanded by the national debt, it feels likewise the loss of the property of which that debt is the representative. Not only has the nation to pay the interest, it has lost the principal also.

Many entertain the opinion that war is essentially beneficial to the community – that it invigorates the social organism; and they refer to the commercial energy, exhibited during the late continental campaigns, in proof of their assertion. But if, on the one hand, they would bear in mind the accidental influences by which such state was induced; whilst, on the other, they turned their attention to the sufferings experienced by the lower orders, during that period, rather than to the aggrandisement of the trading classes, perhaps they would come to a different conclusion. And, even admitting that war produces temporary good, it infallibly inflicts a more than equivalent injury. It acts upon a nation, as wine does upon a man. It creates the same unnatural activity – the same appearance of increased strength. In a similar manner does it call forth the supplies of life and energy provided for the future; in like fashion is the excitement followed by a corresponding depression; and so likewise is the strength of the constitution gradually undermined; and the short-sighted politician, who, judging by the apparent prosperity it produces, pronounces war a benefit to a nation, is falling into the same error, as the man who concludes that a spirituous stimulant is permanently strengthening, because he experiences an accession of vigour whilst under its influence.

War has been the nurse of the feudal spirit so long the curse of all nations; and from that spirit has flowed much of the selfish and tyrannical legislation under which we have so long groaned. If, for the last four or five centuries, the civilised world, instead of having been engaged in invasions and conquests, had directed its attention to the real sources of wealth – industry and commerce, science and the arts – long since would our nobility have found that they were mere drones in the hive, and long since would they have ceased to glory in their shame.

When to the political and commercial evils of war, we add the moral ones, when we remember that it is inconsistent with the spirit of Christianity – that it unduly encourages the animal passions – that it exalts brute courage into the greatest of human virtues – that it tends greatly to retard the civilisation of the world – that it is the grand bar to the extension of that feeling of universal brotherhood with all nations, so essential to the real prosperity of mankind: when, in addition to these collateral evils, we call to mind the immediate ones – the horrors of battle, and the lamentations of kindred – we shall rather feel, that a principle which of necessity excludes these things, should, on that account alone, earnestly commend itself to our notice.

We are told that the time shall come, when nations "shall beat their swords into ploughshares, and their spears into pruning hooks." That time may be yet afar off, but we are advancing towards it – we shall eventually arrive at it, and that too, we may assure ourselves, not by any sudden revolution, but by a continued moral and intellectual progression. We must not wait for a direct interposition of the Almighty to bring about this change; we must use proper means; we must put our shoulders to the wheel, and then look for the fulfilment of the promise as the result of our obedience to the commands. But what are the means? One of them we have before us. Confine the attention of our rulers to their only duty, the administration of justice; and, as far as we are concerned, the prophecy is fulfilled. Many will ask, "What would be the use of our relinquishing war, unless other nations will agree to do so likewise?" The same parties frequently put a similar question, by way of an excuse for not assisting in the reformation of social abuses – What can one man do? Need they be told that men never come unanimously to the same conclusion, at the same time, and that it is impossible they should do so? Need they be told that all great changes have emanated from individuals? Need they be told that what each leaves to the rest, no one does? Would that every man would cease such puerile pretences, and stand boldly forward to do his duty. National evils would then soon be rectified. What is here true of men individually, is true of men in masses. Never need we expect to see all nations abandon war at the same time. One must lead the way. Let England be that one. Let Britain first hold up the fair flag of peace. Let our nation act up to the spirit of its religion, without waiting for others to do the same. Not only would precept and example induce neighbouring states to follow, but new influences would come into play. Steps would quickly be taken to establish the long-talked-of system of national arbitration. Mankind would open their eyes to the advantages of a peaceful decision of state disputes; appeal to arms would become less and less frequent, and soon should we cease to applaud in nations, that litigious and unchristian spirit, and those barbarous notions of "honour," which we have learned to despise in individuals.

"But," I am asked, "is there no such thing as a necessary war?" In theory perhaps there may be; but it is very rarely to be seen in practice. Is our war with China necessary? Is our war with Affghanistan necessary? Was our war with Syria necessary? Was our war with France necessary? Was our war with America necessary? No. In defending ourselves against an invasion, we might perhaps be said to be engaged in a necessary war, but in no other case; and England has but little to fear on that score. Improbable, however, as such an event may be, let us, for the sake of argument, imagine that we involve ourselves in a quarrel with some foreign state, which ends in their attacking us, one of two things must happen. Either we repel the attack, or we do not. Many there are, who, under such circumstances, would look for an intervention of providence; others who would trust to the principle of passive resistance. But, without sheltering under either of these, let us suppose that active defence is necessary. That defence may be conducted in two ways. Either the nation at large must provide for it independently of the state, must call together a council of war, volunteer supplies, and make all other necessary arrangements; or the government must itself, as heretofore, take the affair into its own hands. The first of these alternatives may appear impracticable; but it is questionable whether such impression does not arise from its disagreement with our preconceived notions, rather than from any reasonable conviction. The wars of savage nations have very frequently been carried on without the guidance of any fixed executive power. We have instances, too, in civilised countries, of rebellions in which successful war has been maintained in opposition to the government. How much more, then, might we expect an efficient resistance in such a highly organised social condition as our own? But, admitting the impracticability of this principle – assuming that the interference of the state would be necessary in such cases, what follows? The insufficiency of the original definition, and the consequent sacrifice of the doctrines propounded? No such thing.

Strange as it may seem, the admission of such a necessity is no derogation to the theory before us. The question has hitherto been considered in its application to England only, because the cases brought forward have had exclusive reference to internal policy; but, in the present instance, in which international affairs are involved, we must no longer suppose such a limited sphere of action. Some moral laws cannot receive their perfect development, unless universally acknowledged; they do not agree with the present state of things, and they cannot be measured by an arbitrary standard, with which they are professedly inconsistent. To imagine one part of mankind acting upon a certain principle – to perceive that they will be obliged to infringe that principle, in their intercourse with the rest who are acting under other guidance, and thence to infer that the principle is at fault, is anything but logical. We must give the system fair play, allow it a general application, and test it in accordance with its own conditions. Suppose, then, that all nations confined the attention of their governments, to the administration of justice, aggressive war would cease; but when aggressive war ceases, defensive war becomes unnecessary. We see, therefore, that the concession that it might be requisite for the state to interfere in cases of invasion, implies no error in the definition. The exception would result, not from any inherent imperfection in the principle, but from its confined application.

The positions are these –

1. That war is a great evil, and that the fact of its exclusion by a proposed definition, is a powerful argument in favour of that definition.
2. That depriving our rulers of the power to make war, would be one of the most effectual means within our reach, of hastening that period, when "nation shall not lift up sword against nation."
3. That resistance to invasion is the only war that has any claim to the title of necessary, and that we have little need to fear its requisition.
4. That even assuming the occurrence of a descent upon our shores, and allowing that the interference of the state would in that case be necessary; the exception shows no defect in our principle, but merely a want of extension in its practice.

Letter VI.

Colonisation may possibly appear to some, to be a stumbling-block in their way to the desirable conclusion, that the administration of justice is the only duty of the state. We may anticipate the question – What would the colonies do without our governance and protection? I think facts will bear me out in replying – Far better than they do with them.

The subject naturally ranges itself under three heads – the interests of the mother country, of the emigrants, and of the aborigines. First, then, the interests of the mother country.

The records of ancient nations have ever shown that the riches of a community do not depend upon the acquirement of new territory; our own history bears ample testimony of the same character, and our present experience in every instance confirms that testimony. The well known case of the United States may be cited as an example. Whilst that country was a colony, it was a burden to us; the expenses attending its government were far greater than the profits derived from its trade; but since it has become an independent kingdom, it has been a source of great gain. Canada stands to us in the same position that the United States once did; its distance from us is the same, its commercial advantages are greater, it has the benefit of increased civilisation, and yet, like its prototype, it does not repay the cost of its management. Hindostan may be pointed out as another illustration. The statement of the East India company's profit and loss shows that, in this case also, the balance is against us; and that our enormous oriental possessions have been an injury instead of a benefit. Yet, in spite of these and many similar instances, it is still tacitly assumed that extensive territorial property is synonymous with wealth.

Men argue that, by monopolising the colonial trade, we obtain a more extended market for our produce that we should otherwise have, and that this must needs be a great benefit. The position is a very plausible, but a no less fallacious, one. We monopolise their trade from one of two causes. Either we make the articles they con-sume at a lower rate than any other nation, or we oblige them to buy those articles from us, though they might obtain them for less else-where. If we can undersell other producers, it is plain that we should still exclusively supply the market, were the colonies independent. If we cannot undersell them, it may be made equally clear that we are indirectly injuring ourselves to a greater extent than we are benefited by the monopoly. For, if the colonists take our manufactures, we must take their produce – they cannot pay us in money. Now, the prices of the articles which they barter for our manufactures (the demand remaining constant, as it must) are regulated by the cost of their production; and the cost of their production *other things being the same*, depends upon the prices of the commodities which they have to purchase. If two parties agree to deal exclusively with each other, and one of them doubles his charges, it is clear that the other cannot continue to trade with him, unless he advances his terms in the same ratio. So that by making the colonists pay an extra price for certain merchandise with which we supply them, we do but cause an equivalent increase in the cost of the produce which they send in exchange, and thus entirely neutralise the supposed advantage. Nor is this all. "Each country," says M'Culloch, "has some natural or acquired capabilities that enable her to carry on certain branches of industry more advantageously than any one else. But the fact of a country being undersold in the markets of her colonies, shows con-clusively that, instead of having any superiority, she labours under a disadvantage, as compared with others, in the production of the pecu-liar articles in demand in them. And hence, in providing a forced market in the colonies, for articles that we should not otherwise be able to dispose of, we really engage a portion of the capital and labour of the country in a less advantageous channel than that into which it would naturally have flowed." That system only is beneficial to the world at large, and to each nation individually, under which every commodity is obtained with the least expenditure of time and labour. Were it otherwise, we might as well grow sugar and cotton in English hot-houses, and then flatter ourselves that we were deriving advant-age from the encouragement of home-grown instead of foreign produce!

We come, then, to the conclusion that, in this case, as in every other, the country loses by this exclusive dealing. But who are the gainers? The monopolists. And who are the monopolists? The aristo-cracy. Into their pockets, in the shape of salaries to civil and military officers, dividends of profits, &c., has gone a large part of the enormous revenue of the East India company.[5] Into their pockets goes the great bulk of the extra four millions a year which we pay for Jamaica sugar. Into their pockets has gone the large additional sum annually paid by the nation for coffee and other colonial articles, more than would have been paid but for the protection afforded to West India productions. The colonies, then, do but resolve themselves into another channel, through which the earnings of industry flow into the coffers of idleness. The rich owners of colonial property must have protection, as well as their brethren, the landowners of England – the one their prohibitive duties, the other their corn laws; and the resources of the poor, starved, overburdened people must be still further drained, to augment the overflowing wealth of their rulers.

Secondly, the welfare of the emigrants. In considering this part of the subject, the question may arise – Has not every colonist a claim to protection from the mother country? Custom answers, "Yes." Reason says, "No." Viewed philosophically, a community is a body of men associated together for mutual defence. The members of that community are supposed to occupy a certain territory; and it may be fairly assumed that the privileges conferred are only enjoyed by those residing within that territory. The nation cannot be expected to extend protection to its members wherever they may chance to wander. It cannot be called upon to defend the rights of a citizen in whatever corner of the earth he may choose to locate himself. The natural inference is, that when a man leaves such a community he loses his membership, he forfeits his privileges, and he foregoes all claim to civil assistance. It is presumed that he duly considers, on the one hand, the benefits to be derived by his contemplated emigration, and, on the other, the evils attendant on the loss of citizenship; and that the prospective advantages of a change have the preponderance.

But, waiving the question of right, suppose we examine to what extent the admission of this claim, has, in time past, been of use to the emigrant. Let us inquire how far the history of our colonies, bears evidence of the benefits of this proffered protection. In the declaration of American independence, we have a candid expression

---

[5] See "Wealth of Nations," vol. iii, p. 257. [A. Smith, *An Inquiry into the Nature and Causes of the Wealth of Nations*, London, 1812, 3 Vols.]

of the experience of the settlers on this point; and the document may be referred to, as exhibiting a fair abstract of the effects of home-country governance. Speaking of the king – the personification of the mother country, they say, –

"He has obstructed the administration of justice by refusing his assent to laws for establishing judiciary powers.

"He has erected a multitude of new offices, and sent hither swarms of officers to harass our people, and eat out their substance.

"He has kept among us in times of peace standing armies, without the consent of our legislatures.

"He has combined with others to subject us to a jurisdiction foreign to our constitution, and unacknowledged by our laws: giving his assent to their pretended acts of legislation.

"For quartering large bodies of armed troops among us.

"For protecting them by a mock trial from punishment for any murders which they should commit on the inhabitants of these states.

"For cutting off our trade with all parts of the world.

"For imposing taxes upon us without our consent.

"For depriving us in many cases of the benefits of trial by jury," &c., &c., &c.

Truly we have here, some admirable specimens of the blessings of mother-country protection! Nor are we without analogous instances in our times. The late outbreak in Canada, is a plain indication, of the existence of a similar state of things, to that once experienced by the Americans. And, it is extremely probable, that were we to put it to the Canadians, whether we should continue to take care of them, they would reply, that if it were the same thing to us, they would much rather take care of themselves! We may turn for another example to the settlements in Australia. A living illustration here presents itself, of the evils resulting from the officious interference of our legislature. Thousands of poor emigrants who have been sent out by government, are now without employment, subsisting upon the contributions of the charitable, and almost in a state of starvation. The distress has arisen from the exportation of large bodies of labourers, whilst there has been no corresponding increase in the number of capitalists. Had this colony been left to itself, labour and capital would have kept pace with each other, as they always have done, and always will do; but a meddling state, must needs attempt to regulate the natural laws of society, and hence the calamitous result. Many similar instances,[6] of the injury inflicted upon emigrants, under the pretence of protection, might be quoted, were not those already mentioned sufficiently conclusive.

Thirdly – the interests of the aborigines. A first glance at the bearings of the question, is sufficient to show, that the natives of colonised countries, will meet with much better treatment, at the hands of those settlers, whose emigration has been gradual and unprotected, than from those who are aided by a powerful government, and backed by a military force. In the one case, being the weaker party, the colonists are obliged to stand on their good behaviour, and are induced, through fear, to deal justly with the owners of the soil; in the other, acting upon the barbarous maxim that they have a lawful right to whatever territories they can conquer, forcible possession of the new country, is taken – a continued scene of oppression and bloodshed ensues, and the extermination of the injured race, is, in many cases, the consequence. This is no imaginary picture. Our colonial history, to our shame be it spoken, is full of the injustice and cruelty, to which the original possessors of the soil have been subjected. The extinct tribes of the North American Indians, bear witness of the fact; the gradual retreat of the natives of Australia, may be quoted in support of it; and the miserable condition of the inhabitants of the East Indies, speaks volumes, on the inhumanity attendant upon state colonisation. The ryots, or cultivators of the soil, in Hindostan, are taxed to the extent of nearly one-half of what they produce,[7] and that, by a foreign government, in which they have no voice – which is oppressing them in all directions, and apparently views them as beings created only for the purpose of producing revenue. Another portion of the population is induced to aid our troops, in the support of this despotic government, and whole regiments of them have been put to death, for daring to disobey the tyrannical commands of their oppressors. The recent affair in Affghanistan, affords a further example. Not satisfied with the immense empire

---

[6]   The East and West Indies, cannot be considered as applicable cases, as far as regards the colonists. The greater number of their European inhabitants, are only temporary residents, and nearly all the remainder are either branches of the aristocracy, or their agents, and these are not legislated for as ordinary emigrants.

[7]   See M'Culloch, Art. East India Company. [J. R. McCulloch, 'East India Company's Monopoly – Price of Tea', *Edinburgh Review*, Vol. 39, January 1824, pp. 458–67.]

already within their grasp, our Eastern government, like the wolf in the fable, must needs find a pretext for quarrelling with a neighbouring nation, with the ultimate intention[8] of obtaining possession of their country. And in that war too, some of its officers have been guilty of treachery, of which many a savage would have been ashamed. Thus it is that we exemplify the sublime principles of Christianity.

Having assigned reasons for condemning the artificial system of colonisation, it only remains to inquire, how far the natural system, may be considered feasible. There will be no occasion to enter into any arguments. We may at once appeal to experience, and that experience is conclusive. Pennsylvania affords an admirable example, of a colony originated, and carried out, solely by private enterprise; a colony in which the claims of all parties were duly respected – where natives met with honourable treatment, where strangers as well as friends could obtain justice; a colony that long stood pre-eminent for its prosperity, and which may even now be said to feel the benefits of the liberal conduct of its founders.

The preceding arguments go to prove –

1. That the riches of a country are not increased by great colonial possessions.
2. That the producing classes, both of the colony and the home country, are necessarily injured by any commercial monopoly.
3. That the aristocracy are the only gainers.
4. That emigrants have no claim to protection from the mother country.
5. That where this so-called protection has been given, it has always been converted into an engine for their oppression.
6. That if emigration was carried on by private enterprise, the aborigines, would obviously be less liable to the unjust treatment, which has ever characterised the conduct of civilised settlers towards them.
7. That the case of Pennsylvania, gives ample assurance, of the superiority of the natural system of colonisation.

And hence, that in this case, as well as in those previously discussed, the rejection of legislative interference is eminently desirable.

---

[8] See Sir A. Burns' private and *suppressed* correspondence. [The controversy over Burnes's papers, to which Spencer is referring, is dealt with in J. A. Norris, *The First Afghan War 1838–42*, Cambridge, 1967, pp. 417–22 and 445–8.]

Letter VII.

The question of state interference has been hitherto examined, only in those departments of its application, in which its existing effects are visible – viz., in commerce, religion, charity, war and colonisation. In all of them that interference has been deprecated. It now remains to consider those social institutions which, though at present prospering in their original unfettered simplicity, are threatened by schemes for legislative supervision. Of these the first in importance stands – education.

It is clear that a system of national instruction is excluded by our definition. It cannot be comprehended under the administration of justice. A man can no more call upon the community to educate his children, than he can demand that it shall feed and clothe them. And he may just as fairly claim a continual supply of material food, for the satisfaction of their bodily wants, as of intellectual food, for the satisfaction of their mental ones. It will be the aim of the succeeding arguments to show the advantages of this exclusion.

Mankind are apt to decide upon the means to be employed in the attainment of an end, without sufficient examination into their fitness. Some great object in contemplation, the most obvious mode of securing it is chosen, without duly considering the extreme importance of discovering whether it is the best mode – without ever inquiring whether its ultimate effects may be as good as its immediate ones – without asking what corruptions the machinery of their institution may be liable to – never putting to themselves the question: Is there any other way of arriving at the desideratum? – and neglecting a host of other considerations of like character. Such is the treatment of the question before us. The education of the people is the end in view; an end fraught with results the most momentous – results more intimately connected with the prosperity and happiness of posterity, than, perhaps, any others that may flow from our conduct – results which may accelerate or retard the advancement of mankind for hundreds, perhaps thousands, of years. Yet are there objections, to the method by which this end is to be compassed, of the utmost consequence, that have been entirely overlooked by its advocates – objections fundamentally affecting the principles upon which it rests; and which, if they be admitted as valid, must completely overthrow the whole scheme.

In the first place, national education assumes that a uniform system of instruction is desirable. A general similitude in the kinds of knowledge taught, and the mode of teaching it, must be necessary features in a state-training establishment. The question therefore presents itself – Would a universal fixed plan of intellectual culture be beneficial? After due consideration, I think the general answer will be – No. Almost all men of enlightened views agree that man is essentially a progressive being – that he was intended to be so by the Creator – and that there are implanted in him, desires for improvement, and aspirations after perfection, ultimately tending to produce a higher moral and intellectual condition of the world. The grand facts of history, both sacred and profane – the great principles and promises of revealed religion – the deductions of abstract reasoning – all go to prove that, notwithstanding the oft-repeated falling back, in spite of every difficulty that may be thrown in the way, and in defiance of all apparently adverse circumstances, still, the grand and irresistible law of human existence, is progressive improvement. The very obstacles themselves ultimately serve as stepping stones to a higher condition – the tyranny of an aristocracy is working out the liberties of the people – the corruption of an established church has helped to raise the standard of religious purity – the blindfolding doctrines of priestcraft produce the more perfect discovery, and the still deeper appreciation of the great principles of Christianity – and, as of old, so in our day, the opposition to truth, still tends to accelerate its final triumph. If, then, the belief set forth at the commencement of this essay – that as there are laws for the guidance of the inorganic world – laws for the government of the animate creation – laws for the development of individual mind – so there are laws for the social governance of man – if, I say, this belief be received, it may be fairly assumed, that, in accordance with the great design of human progression, the Almighty has given laws to the general mind, which are ever working together for its advancement. It may be fairly assumed that, in this case as in the more tangible ones, the apparently untoward circumstances are, in reality, eminently conducive to the attainment of the object sought after. That all the prejudices, the mental idiosyncrasies, the love of opposition, the tendencies to peculiar views, and a host of other qualities, in their infinitely varied proportions and combinations, are all conspiring to bring about the intellectual, moral, and social perfection of the human race. If it be granted that man was created a progressive being, it must be granted, also, that the constitution, given to him by his Creator, was the one most perfectly adapted to secure his progression. It may be presumed that, if a uniform construction of mind had been best calculated to attain this end, it would have been adopted; but, as the opposite law has been given – so that, instead of finding minds similar, we find no two alike – unlimited variety, instead of uniformity, being the existing order of things – we must infer that this is the arrangement tending, in the greatest degree, to produce perfection. This conclusion may be supported, not only by abstract reasoning, but by experience. Varied mental constitution produces variety of opinion; different minds take different views of the same subject; hence, every question gets examined in all its bearings; and, out of the general mass of argument, urged forward by antagonist parties, may sound principle be elicited. Truth has ever originated from the conflict of mind with mind; it is the bright spark that emanates from the collision of opposing ideas; like a spiritual Venus, the impersonation of moral beauty, it is born from the foam of the clashing waves of public opinion. Discussion and agitation are the necessary agents of its discovery; and, without a universal dissimilitude in the minds of society, discussion and agitation could never exist.

If, then, it be admitted, that infinite variety in the mental conformation of individuals is essential to the advancement of the general human mind, what shall we say to a system which would train the feelings and intellects of a whole nation after one pattern – which hopes to correct all the irregularities implanted by the Creator, and proposes to take the plastic characters of our youth, and press them, as nearly as possible, into one common mould? And yet this must be the manifest tendency of any uniform routine of education. Natures differently constituted must be gradually brought, by its action, into a condition of similarity. The same influences, working upon successive generations, would presently produce an approximation to a national model. All men would begin to think in the same direction – to form similar opinions upon every subject. One universal bias would affect the mind of society; and, instead of a continual approach to the truth, there would be a gradual divergence from it. Under our present condition, the eccentricities and prejudices induced by one course of education, are neutralised by the opposing tendencies implanted by others; and the growth of the great and truthful features only of the national mind ensues. If, on the other hand, an established system were adopted, however judicious its arrangements might be – notwithstanding it might endeavour to promote liberality and independence of thought, it must eventually produce a general one-sidedness and similarity of character; and inasmuch as it did this, it would dry up the grand source of that spirit of agitation and inquiry, so essential as a stimulus to the improvement of the moral and intellectual man. It matters not what provisions might be made to guard against this evil – what varieties in the mode of instruction might be instituted; such is the general longing after uniformity, and such would be the ignorance of its evils, that we may rest assured no national system would long continue without merging into it.

Nor would this be the only disadvantage arising from a sameness of instruction. It must be remembered, that differently constituted as are the minds of men, each possessing its peculiar perfections and defects, the same mode of culture cannot with any propriety be pursued in all cases. Every character requires a course of treatment somewhat modified to suit its particular circumstances, and no such modifications are ever likely to be made under a national system. It is to be hoped that the time will come, when the wisdom of the teacher will be shown, in adapting his instructions, to the peculiarities of each of his pupils: when it will be his aim to correct this feeling, and to develop the other faculty, and so to train and prune the mind of every scholar, as to send him forth into the world, as perfect a being as possible. Under our present natural arrangement we may one day expect to see this. While the master is amenable to public opinion – while his interests require that he should adopt the most efficient modes of education, we may presume that he will be always zealously endeavouring to improve his methods – ever investigating the principles of his profession, and daily applying the results of those investigations to practice. But no one would ever expect the salaried state-teacher, answerable only to some superior officer, and having no public reputation at stake to stimulate him – no one would expect that he should study the character of each of his scholars, and vary his ordinary routine to suit each case; no one would expect that he should be continually improving, and ever endeavouring to perfect his moral machinery. We may rest assured, that in education as in everything else, the principle of honourable competition, is the only one that can give present satisfaction, or hold out promise of future perfection.

Probably, the existing educational institutions of Prussia and Germany will be appealed to in evidence of the fallacy of these arguments. It may be urged that the plan has been there many years in operation – that no such evils have arisen – that the people are in a comparatively enlightened condition – and that these results, when contrasted with our own, show that we have not made such great advances under the natural system, as they have under the artificial.[9] Strong as this argument may appear, it will be found when closely considered, to be wholly superficial. The foundations of a palace may be hardly above ground, when an ordinary house is nearly complete; but we do not thence infer that the palace will not ultimately be the most magnificent building. It is not argued that because the hothouse plant outstrips its out-door contemporaries, that it will therefore make the most perfect tree; experience teaches the contrary. We do not conclude that the precocious child will make a better man than his less forward companion; we know that the reverse is generally the case. In the same manner, it must be remembered, that although an established education, may, for a time, stimulate the national mind into a rapid growth, we must not therefore presume, that its results will not be ultimately far surpassed by those of the natural system. It is one of the grand laws of creation, that the more perfect the being, the longer must be the time occupied in its development; and analogy would lead us to suppose, that the same may be true of the general mind of man – that the more noble the standard to which it is to attain, the more gradual must be its advancement – the more distant must be the day when it shall arrive at its climax; that the power which is to lead to its highest pinnacle of perfection, must have a broad and deep foundation – must root itself in some fundamental,

---

[9]   Since this was originally published, works have appeared, containing abundant evidence that the boasted intellectual enlightenment produced by government education on the continent, is more than neutralised, by the moral degradation that has accompanied it, and showing that these state-trained nations, are decidedly inferior to the people of this country, in real manliness. Those who are in love with the Prussian system would do well to read Laing's "Notes of a Traveller". [S. Laing, *Notes of a Traveller on the Social and Political State of France, Prussia, Switzerland, Italy, and Other Parts of Europe, During the Present Century*, London, 1842.]

and unchangeable attributes of human nature; and that as its results are to be great, so must its action be slow.

Letter VIII.

An overwhelming prejudice in favour of ancient and existing usages has ever been, and probably will long continue to be, one of the most prominent characteristics of humanity. No matter how totally inconsistent with the existing condition of society – no matter how utterly unreasonable, both in principle and practice – no matter how eminently absurd, in every respect, such institutions or customs may be – still, if they have but the countenance of fashion or antiquity – if they have but been patronised and handed down to us by our forefathers – their glaring inconsistencies, defects, and puerilities, are so completely hidden by the radiant halo wherewith a blind veneration has invested them, that it is almost impossible to open the dazzled eyes of the world, to an unprejudiced view of them. They are reverenced as relics of the so-called "good old times" – reason and philosophy are laid prostrate before them – and the attempt to introduce amendment is akin to sacrilege. Classical education affords a suitable illustration of this. During those dreary times of rampant Roman catholicism, when ecclesiastical dominion had attained its full growth, and all Europe, under its deadly shade, slumbered in dark and debasing ignorance, it became the practice amongst the more enlightened, to make themselves acquainted with the ancient languages, for the purpose of gaining access to the knowledge that was written in them; writings in their own tongue they had none – learning had fallen into neglect, and their only path to a condition above that of the common herd, was through the study of Latin and Greek. In process of time, however, great changes were effected. Man was not doomed to remain for ever in a state of spiritual bondage – the social mind awoke with new vigour from its long sleep – ignorance and bigotry were swept away by the returning tide of intelligence – science and philosophy soared far above the height to which they had before attained – and the knowledge of the ancients dwindled into insignificance, when compared with that of the moderns. It might have been presumed that, under these circumstances, the dead languages would gradually have sunk into disuse. But, no! such is the extreme veneration for precedent – such is the determined adherence to the practices of our ancestors, that, notwithstanding the conditions of the case are entirely altered – although the original necessities no longer exist, still is the same custom persevered in. It boots not to tell them that words are but the signs of ideas, and not the ideas themselves – that language is but a channel for the communication of knowledge – a means to an end; and that it is valuable only in so far as it serves that end. It matters not how clearly it may be shown that he who learns a language for its own sake, is like a workman who constructs a set of tools at immense cost of time and labour, and never afterwards uses them; or like a man who spends the best years of his life in making a ladder, for the purpose of gathering a scanty supply of indifferent fruit from the top of a high tree, when other fruit, of superior quality, is hanging in abundance within reach on a neighbouring one. No matter, I say, how clearly this may be shown, so great is the influence of ancient prescription, and so strong the desire to "do as the world does," that even in this enlightened age, men neglect the rich stores of real knowledge within their grasp, to follow fashion over the barren waste of grammars and lexicons.

Here then stands an example of a system, which, in spite of its many and manifest absurdities, has for centuries bid defiance to the general flood of improvement; and stands in the midst of our progressing social institutions, its main features unaltered from their original condition. What may we infer from this? Does it not warn us of the dangerous consequences that may ensue, from the erection of any lasting scheme of education? If a system, not nationally established, but rooted only in the prejudices, and sheltered by the bias of society, has been able thus to withstand for ages, the assaults of reason and common sense, how much more difficult would it be to reform one, which, in addition to these supporting influences, should receive the protection of the law? It may indeed be provided that the power of remodelling such an establishment be placed in the hands of the people, but practically this would amount to nothing. We have abundant evidence of the almost insuperable difficulties attending the modification of existing institutions, even when the people have theoretically the means of altering them; and we have no right to assume, that these difficulties would not, to a great degree, exist in time to come. Take, for instance, the church. The national body of dissenters are of opinion, that many of its ordinances, services, and ceremonies, require amendment; the great mass of its own communicants think the same; its founders themselves contemplated such a revision; there are no class interests at stake; the amendments alluded to would entail no loss upon the ecclesiastical body; yet, with all these circumstances in favour of a re-arrangement, things remain as they were. How much greater, then, would be the obstacles in reforming an institution, where any extensive change, would probably incapacitate many of its officers?

Even allowing, for a moment, that there would be no great difficulty in introducing improvements into a system of national education; the important question yet remains – Would the people see the necessity for these improvements? Analogy would lead us to answer – No. The blinding effects of prejudice in favour of existing modes of instruction, has already been pointed out, and every day presents us with cases illustrative of the same influence. Ask the classical scholar his opinion of mathematics; or the mathematician what he thinks of geology, chemistry, or physiology, and both their answers will imply a bias in favour of their own kind of education.

It is argued, therefore, that men would never appreciate the imperfections of a mode of teaching, under which they had been brought up; and that even if they did, it would be extremely difficult for them to make any amendments. Should the truth of these conclusions be admitted, there remains but one ground upon which a state education can be defended; namely, the assumption, that it would never require any reform; which is the same thing as saying, that we of the present day, have attained to the pinnacle of mental elevation – that we have duly determined the relative merits of the various kinds of information, and are prepared to point out the most complete scheme of intellectual training – that we are fully competent to decide, not only for ourselves, but for future generations, what are the most valuable branches of knowledge, and what are the best modes of instruction; and that, being perfect masters of the philosophy of mind, we are quite justified in dictating to our successors. Truly a most sensible supposition!

Presuming that all other considerations were favourable, it still behoves us seriously to inquire – What guarantee have we that the beneficial results intended to be secured would, in future ages, be realised? How do we know that the evils and perversions that have never yet been kept out of social institutions by the most perfect human arrangements, would not creep in here also, to the ultimate destruction of the proposed advantages? No satisfactory answer can be given to these questions. We may feel fully convinced, that corruptions and abuses would gradually make their appearance, in defiance of the most carefully regulated provisions for their exclusion – despite of all our endeavours to ensure good management. Again may we turn to the church for an example. Little did our protestant reformers suspect, that the machinery they were about to employ for the support of their religion, was destined to become a tool for political party – an instrument for extortion – a genteel means of gaining a comfortable living – a thing of outside purity and inward depravity – a mere heap of worldliness. True, they had before their eyes the glaring abominations of the church which they had overturned; but they intended to provide against the recurrence of such calamities. And how have they succeeded? As with them, so with us. We may depend upon it that, were the scheme of state instruction carried out, ere a century was expired, we should have educational sinecures, pluralities, non-resident tutors, highly-paid masters, and half-starved teachers, wealthy inspectors, lay patrons, purchasable livings, and numberless other perversions analogous to those of our national church; whilst the whole institution would resolve itself, like its representative, into a field for aristocratic patronage. Surely, if Christianity, the most powerful of all moral antiseptics, has been unable to keep pure, the apparatus devoted to its own ministration; much less can we anticipate freedom from corruption, where the same temptations would exist unopposed by the like preserving influences. It is of no use saying that the people would never again allow such iniquities to be practised. So, in all probability, thought the founders of our state church. But the people *have* allowed them – they *have* had the power to prevent abuses, and have never used it; and we have no right to assume that they would not be equally negligent in time to come.

Another objection, stronger perhaps than any of the foregoing, still remains. The advocates of national education, if they be men who uphold freedom of conscience – if they do not desire one man to pay towards the support of privileges enjoyed only by others – in a word, if they are friends to civil and religious liberty, must necessarily assume that all members of the community, whether churchmen or dissenters, catholics or jews, tories, whigs, radicals, or republicans, will agree, one and all, to support whatever system may be finally adopted. For, if their education is to be truly a national one, it must be managed by the government, and sustained by state funds; those funds must form part of the revenue; that revenue is raised by taxation; that taxation falls upon every individual – upon him that has no children as well as upon him that has; and the result must be, that all would pay towards the maintenance of such an institution, whether they had need of it or not – whether they approved of it or otherwise. Many would, on principle, dissent from a state education, as they would from a state church. Some men would disapprove of the species of instruction – others of the mode of teaching. This man would dislike the moral training – that the intellectual. Here they would disagree upon details – and there protest against the entire system. Would it then be just, would it be reasonable, to let these men bear the burden of an institution from which they derived no benefit? Surely not. Every argument used by religious nonconformists to show the unfairness of calling upon them to uphold doctrines that they cannot countenance, or subscribe towards a ministration which they do not attend, is equally effective in proving the injustice of compelling men to assist in the maintenance of a plan of instruction inconsistent with their principles; and forcing them to pay for teaching, from which neither they nor their children derive any benefit. In the one case, the spread of religious knowledge is the object aimed at – in the other the spread of secular knowledge; and how this difference could affect the right of dissent it would be difficult to discover.

Before dismissing the subject, it may be as well to remark that, rather than see the people educated by means over which they have no control, our government would, no doubt, be very happy to take the task of instruction into their own hands; and we may pretty accurately anticipate what the tendencies of that instruction would be. Bold and independent reasoning, originality of thought, firmness in defence of principles, and all characteristics of that class, we need little expect to be encouraged. Great veneration for authority, a high respect for superiors, and implicit faith in the opinions of the great and learned, would no doubt be studiously inculcated. As for their religious education, we may predict that such virtues as meekness and humility would occupy so much attention as to leave no time for the rest; and we may be sure that the teachers would take especial care to instil into the minds of their pupils all those important and fundamental principles of our religion, such as – "Let every soul be subject to the higher powers" – "Servants be obedient to your masters" – "Learn to be content in that station of life to which it has pleased God to call you;" and other such appropriate selections.[10] An apt illustration of the species of mental training our rulers would patronise, is afforded by the late parliamentary grant for teaching singing. Truly, it would be a lucky thing for the aristocracy, if the people could be persuaded to cultivate their voices instead of their understandings. The nation asks for cheap bread. Their rulers reply – No, we cannot give you cheap bread, because we should lose part of our rents; but, never mind, we will put aside part of your own money to give you lessons in music! We will not give you back your food, but we will teach you to sing! O generous legislators!

The objections to national education are –

1. That it necessarily involves a uniform system of moral and intellectual training, from which the destruction of that variety of character, so essential to a national activity of mind, would inevitably result.

2. That it takes away the grand stimulus to exertion and improvement on the part of the teacher, that must ever exist under the natural arrangement.

3. That, considering the improbability of amendments being introduced in future ages, it practically assumes that we are capable of pointing out to our descendants, what kinds of knowledge are the most valuable, and what are the best modes of acquiring them – an assumption which is anything but true.

4. That it would be liable to the same perversions as a national religion, and would, in all probability, become ultimately as corrupt.

5. That, if it is intended to be an equitable institution, it must be necessarily presumed that all men will agree to adopt it – a presumption which can never be borne out.

6. That it would be used by government as a means of blinding the people – of repressing all aspirations after better things – and of keeping them in a state of subserviency.

From abstract reasoning, and from the evident analogy with existing institutions, it is, therefore, concluded, that national education would, in the end, be a curse, rather than a blessing.

[10] That such prophecies would be realised may be gathered from Sir James Graham's late Education bill, which has run its brief career since these remarks first appeared.

Letter IX.

"That it is the duty of the state to adopt measures for protecting the health, as well as the property, of its subjects," is the fundamental principle espoused by the Eastern Medical association of Scotland. The majority of the medical profession hold the same opinion; a respectable portion of the public at large apparently agree with them; and, judging by the enactments that have from time to time been made, the state itself admits the truth of the doctrine. The position is a very plausible one. Some of the arguments urged on its behalf appear, at first sight, decisive. And great seem the evils that might result from the exclusion of legislative control, over matters affecting the sanitary state of the nation. The question, therefore, demands a careful consideration.

An advocate of an established church, may reasonably support this proposition. He maintains that it is one of the duties of a government, to look after the spiritual welfare of the community; that it ought not to permit unauthorised persons to administer to the religious necessities of their fellow-creatures, lest they should instil false doctrines; that without legislative supervision, the moral atmosphere of society would be vitiated by the contagious breath of wickedness; in short, that state superintendence is essential to the spiritual sanity of the nation. Holding these opinions, he may fairly employ similar arguments in reference to the physical condition of the body politic. He may submit that it is improper to allow unqualified persons to administer to the corporeal ailments of the people lest they should prescribe deleterious medicines, or give dangerous advice; that, in default of legal regulations, the air of our populous towns would become impure from want of ventilation, or be contaminated by the malaria arising from uncleansed sewers, and other sources of corruption; in a word, that government interference is necessary to the preservation of the public health. The analogy between these arguments is obvious. But how stands the dissenter affected towards them? Denying, as he does, their cogency in the one case, he cannot consistently admit it in the other. In the first instance, the spiritual health of the people is the object in view; in the second, their bodily health; and the reasoning that is employed to show that legislation is not required in the one case, will go far to prove its needlessness in the other.

One would have thought that in these anti-monopoly days, when the calamities resulting from selfish legislation have awakened public attention, men would take especial care not to permit anything involving an approach to exclusive privileges, to make its appearance upon the political arena, without raising a vigorous outcry against it. But the expectation is not realised. The doctrine that it is the duty of the state to protect the public health, contains the germ of another gigantic monopoly. Years ago did that germ first show itself, in the shape of an enactment for restricting the prescribing practice of chemists and druggists. Again, is the noxious parasite gathering together its energies, to make another and a stronger shoot, under the form of a more stringent law for the same purpose. That object gained, and some greater extension of power will be its aim. Already do the professional publications of the day, contain rumours of medical directors, medical inspectors, and various grades of officers, to be appointed as overseers of the public health. Willingly will the aristocracy come forward and lend a helping hand to so promising a project – one that holds out so inviting a prospect of more berths for their younger sons; and happy will they be to patronise an institution, which shall thus serve as another medium for the absorption of the nation's wealth. In this way, if the people permit, will the system unfold itself, and may, in the lapse of a few generations, finally saddle itself upon the public after the manner of a national church.

It is needless, however, to enter into any arguments to show that medical men are endeavouring to establish a monopoly, for they publicly acknowledge it. They openly avow that they are seeking for protection, and boldly maintain that they have a right to it. But then, it is all done out of a friendly desire to defend the public against quackery! And, in proof of the benefits that the nation is to derive from this exclusive dealing, these patterns of disinterestedness, hold forth upon the danger of allowing the illiterate to be gulled by unlicensed practitioners. Hear Mr Wakley. Speaking of a recently revived law relating to chemists and druggists – he says, "It must have the effect of checking, to a vast extent, that frightful evil called counter practice, exercised by unqualified persons, which has so long been a disgrace to the operation of the laws relating to medicine in this country, and which, doubtless, has been attended with a dreadful sacrifice of human life." (*Lancet* for Sept. 11, 1841). And again, "There is not a chemist and druggist in the empire who would refuse to prescribe in his own shop in medical cases, or who would hesitate day by day to prescribe simple remedies for the ailments of infants and children." ... "We had previously considered the evil to be of enormous magnitude, but it is quite clear that we had underestimated the extent of the danger to which the public are exposed." (*Lancet* for Oct. 16, 1841.) One hardly knows how sufficiently to admire the great penetration that has discovered this "evil of enormous magnitude," so completely overlooked by society at large. Truly, it affords matter for much wonderment, that the "dreadful sacrifice of human life," resulting from this "frightful evil," has never yet opened men's eyes to a sense of the great "danger" of their situation. But would it not have been more prudent, if this grand discovery had been made public, and the agitation carried forward by unprofessional persons? Mr Wakley should remember, that we are told to avoid the appearance of evil, and he may discover to his cost, that the world is so suspicious, as to ascribe these seeming fruits of patriotic feeling to some less noble origin. And why does Mr Wakley stop short of the full extent of his principle? If it is really the duty of the state to take care of the public health, it is surely bound to adopt the most efficient means of fulfilling that duty. Why not then act upon the old adage, that "prevention is better than cure," endeavour to keep the people always well? Enact a national dietary – prescribe so many meals a day for each individual – fix the quantities and qualities of food, both for men and women, how much animal and how much vegetable – state the proportion of fluids; when to be taken, and of what kind – specify the amount of exercise, and define its character – describe the clothing to be employed – determine the hours of sleep, allowing for the difference of age and sex, and so on with all other particulars, necessary to complete a perfect synopsis, for the daily guidance of the nation. Surely this would be much more efficient than any of these half measures, and, in principle, much about as reasonable. If you insist upon a man getting rid of his ailments according to law, you may as well endeavour to keep him in health by law also.

But seriously, all legislation of the kind desired by Mr Wakley and his colleagues, virtually, rests upon the assumption, that men are not fitted to take care of themselves. It treats them as so many children. It puts the people into leading strings. Poor things! if we do not look after them, they will be going to ignorant quacks for advice, and, perhaps, get poisoned! Such is practically the language of the state towards its subjects, and the longer they are treated in this manner, the more helpless will they become. If any one foolishly chooses, for the sake of saving a little money, to employ an uneducated empiric he must take the consequences, be they what they may. He has acted under the guidance of his own free will, and, if he suffers, he has no one to blame but himself. Imagine a man to have a watch that wants repairing; and, suppose that, from considerations of economy, he takes it to a blacksmith, who tells him that he can rectify it – the blacksmith spoils it – the man is angry – complains that he has been ill used – enlists a number of the mawkishly benevolent upon his side, and gets them to petition parliament, that all blacksmiths be in future prevented from repairing watches. Who would not laugh at such foolishness? The man was in fault for putting his watch into such hands, and richly deserved the reward of his stupidity. Yet the case is perfectly parallel to the one before us. Instead of his timepiece, he takes himself (a much more complicated machine) to be repaired – he applies to one who knows as little about the human frame, as a blacksmith does about a watch – the ignorant pretender prescribes – the patient gets no better – by and by his constitution is permanently injured, and perhaps he becomes an invalid for life – that is, instead of having his watch spoiled, he has been spoiled himself. But what then? The consequence may be more serious in the one case than in the other, but the man has no greater right to complain. If he had exercised his reason, he might have known, that it was as silly to put his body under the care of one who did not understand its mechanism, as to give a chronometer into the hands of a blacksmith; and there is abstractly no more ground for legislative interference to guard against such imprudence in the one instance than in the other.

A large class of officiously humane people, can never see any social evil, but they propose to pass some law for its future prevention. It never strikes them that the misfortunes of one are lessons for thousands – that the world generally learns more by its mistakes than by its successes – and that it is by the continual endeavour to avoid errors, difficulties, and dangers, that society is to become wiser. It is not for a moment denied that many individuals have been injured by druggists' prescriptions, and quack medicines – some temporarily weakened – others permanently debilitated – and a few perhaps killed outright. But, admitting this, it does not follow that it is not the wisest in the end, to let things take their own course. Such conduct may at first sight appear unkind, but when its effects upon future generations are considered, it will be found to be the reverse. Many arrangements in the animal creation cause much suffering and death; but we do not thence infer that the Almighty is unmerciful. Investigation explains the anomaly, and shows us that these apparent evils are collateral results of laws, ultimately tending to produce the greatest amount of health and happiness, and a careful consideration will satisfy us, that the pains inflicted upon human beings by their own imprudence, are of like character.

There is yet another position from which this question may be considered, and one, perhaps, whence the clearest and most extended view of it can be obtained. All legislation which assists the people in the satisfaction of their natural wants – which provides a fund for their maintenance in illness and old age, educates their children, takes care of their religious instruction, looks after their bodily health, or in any other way does for them what they may be fairly expected to do for themselves, arises from a radically wrong understanding of human existence. It wholly neglects the condition of man's earthly being, and altogether loses sight of one of the great and universal laws of creation.

Every animate creature stands in a specific relation to the external world in which it lives. From the meanest zoophyte, up to the most highly organised of the vertebrata, one and all have certain fixed principles of existence. Each has its varied bodily wants to be satisfied – food to be provided for its proper nourishment – a habitation to be constructed for shelter from the cold, or for defence against enemies – now arrangements to be made for bringing up a brood of young, nests to be built, little ones to be fed and fostered – then a store of provisions to be laid in against winter, and so on, with a variety of other natural desires to be gratified. For the performance of all these operations, every creature has its appropriate organs and instincts – external apparatus and internal faculties; and the health and happiness of each being, are bound up with the perfection and activity of these powers. They, in their turn, are dependent upon the position in which the creature is placed. Surround it with circumstances which preclude the necessity for any one of its faculties, and that faculty will become gradually impaired. Nature provides nothing in vain. Instincts and organs are only preserved so long as they are required. Place a tribe of animals in a situation where one of their attributes is unnecessary – take away its natural exercise – diminish its activity, and you will gradually destroy its power. Successive generations will see the faculty, or instinct, or whatever it may be, become gradually weaker, and an ultimate degeneracy of the race will inevitably ensue. All this is true of man. He, in like manner, has wants, many and varied – he is provided with moral and intellectual faculties, commensurate with the complexity of his relation to the external world – his happiness essentially depends upon the activity of those faculties; and with him, as with all the rest of the creation, that activity is chiefly influenced by the requirements of his condition. The demands made upon his mental powers by his every day wants – by the endeavour to overcome difficulties or avoid dangers, and by the desire to secure a comfortable provision for the decline of life, are so many natural and salutary incentives to the exercise of those powers. Imperious necessity is the grand stimulus to man's physical and mental endowments, and without it he would sink into a state of hopeless torpidity. Establish a poor law to render his forethought and self-denial unnecessary – enact a system of national education to take the care of his children off his hands – set up a national church to look after his religious wants – make laws for the preservation of his health, that he may have less occasion to look after it himself – do all this, and he may then, to a great extent, dispense with the faculties that the Almighty has given to him. Every powerful spring of action is destroyed – acuteness of intellect is not wanted – force of moral feeling is never called for – the higher powers of his mind are deprived of their natural exercise, and a gradual deterioration of character must ensue. Take away the demand for exertion, and you will ensure inactivity. Induce inactivity, and you will soon have degradation.

The reader will therefore observe –

1. That the dissenter cannot consistently admit that the state should have the care of the bodily health of the people, when he denies that it has anything to do with their spiritual health.
2. That the warmest supporters of this theory of government superintendence, are only making it a blind for another monopoly.
3. That no man has a claim upon the legislature to take that care of his health which he will not take himself.
4. That in this case, as in every other, to do for the people what

they are naturally fitted to do for themselves, is to adopt one of the most efficient means of lowering the standard of national character.

Letter X.

Had our governors always taken care, duly to perform their original, and all-important functions – had the administration of justice ever stood pre-eminent in their eyes – had it at all times been considered as the one thing needful – and had no other questions ever been entertained at its expense, then might their interference, in matters with which they had no concern, have been more excusable. But it is not so. To the long list of their sins of commission, we have to add the sin of omission; and most grievously has the nation suffered from their neglect, as well as from their officiousness.

Describe to an unbiassed arbitrator the relationship existing between a people and a government. Tell him that the legislature is a body deputed by the nation to keep order, to protect person and property, and that these are its most important, if not its only duties. Tell him that every man practically gives in his allegiance to this body – that he annually pays towards its support a considerable portion of his earnings – that he sacrifices to it his personal independence – and that he does these things, in the expectation of receiving from it, the advantages of that protection, which it is presumed to give in return for such deprivations. Explain all this, and then ask him to state, in what manner he should expect the government, to fulfil its part of the contract. He would say that when the subjects had paid their taxes, and submitted themselves to the authorities, they had done all that could be required of them – that it remained with those authorities to carry home to every man the benefits of civil order – that the revenue was subscribed by the people for the express purpose of defraying the charges of this protective establishment – and that, after men had thus prepaid the government, it would be a most unjust proceeding for that government to put them to additional expense whenever it was called upon to perform its duty towards them. From these considerations he would infer that it behoved the state to establish courts of justice, which should be easy of access, speedy in their decisions, and in which every man should be able to obtain the protection of the law, free of cost. Such is the obviously equitable conclusion at which a conscientious umpire would arrive. How widely different from the reality! Our legislators tax the people to a most exorbitant extent; squander the money thus wrested from the toiling artisan in the support of institutions for the benefit of the rich; maintain, by its aid, standing armies to ensure popular subjection; and, when the misused subject demands of the government that it defend him in the exercise of his rights and privileges – when he asks it to fulfil the duties for which it was instituted – when he requests it to do for him that for which he has already paid it so extravagantly – what is its conduct? Does it willingly and efficiently respond to his demand? Does it, without further reward, fully and fairly administer the laws? Does it send forth its officers, commanding them diligently to secure to every one, that protection, which he has sacrificed so much to obtain? Does it take up the cause of the poor man, and defend him against the aggressions of his rich neighbour? No! it does none of these things. It turns over the complainant to the tender mercies of solicitors, attorneys, barristers, and a whole legion of law officers. It drains his purse with charges for writs, briefs, affidavits, subpœnas, fees of all kinds, and expenses innumerable. It involves him in all the mazy intricacies of common courts, chancery courts, suits, counter-suits, and appeals; and thousands of times has it overwhelmed with irretrievable ruin, the man whose person and property it was bound to defend. And this is our "glorious constitution!"

We pity the poor subjects of oriental despotism. We view their absolute form of government with contempt. We turn from it to contemplate what we call our "free institutions" with pride, and congratulate ourselves upon the superiority of our condition. Yet might these autocrat-ridden people hold up to the world's scorn, the results of our seemingly "free institutions." Many and many a case could they point out in this "land of liberty," of misery and famine, inflicted by the rich man's tyranny – of wrongs endured, because money was wanting wherewith to purchase redress – of rights unclaimed, because contention with the powerful usurper was useless – aye, hundreds upon hundreds might they find, whose hollow cheeks and tattered clothing, could bear testimony to the delusiveness of English justice. And then, by way of contrast, they could tell of the active and even-handed legislation of many an absolute monarch. Countless examples might they point out, of justice freely and fairly administered by Eastern sultans – instances where the poor and weak could pour their tales of tyranny into the ear of the monarch himself, and obtain assistance – where wealth and interest were not required to secure protection; neither were any shield to the oppressor. Fie upon Englishmen that they should still continue to praise and venerate a mere shadow – to pride and congratulate themselves upon the possession of what is daily demonstrated to be a hollow mockery! How long will men allow themselves to be cheated by an empty name? Not only has our government done those things which it ought not to have done, but it has left undone those things which it ought to have done; and truly may it be said that there is no health in it.

Let us, therefore, bear in mind that, by permitting our rulers to spend their time and our money in the management of matters over which they ought to have no control, we not only entail upon ourselves, the evils arising from their mischievous legislation, but likewise those resulting from the neglect of their real duties.

Letter XI.

A few remarks upon an important collateral topic, in so far as it is affected by the solution of the question in hand, may not be here out of place. The enfranchisement of the working classes is the topic alluded to.

With that large class of men, whose conclusions are determined by the dictates of expediency, rather than by the demands of justice, one of the objections to an investment of power in the hands of the people, is this – "Society is a complicated machine; the interests of its members are many and various, and so mysteriously connected and intertwined with each other, that it requires deep sagacity, and clearness of intellect, fully to comprehend and appreciate their multiplied relations. Legislation has for one of its objects, the proper regulation of these conflicting interests; and such is the difficulty of keeping everything in equilibrium, that even our most profound statesmen have been baffled in the attempt, Would it then, be prudent, to give to the uneducated classes, the power of directing the legislature in matters so difficult to understand, yet so important to the public welfare?"

Now, if it should turn out that these complex and manifold interests require no regulation at all, but that they are originally so arranged as to regulate themselves – if it should be discovered that the great difficulties encountered in the management of social concerns, arise from the disturbance of natural laws, and that governments have been foolishly endeavouring to maintain, in a condition of *unstable* equilibrium, things which, if let alone, would of themselves assume a condition of *stable* equilibrium; then must the objection be to a great extent invalidated. That the affairs of the nation are in circumstances of dreadful embarrassment, and that it may take some skill to bring them back to their normal state, is not denied; but, whilst it can be shown that this disastrous effect has resulted – not from want of legislation, but from over legislation – not from any intellectual deficiency on the part of our law-makers, but from their everlasting selfish interference – the fact can afford no argument against complete suffrage. Take an illustration. Imagine some poor unlucky wight to be persuaded by his doctor that he could never enjoy perfect health without medical superintendence – that his digestion would not go on properly without stimulants – that he must take pectoral pills to keep his lungs in order – that he must swallow, now and then, a sudorific, to sustain the functions of his skin, and so on: and suppose that, in the abundance of his faith, our patient puts himself under the direction of this learned physician; and, in obedience to his orders, gulps down, day by day, one dose of medicine after another – first, an aperient to rectify his digestive organs, and then a tonic to strengthen them – now a vapour bath to augment his perspiration, and again a diuretic to diminish it – this week eats abundance of nourishing food to increase his energies, and the next parts with a few ounces of blood to guard against plethora – and so on, through a long course of medical treatment, taking in their turns, emetics, anodynes, cathartics, opiates, febrifuges, and alternatives, together with a due proportion of topical applications, such as plasters, blisters, liniments, emollients, and so forth. And when, after all this doctoring, the poor fellow has been brought to such a pass, as to be for ever going wrong in some way or other, and is continually requiring the attendance of his physician, to remove this pain and to rectify the other distemper – when he has come to such a state, that he no sooner gets rid of one malady, than he is seized with another, imagine this professor of the healing art to gather round the sick man's bed-side a cluster of country clowns, and begin to harangue them upon the various and complicated functions of the human body, describing to them its numerous organs, and their individual duties, the manifold disorders to which they are liable, and the difficulties of their cure; and then, to add point to his lecture, fancy him turning to his patient, and saying, "See what a difficult thing it is to keep a man in health!" Why, even John Bull, with all his gullibility, would smile at this. And yet, when the same thing is said of society – when the invalid is a nation instead of a man, he believes it. Our state physicians have, from time immemorial, persuaded the people that social affairs would never go right without their interference; that a vigilant supervision was necessary to secure the healthy fulfilment of all the national functions; and, in accordance with all these notions, they have been for ever doctoring the affairs of the country; now prescribing a lower diet under the name of "restrictive duties," and then letting in a surfeit of food to make up for past privations – at one time administering a stimulus to exercise, styled "encouragement to home manufactures," and at another, raising an outcry for some remedy against over-production – here providing a tonic for the nation's morals, called a "national church," and there creating a war, to prevent those morals acquiring undue strength – on one part of the social body, applying a soothing ointment, in the shape of a 'poor law,' and on another, inflicting an extensive bleeding, under the form of an "income tax." And when, after all these transcendently skilful operations, the nation has been brought almost to the brink of dissolution – when its debility is showing itself in the most alarming forms – when its constitution is so weakened that it is hardly possible to cure one of its disorders without producing a worse – when, in short, it is in the state in which we now see it, we hear these sage and self-complacent legislators exclaim, "See what a difficult thing it is to govern a country!"

If, then, it be admitted, that our national misfortunes have not arisen from the difficulties inherent in the nature of government, but from the determination to legislate when no legislation was required, that is, if it be admitted that the administration of justice, is the sole duty of the state, we are at once relieved from one of the greatest objections, to the enfranchisement of the working classes.

Letter XII.

A brief review of the arguments that have been set forth in the foregoing letters many serve to place the general question more distinctly before the mind.

Having shown that the proposed definition of state duties was in exact accordance with the primitive requirements of society – was, in fact, theoretically derived from them, and that its derivation did not countenance the universal interference now permitted; an attempt was made to exhibit some of the chief advantages that would arise out of the restoration of our various social institutions to their original freedom from legislative control; in the course of which it was argued:–

1. That all commercial restrictions have been proved, both by past and present experience, to be eminently inimical to social prosperity; that necessity is fast forcing us towards free trade, and that we must ultimately return to the perfect commercial liberty dictated by nature, from which we should never have diverged, had there been a proper limitation of state power.

2. That a national church is to be deprecated, not only as being unnecessary to the spread of religion, but as opposing, by its worldliness, corruption, and uncharitableness, a barrier to its progress; that, on the showing of its own ministers, it is totally incapable of Christianising the nation, seeing that by the vital importance they attach to a state-paid priesthood, they practically admit that they have themselves imbibed so little Christian spirit that their own ministry would cease were it not for its emoluments; and hence in so far as the definition involves the disseverment of church and state, it is advantageous.

3. That a poor law, though apparently a boon to the working classes, is in reality a burden to them; that it delays the rectification of social abuses; that it discourages the exercise of genuine benevolence; that compulsory relief is degrading alike to the giver and to the receiver; that voluntaryism is equally applicable in the practice of religion as in its ministry; and that the blessings of charity would be secured unaccompanied by the evils of pauperism were the legislature prevented from meddling.

4. That war is universally admitted to be a great evil; that it is our duty as Christians to adopt all feasible means of putting an end

to it; and that restricting governments, to the fulfilment of their primitive functions, and thereby depriving them of the power of invasion, would be the most effectual means of preventing it.

5. That artificial colonisation is injurious in each of its several influences; that colonial trade has always been turned into a monopoly for the benefit of the aristocracy; that the pretended protection given to the settlers has generally proved a great curse to them; that the original possessors of the soil have ever been cruelly persecuted in state-established colonies; and that the case of Pennsylvania affords satisfactory evidence of the superiority of that voluntary, unprotected, emigration, that must follow from the recognition of the proposed principle.

6. That a national education would tend to destroy that variety and originality of mind so essential to social progress; that it would discourage improvement by annihilating healthy competition, and by placing in the way of reform the difficulties of institutional changes, in addition to the obstacles arising from natural prejudice in favour of existing modes of instruction; that we have no guarantee for its future efficiency, and have every reason to believe that it would ultimately become as corrupt as a national religion: that the mode of its support, involving as it must, the taxation of the whole community, consentients and dissentients, would be manifestly unjust; and that a constitution which necessarily excludes it, thereby commends itself to our adoption.

7. That the zealous advocacy, by certain medical men, of enactments for the preservation of the public health, arises from interested motives; that the health of the people is no more a subject for legislation than their religion; that no man can reasonably require the state to take that care of his body which he will not take himself; and that in this case as in every other, to do for the people what the Almighty has intended them to do for themselves, is infallibly to lower them in the scale of creation.

8. That by confining the attention of government to the preservation of order, and the protection of person and property, we should not only avoid the many injuries inflicted on us by its officious interferences, but should likewise secure the proper performance of its all-important, though now neglected duties.

Such are the evidences which have been adduced in favour of the theorem, that the administration of justice is the sole duty of the state. Others might be added, did it seem desirable. It is hoped, however, that those already set forth, if not of themselves sufficient to create in candid minds the conviction of its truth, will at least so far serve to exhibit its probability, as to beget for it a serious examination.

In conclusion, it will be well to remind the reader, that whatever may be the result of his deliberations upon this momentous question – whether he agrees with the arguments that have been brought forward, or dissents from them – whether he acknowledges the legitimacy of the deductions, or decides against them – one thing is certain. A definition of the duty of the state there must be. It needs no argument to prove that there is a boundary beyond which no legislative control should pass – that there are individual and social requirements whose fulfilment will be better secured by moral stimulus and voluntary exertion, than by any artificial regulations – that between the two extremes of its possible power, the *everything* and the *nothing* with which a government might be entrusted, there must be some point which both principle and policy indicate as its proper limitation. This point, this boundary, it behoves every man to fix for himself; and if he disagrees with the definition, as above expressed, consistency demands that he should make one for himself. If he wishes to avoid the imputation of political empiricism, he must ascertain the nature and intent of that national organ called the legislature, ere he seeks to prescribe its actions. Before he ventures to entertain another opinion upon what a government should *do*, he must first settle for himself the question – What is a government *for?*

THE MAN *VERSUS* THE STATE

Preface

The *Westminster Review* for April 1860, contained an article entitled "Parliamentary Reform: the Dangers and the Safeguards." In that article I ventured to predict some results of political changes then proposed.

Reduced to its simplest expression, the thesis maintained was that, unless due precautions were taken, increase of freedom in form would be followed by decrease of freedom in fact. Nothing has occurred to alter the belief I then expressed. The drift of legislation since that time has been of the kind anticipated. Dictatorial measures, rapidly multiplied, have tended continually to narrow the liberties of individuals; and have done this in a double way. Regulations have been made in yearly-growing numbers, restraining the citizen in directions where his actions were previously unchecked, and compelling actions which previously he might perform or not as he liked; and at the same time heavier public burdens, chiefly local, have further restricted his freedom, by lessening that portion of his earnings which he can spend as he pleases, and augmenting the portion taken from him to be spent as public agents please.

The causes of these foretold effects, then in operation, continue in operation – are, indeed, likely to be strengthened; and finding that the conclusions drawn respecting these causes and effects have proved true, I have been prompted to set forth and emphasize kindred conclusions respecting the future, and do what little may be done towards awakening attention to threatened evils.

For this purpose were written the four following articles, originally published in the *Contemporary Review* for February, April, May, June and July of this year. To meet certain criticisms and to remove some of the objections likely to be raised, I have now added a postscript.

Bayswater, July, 1884

The New Toryism

Most of those who now pass as Liberals, are Tories of a new type. This is a paradox which I propose to justify. That I may justify it, I must first point out what the two political parties originally were; and I must then ask the reader to bear with me while I remind him of facts he is familiar with, that I may impress on him the intrinsic natures of Toryism and Liberalism properly so called.

Dating back to an earlier period than their names, the two political parties at first stood respectively for two opposed types of social organization, broadly distinguishable as the militant and the industrial – types which are characterized, the one by the *régime* of status, almost universal in ancient days, and the other by the *régime* of contract, which has become general in modern days, chiefly among the Western nations, and especially among ourselves and the Americans. If, instead of using the word "co-operation" in a limited sense, we use it in its widest sense, as signifying the combined activities of citizens under whatever system of regulation; then these two are definable as the system of compulsory co-operation and the system of voluntary co-operation. The typical structure of the one we see in an army formed of conscripts, in which the units in their several grades have to fulfil commands under pain of death, and receive food and clothing and pay, arbitrarily apportioned; while the typical structure of the other we see in a body of producers or distributors, who severally agree to specified payments in return for specified services, and may at will, after due notice, leave the organization if they do not like it.

During social evolution in England, the distinction between these two fundamentally-opposed forms of co-operation, made its appearance gradually; but long before the names Tory and Whig came into use, the parties were becoming traceable, and their connexions with militancy and industrialism respectively, were vaguely shown. The truth is familiar that, here as elsewhere, it was habitually by town-populations, formed of workers and traders accustomed to co-operate under contract, that resistances were made to that coercive rule which characterizes co-operation under status. While, conversely, co-operation under status, arising from, and adjusted to, chronic warfare, was supported in rural districts, originally peopled by military chiefs and their dependents, where the primitive ideas and traditions survived. Moreover, this contrast in political leanings, shown before Whig and Tory principles became clearly distinguished, continued to be shown afterwards. At the period of the Revolution, "while the villages and smaller towns were monopolized by Tories, the larger cities, the manufacturing districts, and the ports of commerce, formed the strongholds of the Whigs." And that, spite of exceptions, the like general relation still exists, needs no proving.

Such were the natures of the two parties as indicated by their origins. Observe, now, how their natures were indicated by their early doctrines and deeds. Whiggism began with resistance to Charles II. and his cabal, in their efforts to re-establish unchecked monarchical power. The Whigs "regarded the monarchy as a civil institution, established by the nation for the benefit of all its members;" while with the Tories "the monarch was the delegate of heaven." And these doctrines involved the beliefs, the one that subjection of citizen to ruler was conditional, and the other that it was unconditional. Describing Whig and Tory as conceived at the end of the seventeenth century, some fifty years before he wrote his *Dissertation on Parties*, Bolingbroke says:–

"The power and majesty of the people, an original contract, the authority and independency of Parliaments, liberty, resistance, exclusion, abdication, deposition; these were ideas associated, at that time, to the idea of a Whig, and supposed by every Whig to be incommunicable, and inconsistent with the idea of a Tory.

"Divine, hereditary, indefeasible right, lineal succession, passive-obedience, prerogative, non-resistance, slavery, nay, and sometimes popery too, were associated in many minds to the idea of a Tory, and deemed incommunicable and inconsistent, in the same manner, with the idea of a Whig."

Dissertation on Parties, p. 5 [1735, p. 4].

And if we compare these descriptions, we see that in the one party there was a desire to resist and decrease the coercive power of the ruler over the subject, and in the other party to maintain or increase his coercive power. This distinction in their aims – a distinction which transcends in meaning and importance all other political distinctions – was displayed in their early doings. Whig principles were exemplified in the Habeas Corpus Act, and in the measure by which judges were made independent of the Crown; in defeat of the Non-Resisting Test Bill, which proposed for legislators and officials a compulsory oath that they would in no case resist the king by arms; and, later, they were exemplified in the Bill of Rights, framed to secure subjects against monarchical aggressions. These Acts had the same intrinsic nature. The principle of compulsory co-operation throughout social life was weakened by them, and the principle of voluntary co-operation strengthened. That at a subsequent period the policy of the party had the same general tendency, is well shown by a remark of Mr. Green concerning the period of Whig power after the death of Anne:–

"Before the fifty years of their rule had passed, Englishmen had forgotten that it was possible to persecute for differences of religion, or to put down the liberty of the press, or to tamper with the administration of justice, or to rule without a Parliament."

Short History, p. 705.
[J. R. Green, *Short History of the English People*, London, 1874. The (later) editions which I have been able to consult have 'opinion' in place of 'religion'.]

And now, passing over the war-period which closed the last century and began this, during which that extension of individual freedom previously gained was lost, and the retrograde movement towards the social type proper to militancy was shown by all kinds of coercive measures, from those which took by force the persons and property of citizens for war-purposes to those which suppressed public meetings and sought to gag the press, let us recall the general characters of those changes effected by Whigs or Liberals after the re-establishment of peace permitted revival of the industrial *régime* and return to its appropriate type of structure. Under growing Whig influence there came repeal of the laws forbidding combinations among artisans, as well as of those which interfered with their freedom of travelling. There was the measure by which, under Whig pressure, Dissenters were allowed to believe as they pleased without suffering certain civil penalties; and there was the Whig measure, carried by Tories under compulsion, which enabled Catholics to profess their religion without losing part of their freedom. The area of liberty was extended by Acts which forbade the buying of negroes and the holding of them in bondage. The East India Company's monopoly was abolished, and trade with the East made open to all. The political serfdom of the unrepresented was narrowed in area, both by the Reform Bill and the Municipal Reform Bill; so that alike generally and locally, the many were less under the coercion of the few. Dissenters, no longer obliged to submit to the ecclesiastical form of marriage, were made free to wed by a purely civil rite. Later came diminution and removal of restraints on the buying of foreign commodities and the employment of foreign vessels and foreign sailors; and later still the removal of those burdens on the press which were originally imposed to hinder the diffusion of opinion. And of all these changes it is unquestionable that, whether made or not by Liberals themselves, they were made in conformity with principles professed and urged by Liberals.

But why do I enumerate facts so well known to all? Simply because, as intimated at the outset, it seems needful to remind everybody what Liberalism was in the past, that they may perceive its unlikeness to the so-called Liberalism of the present. It would be inexcusable to name these various measures for the purpose of pointing out the character common to them, were it not that in our day men have forgotten their common character. They do not remember that, in one or other way, all these truly Liberal changes diminished compulsory co-operation throughout social life and increased voluntary co-operation. They have forgotten that, in one direction or other, they diminished the range of governmental authority, and increased the area within which each citizen may act unchecked. They have lost sight of the truth that in past times Liberalism habitually stood for individual freedom *versus* State-coercion.

And now comes the inquiry – How is it that Liberals have lost sight of this? How is it that Liberalism, getting more and more into power, has grown more and more coercive in its legislation? How is it that, either directly through its own majorities or indirectly through aid given in such cases to the majorities of its opponents, Liberalism has to an increasing extent adopted the policy of dictating the actions of citizens, and, by consequence, diminishing the range throughout which their actions remain free? How are we to explain this spreading confusion of thought which has led it, in pursuit of what appears to be public good, to invert the method by which in earlier days it achieved public good?

Unaccountable as at first sight this unconscious change of policy seems, we shall find that it has arisen quite naturally. Given the unanalytical thought ordinarily brought to bear on political matters, and, under existing conditions, nothing else was to be expected. To make this clear some parenthetic explanations are needful.

From the lowest to the highest creatures, intelligence progresses by acts of discrimination; and it continues so to progress among men, from the most ignorant to the most cultured. To class rightly – to put in the same group things which are of essentially the same natures, and in other groups things of natures essentially different – is the fundamental condition to right guidance of actions. Beginning with rudimentary vision, which gives warning that some large opaque body is passing near (just as closed eyes turned to the window, perceiving the shade caused by a hand put before them, tells us of something moving in front), the advance is to developed vision, which, by exactly-appreciated combinations of forms, colours, and motions, identifies objects at great distances as prey or enemies, and so makes it possible to improve the adjustments of conduct for securing food or evading death. That progressing perception of differences and consequent greater correctness of classing, constitutes, under one of its chief aspects, the growth of intelligence, is equally seen when we pass from the relatively simple physical vision to the relatively complex intellectual vision – the vision through the agency of which, things previously grouped by certain external resemblances or by certain extrinsic circumstances, come to be more truly grouped in conformity with their intrinsic structures or natures. Undeveloped intellectual vision is just as indiscriminating and erroneous in its classings as undeveloped physical vision. Instance the early arrangement of plants into the groups, trees, shrubs, and herbs: size, the most conspicuous trait, being the ground of distinction; and the assemblages formed being such as united many plants extremely unlike in their natures, and separated others that are near akin. Or still better, take the popular classification which puts together under the same general name, fish and shell-fish, and under the sub-name, shell-fish, puts together crustaceans and molluscs; nay, which goes further, and regards as fish the cetacean mammals. Partly because of the likeness in their modes of life as inhabiting the water, and partly because of some general resemblance in their flavours, creatures that are in their essential natures far more widely separated than a fish is from a bird, are associated in the same class and in the same sub-class.

Now the general truth thus exemplified, holds throughout those higher ranges of intellectual vision concerned with things not presentable to the senses, and, among others, such things as political institutions and political measures. For when thinking of these, too, the results of inadequate intellectual faculty, or inadequate culture of it, or both, are erroneous classings and consequent erroneous conclusions. Indeed, the liability to error is here much greater; since the things with which the intellect is concerned do not admit of examination in the same easy way. You cannot touch or see a political institution: it can be known only by an effort of constructive imagination. Neither can you apprehend by physical perception a political measure: this no less requires a process of mental representation by which its elements are put together in thought, and the essential nature of the combination conceived. Here, therefore, still more than in the cases above named, defective intellectual vision is shown in grouping by external characters, or extrinsic circumstances. How institutions are wrongly classed from this cause, we see in the common notion that the Roman Republic was a popular form of government. Look into the early ideas of the French revolutionists who aimed at an ideal state of freedom, and you find that the political forms and deeds of the Romans were their models; and even now a historian might be named who instances the corruptions of the Roman Republic as showing us what popular government leads to. Yet the resemblance between the institutions of the Romans and free institutions properly so-called, was less than that between a shark and a porpoise – a resemblance of general external form accompanying widely different internal structures. For the Roman Government was that of a small oligarchy within a larger oligarchy: the members of each being unchecked autocrats. A society in which the relatively few men who had political power, and were in a qualified sense free, were so many petty despots, holding not only slaves and dependents but even children in a bondage no less absolute than that in which they held their cattle, was, by its intrinsic nature, more nearly allied to an ordinary despotism than to a society of citizens politically equal.

Passing now to our special question, we may understand the kind of confusion in which Liberalism has lost itself; and the origin of those mistaken classings of political measures which have misled it – classings, as we shall see, by conspicuous external traits instead of by internal natures. For what, in the popular apprehension and in the apprehension of those who effected them, were the changes made by Liberals in the past? They were abolitions of grievances suffered by the people, or by portions of them: this was the common trait they had which most impressed itself on men's minds. They were mitigations of evils which had directly or indirectly been felt by large classes of citizens, as causes of misery or as hindrances to happiness. And since, in the minds of most, a rectified evil is equivalent to an achieved good, these measures came to be thought of as so many positive benefits; and the welfare of the many came to be conceived alike by Liberal statesmen and Liberal voters as the aim of Liberalism. Hence the confusion. The gaining of a popular good, being the external conspicuous trait common to Liberal measures in earlier days (then in each case gained by a relaxation of restraints), it has happened that popular good has come to be sought by Liberals, not as an end to be indirectly gained by relaxations of restraints, but as the end to be directly gained. And seeking to gain it directly, they have used methods intrinsically opposed to those originally used.

And now, having seen how this reversal of policy has arisen (or partial reversal, I should say, for the recent Burials Act and the efforts to remove all remaining religious inequalities, show continuance of the original policy in certain directions), let us proceed to contemplate the extent to which it has been carried during recent times, and the still greater extent to which the future will see it carried if current ideas and feelings continue to predominate.

Before proceeding, it may be well to say that no reflections are intended on the motives which prompted one after another of these various restraints and dictations. These motives were doubtless in nearly all cases good. It must be admitted that the restrictions placed by an Act of 1870, on the employment of women and children in Turkey-red dyeing works, were, in intention, no less philanthropic than those of Edward VI., which prescribed the minimum time for which a journeyman should be retained. Without question, the Seed Supply (Ireland) Act of 1880, which empowered guardians to buy seed for poor tenants, and then to see it properly planted, was moved by a desire for public welfare no less great than that which in 1533 pre-scribed the number of sheep a tenant might keep, or that of 1597, which commanded that decayed houses of husbandry should be rebuilt. Nobody will dispute that the various measures of late years taken for restricting the sale of intoxicating liquors, have been taken as much with a view to public morals as were the measures taken of old for checking the evils of luxury; as, for instance, in the fourteenth century, when diet as well as dress was restricted. Everyone must see that the edicts issued by Henry VIII. to prevent the lower classes from playing dice, cards, bowls, &c., were not more prompted by desire for popular welfare than were the Acts passed of late to check gambling.

Further, I do not intend here to question the wisdom of these modern interferences, which Conservatives and Liberals vie with one another in multiplying, any more than to question the wisdom of those ancient ones which they in many cases resemble. We will not now consider whether the plans of late adopted for preserving the lives of sailors, are or are not more judicious than that sweeping Scotch measure which, in the middle of the fifteenth century, prohib-ited captains from leaving harbour during the winter. For the present, it shall remain undebated whether there is a better warrant for giving sanitary officers powers to search certain premises for unfit food, than there was for the law of Edward III., under which innkeepers at seaports were sworn to search their guests to prevent the exporta-tion of money or plate. We will assume that there is no less sense in that clause of the Canal-boat Act, which forbids an owner to board gratuitously the children of the boatmen, than there was in the Spital-fields Acts, which, up to 1824, for the benefit of the artisans, forbade the manufacturers to fix their factories more than ten miles from the Royal Exchange.

We exclude, then, these questions of philanthropic motive and wise judgement, taking both of them for granted; and have here to concern ourselves solely with the compulsory nature of the measures which, for good or evil as the case may be, have been put in force during periods of Liberal ascendancy.

To bring the illustrations within compass, let us commence with 1860, under the second administration of Lord Palmerston. In that year, the restrictions of the Factories Act were extended to bleaching and dyeing works; authority was given to provide analysts of food and drink, to be paid out of local rates; there was an Act providing for inspection of gas-works, as well as for fixing quality of gas and limiting price; there was the Act which, in addition to further mine-inspection, made it penal to employ boys under twelve not attending school and unable to read and write. In 1861 occurred an extension of the compulsory provisions of the Factories Act to lace-works; power was given to poor-law guardians, &c., to enforce vaccination; local boards were authorized to fix rates of hire for horses, ponies, mules, asses, and boats; and certain locally-formed bodies had given to them powers of taxing the locality for rural drainage and irrigation works, and for supplying water to cattle. In 1862 an Act was passed for restricting the employment of women and children in open-air bleaching; and an Act for making illegal a coal-mine with a single shaft, or with shafts separated by less than a specified space; as well as an Act giving the Council of Medical Education the exclusive right to publish a Pharmacopœia, the price of which is to be fixed by the Treasury. In 1863 came the extension of compulsory vaccination to Scotland, and also to Ireland; there came the empowering of certain boards to borrow money repayable from the local rates, to employ and pay those out of work; there came the authorizing of town-authorities to take possession of neglected ornamental spaces, and rate the inhabitants for their support; there came the Bakehouses Regulation Act, which, besides specifying minimum age of employés occupied between certain hours, prescribed periodical lime-washing, three coats of paint when painted, and cleaning with hot water and soap at least once in six months; and there came also an Act giving a magistrate authority to decide on the wholesomeness or unwholesomeness of food brought before him by an inspector. Of compulsory legislation dating from 1864, may be named an extension of the Factories Act to various additional trades, including regulations for cleansing and ventilation, and specifying of certain employés in match-works, that they might not take meals on the premises except in the wood-cutting places. Also there were passed a Chimney-Sweepers Act, an Act for further regulating the sale of beer in Ireland, an Act for compulsory testing of cables and anchors, an Act extending the Public Works Act of 1863, and the Contagious Diseases Act: which last gave the police, in specified places, powers which, in respect of certain classes of women, abolished sundry of those safeguards to individual freedom established in past times. The year 1865 witnessed further provision for the reception and temporary relief of wanderers at the cost of ratepayers; another public-house closing Act; and an Act making compulsory regulations for extinguishing fires in London. Then, under the Ministry of Lord John Russell, in 1866, have to be named an Act to regulate cattle-sheds, &c., in Scotland, giving local authorities powers to inspect sanitary conditions and fix the numbers of cattle; an Act forcing hop-growers to label their bags with the year and place of growth and the true weight, and giving police powers of search; an Act to facilitate the building of lodging-houses in Ireland, and providing for regulation of the inmates; a Public Health Act, under which there is registration of lodging-houses and limitation of occupants, with inspection and directions for lime-washing, &c.; and a Public Libraries Act, giving local powers by which a majority can tax a minority for their books.

Passing now to the legislation under the first Ministry of Mr. Gladstone, we have, in 1869, the establishment of State-telegraphy, with the accompanying interdict on telegraphing through any other agency; we have the empowering a Secretary of State to regulate hired conveyances in London; we have further and more stringent regulations to prevent cattle-diseases from spreading, another Beerhouse Regulation Act, and a Sea-birds Preservation Act (ensuring greater mortality of fish). In 1870 we have a law authorizing the Board of Public Works to make advances for landlords' improvements and for purchase by tenants; we have the Act which enables the Education Department to form school-boards which shall purchase sites for schools, and may provide free schools supported by local rates, and enabling school-boards to pay a child's fees, to compel parents to send their children, &c., &c.; we have a further Factories and Workshops Act, making, among other restrictions, some on the employment of women and children in fruit-preserving and fish-curing works. In 1871 we meet with an amended Merchant Shipping Act, directing officers of the Board of Trade to record the draught of sea-going vessels leaving port; there is another Factory and Work-shops Act, making further restrictions; there is a Pedlar's Act, inflicting penalties for hawking without a certificate, and limiting the district within which the certificate holds, as well as giving the police power to search pedlars' packs; and there are further measures for enforcing vaccination. The year 1872 had, among other Acts, one which makes it illegal to take for hire more than one child to nurse, unless in a house registered by the authorities, who prescribe the number of infants to be received; it had a Licensing Act, interdicting sale of spirits to those apparently under sixteen; and it had another Merchant Shipping Act, establishing an annual survey of passenger steamers. Then in 1873 was passed the Agricultural Children's Act, which makes it penal for a farmer to employ a child who has neither certificate of elementary education nor of certain prescribed school-attendances; and there was passed a Merchant Shipping Act, requir-ing on each vessel a scale showing draught and giving the Board of Trade power to fix the numbers of boats and life-saving appliances to be carried.

Turn now to Liberal law-making under the present Ministry. We have, in 1880, a law which forbids conditional advance-notes in pay-ment of sailors' wages; also a law which dictates certain arrangements for the safe carriage of grain-cargoes; also a law increasing local coercion over parents to send their children to school. In 1881 comes legislation to prevent trawling over clam-beds and bait-beds, and an interdict making it impossible to buy a glass of beer on Sunday in Wales. In 1882 the Board of Trade was authorized to grant licences to generate and sell electricity, and municipal bodies were enabled to levy rates for electric-lighting; further exactions from ratepayers were authorized for facilitating more accessible baths and wash-houses; and local authorities were empowered to make bye-laws for securing the decent lodging of persons engaged in picking fruit and vegetables. Of such legislation during 1883 may be named the Cheap Trains Act, which, partly by taxing the nation to the extent of £400,000 a year (in the shape of relinquished passenger duty), and partly at the cost of railway-proprietors, still further cheapens travel-ling for workmen: the Board of Trade, through the Railway Commis-sioners, being empowered to ensure sufficiently good and frequent accommodation. Again, there is the Act which, under penalty of £10 for disobedience, forbids the payment of wages to workmen at or within public-houses; there is another Factory and Workshops Act, commanding inspection of white lead works (to see that there are provided overalls, respirators, baths, acidulated drinks, &c.) and of bake-houses, regulating times of employment in both, and prescribing in detail some constructions for the last, which are to be kept in a condition satisfactory to the inspectors.

But we are far from forming an adequate conception if we look only at the compulsory legislation which has actually been established of late years. We must look also at that which is advocated, and which threatens to be far more sweeping in range and stringent in character. We have lately had a Cabinet Minister, one of the most advanced Liberals, so-called, who pooh-poohs the plans of the late Government for improving industrial dwellings as so much "tinkering;" and contends for effectual coercion to be exercised over owners of small houses, over land-owners, and over rate-payers. Here is another Cabinet Minister who, addressing his constituents, speaks slightingly of the doings of philanthropic societies and religious bodies to help the poor, and says that "the whole of the people of this country ought to look upon this work as being their own work:" that is to say, some extensive Government measure is called for. Again, we have a Radical member of Parliament who leads a large and powerful body, aiming with annually-increasing promise of success, to enforce sobriety by giving to local majorities powers to prevent freedom of exchange in respect of certain commodities. Regulation of the hours of labour for certain classes, which has been made more and more general by successive extensions of the Factories Acts, is likely now to be made still more general: a measure is to be proposed bringing the employés in all shops under such regulation. There is a rising demand, too, that education shall be made gratis for all. The payment of school-fees is beginning to be denounced as a wrong: the State must take the whole burden. Moreover, it is proposed by many that the State, regarded as an undoubtedly competent judge of what constitutes good education for the poor, shall undertake also to prescribe good education for the middle classes – shall stamp the children of these, too, after a State pattern, concerning the goodness of which they have no more doubt than the Chinese had when they fixed theirs. Then there is the "endowment of research," of late energetically urged. Already the Government gives every year the sum of £4,000 for this purpose, to be distributed through the Royal Society; and in the absence of those who have strong motives for resisting the pressure of the interested backed by those they easily persuade, it may by-and-by establish that paid "priesthood of science" long ago advocated by Sir David Brewster. Once more, plausible proposals are made that there should be organized a system of compulsory insurance, by which men during their early lives shall be forced to provide for the time when they will be incapacitated.

Nor does enumeration of these further measures of coercive rule, looming on us near at hand or in the distance, complete the account. Nothing more than cursory allusion has yet been made to that accompanying compulsion which takes the form of increased taxation, general and local. Partly for defraying the costs of carrying out these ever-multiplying coercive measures, each of which requires an additional staff of officers, and partly to meet the outlay for new public institutions, such as board-schools, free libraries, public museums, baths and wash-houses, recreation grounds, &c., &c., local rates are year after year increased; as the general taxation is increased by grants for education and to the departments of science and art, &c. Every one of these involves further coercion – restricts still more the freedom of the citizen. For the implied address accompanying every additional exaction is – "Hitherto you have been free to spend this portion of your earnings in any way which pleased you; hereafter you shall not be free so to spend it, but we will spend it for the general benefit." Thus, either directly or indirectly, and in most cases both at once, the citizen is at each further stage in the growth of this compulsory legislation, deprived of some liberty which he previously had.

Such, then, are the doings of the party which claims the name of Liberal; and which calls itself Liberal as being the advocate of extended freedom.

I doubt not that many a member of the party has read the preceding section with impatience; wanting, as he does, to point out an immense oversight which he thinks destroys the validity of the argument. "You forget," he wishes to say, "the fundamental difference between the power which, in the past, established those restraints that Liberalism abolished, and the power which, in the present, establishes the restraints you call anti-Liberal. You forget that the one was an irresponsible power, while the other is a responsible power. You forget that if by the recent legislation of Liberals, people are variously regulated, the body which regulates them is of their own creating, and has their warrant for its acts."

My answer is, that I have not forgotten this difference, but am prepared to contend that the difference is in large measure irrelevant to the issue.

In the first place, the real issue is whether the lives of citizens are more interfered with than they were; not the nature of the agency which interferes with them. Take a simpler case. A member of a trades' union has joined others in establishing an organization of a purely representative character. By it he is compelled to strike if a majority so decide; he is forbidden to accept work save under the conditions they dictate; he is prevented from profiting by his superior ability or energy to the extent he might do were it not for their interdict. He cannot disobey without abandoning those pecuniary benefits of the organization for which he has subscribed, and bringing on himself the persecution, and perhaps violence, of his fellows. Is he any the less coerced because the body coercing him is one which he had an equal voice with the rest in forming?

In the second place, if it be objected that the analogy is faulty, since the governing body of a nation, to which, as protector of the national life and interests, all must submit under penalty of social disorganization, has a far higher authority over citizens than the government of any private organization can have over its members; then the reply is that, granting the difference, the answer made continues valid. If men use their liberty in such a way as to surrender their liberty, are they thereafter any the less slaves? If people by a *plébiscite* elect a man despot over them, do they remain free because the despotism was of their own making? Are the coercive edicts issued by him to be regarded as legitimate because they are the ultimate outcome of their own votes? As well might it be argued that the East African, who breaks a spear in another's presence that he may so become bondsman to him, still retains his liberty because he freely chose his master.

Finally if any, not without marks of irritation as I can imagine, repudiate this reasoning, and say that there is no true parallelism between the relation of people to government where an irresponsible single ruler has been permanently elected, and the relation where a responsible representative body is maintained, and from time to time re-elected; then there comes the ultimate reply – an altogether het-

erodox reply – by which most will be greatly astonished. This reply
is, that these multitudinous restraining acts are not defensible on the
ground that they proceed from a popularly-chosen body; for that the
authority of a popularly-chosen body is no more to be regarded as
an unlimited authority than the authority of a monarch; and that as
true Liberalism in the past disputed the assumption of a monarch's
unlimited authority, so true Liberalism in the present will dispute the
assumption of unlimited parliamentary authority. Of this, however,
more anon. Here I merely indicate it as an ultimate answer.

Meanwhile it suffices to point out that until recently, just as of old,
true Liberalism was shown by its acts to be moving towards the theory
of a limited parliamentary authority. All these abolitions of restraints
over religious beliefs and observances, over exchange and transit,
over trade-combinations and the travelling of artisans, over the publication of opinions, theological or political, &c., &c., were tacit assertions of the desirableness of limitation. In the same way that the
abandonment of sumptuary laws, of laws forbidding this or that kind
of amusement, of laws dictating modes of farming, and many others
of like meddling nature, which took place in early days, was an
implied admission that the State ought not to interfere in such matters; so those removals of hindrances to individual activities of one
or other kind, which the Liberalism of the last generation effected,
were practical confessions that in these directions, too, the sphere of
governmental action should be narrowed. And this recognition of the
propriety of restricting governmental action was a preparation for
restricting it in theory. One of the most familiar political truths is
that, in the course of social evolution, usage precedes law; and that
when usage has been well established it becomes law by receiving
authoritative endorsement and defined form. Manifestly then, Liberalism in the past, by its practice of limitation, was preparing the way
for the principle of limitation.

But returning from these more general considerations to the special question, I emphasize the reply that the liberty which a citizen
enjoys is to be measured, not by the nature of the governmental
machinery he lives under, whether representative or other, but by the
relative paucity of the restraints it imposes on him; and that, whether
this machinery is or is not one that he has shared in making, its
actions are not of the kind proper to Liberalism if they increase such
restraints beyond those which are needful for preventing him from

directly or indirectly aggressing on his fellows – needful, that is, for maintaining the liberties of his fellows against his invasions of them: restraints which are, therefore, to be distinguished as negatively coercive, not positively coercive.

Probably, however, the Liberal, and still more the sub-species Radical, who more than any other in these latter days seems under the impression that so long as he has a good end in view he is warranted in exercising over men all the coercion he is able, will continue to protest. Knowing that his aim is popular benefit of some kind, to be achieved in some way, and believing that the Tory is, contrariwise, prompted by class-interest and the desire to maintain class-power, he will regard it as palpably absurd to group him as one of the same genus, and will scorn the reasoning used to prove that he belongs to it.

Perhaps an analogy will help him to see its validity. If, away in the far East, where personal government is the only form of government known, he heard from the inhabitants an account of a struggle by which they had deposed a cruel and vicious despot, and put in his place one whose acts proved his desire for their welfare – if, after listening to their self-gratulations, he told them that they had not essentially changed the nature of their government, he would greatly astonish them; and probably he would have difficulty in making them understand that the substitution of a benevolent despot for a malevolent despot, still left the government a despotism. Similarly with Toryism as rightly conceived. Standing as it does for coercion by the State *versus* the freedom of the individual, Toryism remains Toryism, whether it extends this coercion for selfish or unselfish reasons. As certainly as the despot is still a despot, whether his motives for arbitrary rule are good or bad; so certainly is the Tory still a Tory, whether he has egoistic or altruistic motives for using State-power to restrict the liberty of the citizen, beyond the degree required for maintaining the liberties of other citizens. The altruistic Tory as well as the egoistic Tory belongs to the genus Tory; though he forms a new species of the genus. And both stand in distinct contrast with the Liberal as defined in the days when Liberals were rightly so called, and when the definition was – "one who advocates greater freedom from restraint, especially in political institutions."

Thus, then, is justified the paradox I set out with. As we have seen, Toryism and Liberalism originally emerged, the one from militancy and the other from industrialism. The one stood for the *régime* of status and the other for the *régime* of contract – the one for that system of compulsory co-operation which accompanies the legal inequality of classes, and the other for that voluntary co-operation which accompanies their legal equality; and beyond all question the early acts of the two parties were respectively for the maintenance of agencies which effect this compulsory co-operation, and for the weakening or curbing of them. Manifestly the implication is that, in so far as it has been extending the system of compulsion, what is now called Liberalism is a new form of Toryism.

How truly this is so, we shall see still more clearly on looking at the facts the other side upwards, which we will presently do.

NOTE – By sundry newspapers which noticed this article when it was originally published, the meaning of the above paragraphs was supposed to be that Liberals and Tories have changed places. This, however, is by no means the implication. A new species of Tory may arise without disappearance of the original species. When saying, as on page 70, that in our days "Conservatives and Liberals vie with one another in multiplying" interferences, I clearly implied the belief that while Liberals have taken to coercive legislation, Conservatives have not abandoned it. Nevertheless, it is true that the laws made by Liberals are so greatly increasing the compulsions and restraints exercised over citizens, that among Conservatives who suffer from this aggressiveness there is growing up a tendency to resist it. Proof is furnished by the fact that the "Liberty and Property Defence League," largely consisting of Conservatives, has taken for its motto "Individualism *versus* Socialism." So that if the present drift of things continues, it may by and by really happen that the Tories will be defenders of liberties which the Liberals, in pursuit of what they think popular welfare, trample under foot.

The Coming Slavery

The kinship of pity to love is shown among other ways in this, that it idealizes its object. Sympathy with one in suffering suppresses, for the time being, remembrance of his transgressions. The feeling which vents itself in "poor fellow!" on seeing one in agony, excludes the thought of "bad fellow," which might at another time arise. Naturally, then, if the wretched are unknown or but vaguely known, all the demerits they may have are ignored; and thus it happens that when, as just now, the miseries of the poor are depicted, they are thought of as the miseries of the deserving poor, instead of being thought of, as in large measure they should be, as the miseries of the undeserving poor. Those whose hardships are set forth in pamphlets and proclaimed in sermons and speeches which echo throughout society, are assumed to be all worthy souls, grievously wronged; and none of them are thought of as bearing the penalties of their own misdeeds.

On hailing a cab in a London street, it is surprising how frequently the door is officiously opened by one who expects to get something for his trouble. The surprise lessens after counting the many loungers about tavern-doors, or after observing the quickness with which a street-performance, or procession, draws from neighbouring slums and stable-yards a group of idlers. Seeing how numerous they are in every small area, it becomes manifest that tens of thousands of such swarm through London. "They have no work," you say. Say rather that they either refuse work or quickly turn themselves out of it. They are simply good-for-nothings, who in one way or other live on the good-for-somethings – vagrants and sots, criminals and those on the way to crime, youths who are burdens on hard-worked parents, men who appropriate the wages of their wives, fellows who share the gains of prostitutes; and then, less visible and less numerous, there is a corresponding class of women.

Is it natural that happiness should be the lot of such? or is it natural that they should bring unhappiness on themselves and those connected with them? Is it not manifest that there must exist in our midst an immense amount of misery which is a normal result of misconduct, and ought not to be dissociated from it? There is a notion, always more or less prevalent and just now vociferously expressed, that all social suffering is removable, and that it is the duty of somebody or other to remove it. Both these beliefs are false. To separate pain from ill-doing is to fight against the constitution of things, and will be followed by far more pain. Saving men from the natural penalties of dissolute living, eventually necessitates the infliction of artificial penalties in solitary cells, on tread-wheels, and by the lash. I suppose a dictum, on which the current creed and the creed of science are at one, may be considered to have as high an authority as can be found. Well, the command "if any would not work neither should he eat," is simply a Christian enunciation of that universal law of Nature under which life has reached its present height – the law that a creature not energetic enough to maintain itself must die: the sole difference being that the law which in the one case is to be artificially enforced, is, in the other case, a natural necessity. And yet this particular tenet of their religion which science so manifestly justifies, is the one which Christians seem least inclined to accept. The current assumption is that there should be no suffering, and that society is to blame for that which exists.

"But surely we are not without responsibilities, even when the suffering is that of the unworthy?"

If the meaning of the word "we" be so expanded as to include with ourselves our ancestors, and especially our ancestral legislators, I agree. I admit that those who made, and modified, and administered, the old Poor Law, were responsible for producing an appalling amount of demoralization, which it will take more than one generation to remove. I admit, too, the partial responsibility of recent and present law-makers for regulations which have brought into being a permanent body of tramps, who ramble from union to union; and also their responsibility for maintaining a constant supply of felons by sending back convicts into society under such conditions that they are almost compelled again to commit crimes. Moreover, I admit that the philanthropic are not without their share of responsibility; since, that they may aid the offspring of the unworthy, they disadvantage the offspring of the worthy through burdening their parents by increased local rates. Nay, I even admit that these swarms of good-for-nothings, fostered and multiplied by public and private agencies, have, by sundry mischievous meddlings, been made to suffer more than they would otherwise have suffered. Are these the responsibilities meant? I suspect not.

But now, leaving the question of responsibilities, however conceived, and considering only the evil itself, what shall we say of its treatment? Let me begin with a fact.

A late uncle of mine, the Rev. Thomas Spencer, for some twenty years incumbent of Hinton Charterhouse, near Bath, no sooner entered on his parish duties than he proved himself anxious for the welfare of the poor, by establishing a school, a library, a clothing club and land-allotments, besides building some model cottages. Moreover, up to 1833 he was a pauper's friend – always for the pauper against the overseer. There presently came, however, the debates on the Poor Law, which impressed him with the evils of the system then in force. Though an ardent philanthropist he was not a timid sentimentalist. The result was that, immediately the new Poor Law was passed, he proceeded to carry out its provisions in his parish. Almost universal opposition was encountered by him: not the poor only being his opponents, but even the farmers on whom came the burden of heavy poor-rates. For, strange to say, their interests had become apparently identified with the maintenance of this system which taxed them so largely. The explanation is that there had grown up the practice of paying out of the rates a part of the wages of each farm-servant – "make-wages," as the sum was called. And though the farmers contributed most of the fund from which "make-wages" were paid, yet, since all other ratepayers contributed, the farmers seemed to gain by the arrangement. My uncle, however, not easily deterred, faced all this opposition and enforced the law. The result was that in two years the rates were reduced from £700 a year to £200 a year; while the condition of the parish was greatly improved. "Those who had hitherto loitered at the corners of the streets, or at the doors of the beer-shops, had something else to do, and one after another they obtained employment;" so that out of a population of 800, only 15 had to be sent as incapable paupers to the Bath Union (when that was formed), in place of the 100 who received out-door relief a short time before. If it be said that the £20 telescope which, a few years after, his parishioners presented to my uncle, marked only the gratitude of the ratepayers; then my reply is the fact that when, some years later still, having killed himself by overwork in pursuit of popular welfare, he was taken to Hinton to be buried, the procession which followed him to the grave included not the well-to-do only but the poor.

Several motives have prompted this brief narrative. One is the wish to prove that sympathy with the people and self-sacrificing efforts on their behalf, do not necessarily imply approval of gratuitous aids. Another is the desire to show that benefit may result, not from multiplication of artificial appliances to mitigate distress, but, contrariwise, from diminution of them. And a further purpose I have in view is that of preparing the way for an analogy.

Under another form and in a different sphere, we are now yearly extending a system which is identical in nature with the system of "make-wages" under the old Poor Law. Little as politicians recognize the fact, it is nevertheless demonstrable that these various public appliances for working-class comfort, which they are supplying at the cost of ratepayers, are intrinsically of the same nature as those which, in past times, treated the farmer's man as half-labourer and half-pauper. In either case the worker receives in return for what he does, money wherewith to buy certain of the things he wants; while, to procure the rest of them for him, money is furnished out of a common fund raised by taxes. What matters it whether the things supplied by ratepayers for nothing, instead of by the employer in payment, are of this kind or that kind? The principle is the same. For sums received let us substitute the commodities and benefits purchased; and then see how the matter stands. In old Poor-Law times, the farmer gave for work done the equivalent, say of house-rent, bread, clothes, and fire; while the ratepayers practically supplied the man and his family with their shoes, tea, sugar, candles, a little bacon, &c. The division is, of course, arbitrary; but unquestionably the farmer and the rate-payers furnished these things between them. At the present time the artisan receives from his employer in wages, the equivalent of the consumable commodities he wants; while from the public comes satisfaction for others of his needs and desires. At the cost of ratepayers he has in some cases, and will presently have in more, a house at less than its commercial value; for of course when, as in Liverpool, a municipality spends nearly £200,000 in pulling down and reconstructing low-class dwellings, and is about to spend as much again, the implication is that in some way the ratepayers supply the poor with more accommodation than the rents they pay would otherwise have brought. The artisan further receives from them, in schooling for his children, much more than he pays for; and there is every probability that he will presently receive it from them gratis. The ratepayers also satisfy what desire he may have for books and newspapers, and comfortable places to read them in. In some cases too, as in Manchester, gymnasia for his children of both sexes, as well as recreation grounds, are provided. That is to say, he obtains from a fund raised by local taxes, certain benefits beyond those which the sum received for his labour enables him to purchase. The sole difference, then, between this system and the old system of "make-wages," is between the kinds of satisfactions obtained; and this difference does not in the least affect the nature of the arrangement.

Moreover, the two are pervaded by substantially the same illusion. In the one case, as in the other, what looks like a gratis benefit is not a gratis benefit. The amount which, under the old Poor Law, the half-pauperized labourer received from the parish to eke out his weekly income, was not really, as it appeared, a bonus; for it was accompanied by a substantially-equivalent decrease in his wages, as was quickly proved when the system was abolished and the wages rose. Just so is it with these seeming boons received by working people in towns. I do not refer only to the fact that they unawares pay in part through the raised rents of their dwellings (when they are not actual ratepayers); but I refer to the fact that the wages received by them are, like the wages of the farm-labourer, diminished by these public burdens falling on employers. Read the accounts coming of late from Lancashire concerning the cotton strike, containing proofs, given by artisans themselves, that the margin of profit is so narrow that the less skilful manufacturers, as well as those with deficient capital, fail, and that the companies of co-operators who compete with them can rarely hold their own; and then consider what is the implication respecting wages. Among the costs of production have to be reckoned taxes, general and local. If, as in our large towns, the local rates now amount to one-third of the rental or more – if the employer has to pay this, not on his private dwelling only, but on his business-premises, factories, warehouses, or the like; it results that the interest on his capital must be diminished by that amount, or the amount must be taken from the wages-fund, or partly one and partly the other. And if competition among capitalists in the same business and in other businesses, has the effect of so keeping down interest that while some gain others lose, and not a few are ruined – if capital, not getting adequate interest, flows elsewhere and leaves labour unemployed; then it is manifest that the choice for the artisan under such conditions, lies between diminished amount of work or diminished rate of payment for it. Moreover, for kindred reasons these local burdens raise the costs of the things he consumes. The charges made by distributors are, on the average, determined by the current rates of interest on capital used in distributing businesses; and the extra costs of carrying on such businesses have to be paid for by extra prices. So that as in the past the rural worker lost in one way what he gained in another, so in the present does the urban worker: there being too, in both cases, the loss entailed on him by the cost of administration and the waste accompanying it.

"But what has all this to do with 'the coming slavery'?" will perhaps be asked. Nothing directly, but a good deal indirectly, as we shall see after yet another preliminary section.

It is said that when railways were first opened in Spain, peasants standing on the tracks were not unfrequently run over; and that the blame fell on the engine-drivers for not stopping: rural experiences having yielded no conception of the momentum of a large mass moving at a high velocity.

The incident is recalled to me on contemplating the ideas of the so-called "practical" politician, into whose mind there enters no thought of such a thing as political momentum, still less of a political momentum which, instead of diminishing or remaining constant, increases. The theory on which he daily proceeds is that the change caused by his measure will stop where he intends it to stop. He contemplates intently the things his act will achieve, but thinks little of the remoter issues of the movement his act sets up, and still less of its collateral issues. When, in war-time, "food for powder" was to be provided by encouraging population – when Mr. Pitt said, "Let us make relief in cases where there are a number of children a matter of right and honour, instead of a ground for opprobrium and contempt;"[1] it was not expected that the poor-rates would be quadrupled in fifty years, that women with many bastards would be preferred as wives to modest women, because of their incomes from the parish, and that hosts of ratepayers would be pulled down into the ranks of pauperism. Legislators who in 1833 voted £20,000 a year to aid in building school-houses, never supposed that the step they then took would lead to forced contributions, local and general, now amounting to £6,000,000; they did not intend to establish the principle that A should be made responsible for educating B's offspring; they did not dream of a compulsion which would deprive poor widows of the help of their elder children; and still less did they dream that their successors, by requiring impoverished parents to apply to Boards of Guardians to pay the fees which School Boards would not remit, would initiate a habit of applying to Boards of Guardians and so cause pauperization.[2] Neither did those who in 1834 passed an Act regulating the labour of women and children in certain factories, imagine that the system they were beginning would end in the restriction and inspection of labour in all kinds of producing establishments where more than fifty people are employed; nor did they conceive that the inspection provided would grow to the extent of requiring that before a "young person" is employed in a factory, authority must be given by a certifying surgeon, who, by personal examination (to which no limit is placed) has satisfied himself that there is no incapacitating disease or bodily infirmity: his verdict determining whether the "young person" shall earn wages or not.[3] Even less, as I say, does the politician who plumes himself on the practicalness of his aims, conceive the indirect results which will follow the direct results of his measures. Thus, to take a case connected with one named above, it was not intended through the system of "payment by results," to do anything more than give teachers an efficient stimulus: it was not supposed that in numerous cases their health would give way under the stimulus; it was not expected that they would be led to adopt a cramming system and to put undue pressure on dull and weak children, often to their great injury; it was not foreseen that in many

---

[1] Hansard's *Parliamentary History*, 32, p. 710.
[2] *Fortnightly Review*, January, 1884, p. 17. [F. Adams, 'The Radical Programme (No. v): Free Schools', *Fortnightly Review*, Vol. 41, January 1884, pp. 1–20.]
[3] Factories and Workshops Act, 41 and 42 Vic., cap. 16.

cases a bodily enfeeblement would be caused which no amount of grammar and geography can compensate for. The licensing of public-houses was simply for maintaining public order: those who devised it never imagined that there would result an organized interest powerfully influencing elections in an unwholesome way. Nor did it occur to the "practical" politicians who provided a compulsory load-line for merchant vessels, that the pressure of shipowners' interests would habitually cause the putting of the load-line at the very highest limit, and that from precedent to precedent, tending ever in the same direction, the load-line would gradually rise in the better class of ships; as from good authority I learn that it has already done. Legislators who, some forty years ago, by Act of Parliament compelled railway-companies to supply cheap locomotion, would have ridiculed the belief, had it been expressed, that eventually their Act would punish the companies which improved the supply; and yet this was the result to companies which began to carry third-class passengers by fast trains; since a penalty to the amount of the passenger-duty was inflicted on them for every third-class passenger so carried. To which instance concerning railways, add a far more striking one disclosed by comparing the railway policies of England and France. The law-makers who provided for the ultimate lapsing of French railways to the State, never conceived the possibility that inferior travelling facilities would result – did not foresee that reluctance to depreciate the value of property eventually coming to the State, would negative the authorization of competing lines and that in the absence of competing lines locomotion would be relatively costly, slow, and infrequent; for, as Sir Thomas Farrer has lately shown, the traveller in England has great advantages over the French traveller in the economy, swiftness, and frequency with which his journeys can be made.

But the "practical" politician who, in spite of such experiences repeated generation after generation, goes on thinking only of proximate results, naturally never thinks of results still more remote, still more general, and still more important than those just exemplified. To repeat the metaphor used above – he never asks whether the political momentum set up by his measure, in some cases decreasing but in other cases greatly increasing, will or will not have the same general direction with other like momenta; and whether it may not join them in presently producing an aggregate energy working changes never thought of. Dwelling only on the effects of his particular stream of legislation, and not observing how other such streams already existing, and still other streams which will follow his initiative, pursue the same average course, it never occurs to him that they may presently unite into a voluminous flood utterly changing the face of things. Or to leave figures for a more literal statement, he is unconscious of the truth that he is helping to form a certain type of social organization, and that kindred measures, effecting kindred changes of organization, tend with ever-increasing force to make that type general; until, passing a certain point, the proclivity towards it becomes irresistible. Just as each society aims when possible to produce in other societies a structure akin to its own – just as among the Greeks, the Spartans and the Athenians struggled to spread their respective political institutions, or as, at the time of the French Revolution, the European absolute monarchies aimed to re-establish absolute monarchy in France while the Republic encouraged the formation of other republics; so within every society, each species of structure tends to propagate itself. Just as the system of voluntary co-operation by companies, associations, unions, to achieve business ends and other ends, spreads throughout a community; so does the antagonistic system of compulsory co-operation under State-agencies spread; and the larger becomes its extension the more power of spreading it gets. The question of questions for the politician should ever be – "What type of social structure am I tending to produce?" But this is a question he never entertains.

Here we will entertain it for him. Let us now observe the general course of recent changes, with the accompanying current of ideas, and see whither they are carrying us.

The blank form of a question daily asked is – "We have already done this; why should we not do that?" And the regard for precedent suggested by it, is ever pushing on regulative legislation. Having had brought within their sphere of operation more and more numerous businesses, the Acts restricting hours of employment and dictating the treatment of workers are now to be made applicable to shops. From inspecting lodging-houses to limit the number of occupants and enforce sanitary conditions, we have passed to inspecting all houses below a certain rent in which there are members of more than one family, and are now passing to a kindred inspection of all small houses.[4] The buying and working of telegraphs by the State is made a reason for urging that the State should buy and work the railways. Supplying children with food for their minds by public agency is being followed in some cases by supplying food for their bodies; and after the practice has been made gradually more general, we may anticipate that the supply, now proposed to be made gratis in the one case, will eventually be proposed to be made gratis in the other: the argument that good bodies as well as good minds are needful to make good citizens, being logically urged as a reason for the extension.[5] And then, avowedly proceeding on the precedents furnished by the church, the school, and the reading-room, all publicly provided, it is contended that "pleasure, in the sense it is now generally admitted, needs legislating for and organizing at least as much as work."[6]

Not precedent only prompts this spread, but also the necessity which arises for supplementing ineffective measures, and for dealing with the artificial evils continually caused. Failure does not destroy faith in the agencies employed, but merely suggests more stringent use of such agencies or wider ramifications of them. Laws to check intemperance, beginning in early times and coming down to our own times, when further restraints on the sale of intoxicating liquors occupy nights every session, not having done what was expected, there come demands for more thorough-going laws, locally preventing the sale altogether; and here, as in America, these will doubtless be followed by demands that prevention shall be made universal. All the many appliances for "stamping out" epidemic diseases not having succeeded in preventing outbreaks of small-pox, fevers, and the like, a further remedy is applied for in the shape of police-power, to search houses for diseased persons, and authority for medical officers to examine any one they think fit, to see whether he or she

[4] See letter of Local Government Board, *Times*, January 2, 1884.
[5] Verification comes more promptly than I expected. This article has been standing in type since January 30, and in the interval, namely on March 13 [the article was published on April 1], the London School Board resolved to apply for authority to use local charitable funds for supplying gratis meals and clothing to indigent children. Presently the definition of "indigent" will be widened; more children will be included, and more funds asked for.
[6] *Fortnightly Review*, January, 1884, p. 21. [V. Greville, 'Social Reforms for the London Poor' , *Fortnightly Review*, Vol. 41, January 1884, pp. 21–30.]

is suffering from an infectious or contagious malady. Habits of improvidence having for generations been cultivated by the Poor Law, and the improvident enabled to multiply, the evils produced by compulsory charity are now proposed to be met by compulsory insurance.

The extension of this policy, causing extension of corresponding ideas, fosters everywhere the tacit assumption that Government should step in whenever anything is not going right. "Surely you would not have this misery continue!" exclaims someone, if you hint a demurrer to much that is now being said and done. Observe what is implied by this exclamation. It takes for granted, first, that all suffering ought to be prevented, which is not true: much suffering is curative, and prevention of it is prevention of a remedy. In the second place, it takes for granted that every evil can be removed: the truth being that with the existing defects of human nature, many evils can only be thrust out of one place or form into another place or form – often being increased by the change. The exclamation also implies the unhesitating belief, here especially concerning us, that evils of all kinds should be dealt with by the State. There does not occur the inquiry whether there are at work other agencies capable of dealing with evils, and whether the evils in question may not be among those which are best dealt with by these other agencies. And obviously, the more numerous governmental interventions become, the more confirmed does this habit of thought grow, and the more loud and perpetual the demands for intervention.

Every extension of the regulative policy involves an addition to the regulative agents – a further growth of officialism and an increasing power of the organization formed of officials. Take a pair of scales with many shot in the one and a few in the other. Lift shot after shot out of the loaded scale and put it into the unloaded scale. Presently you will produce a balance; and if you go on, the position of the scales will be reversed. Suppose the beam to be unequally divided, and let the lightly loaded scale be at the end of a very long arm; then the transfer of each shot, producing a much greater effect, will far sooner bring about a change of position. I use the figure to illustrate what results from transferring one individual after another from the regulated mass of the community to the regulating structures. The transfer weakens the one and strengthens the other in a far greater degree than is implied by the relative change of numbers. A comparatively small body of officials, coherent, having common interests, and acting under central authority, has an immense advantage over an incoherent public which has no settled policy, and can be brought to act unitedly only under strong provocation. Hence an organization of officials, once passing a certain stage of growth, becomes less and less resistible; as we see in the bureaucracies of the Continent. Not only does the power of resistance of the regulated part decrease in a geometrical ratio as the regulating part increases, but the private interests of many in the regulated part itself, make the change of ratio still more rapid. In every circle conversations show that now, when the passing of competitive examinations renders them eligible for the public service, youths are being educated in such ways that they may pass them and get employment under Government. One consequence is that men who might otherwise reprobate some further growth of officialism, are led to look on it with tolerance, if not favourably, as offering possible careers for those dependent on them and those related to them. Any one who remembers the numbers of upper-class and middle-class families anxious to place their children, will see that no small encouragement to the spread of legislative control is now coming from those who, but for the personal interests thus arising, would be hostile to it.

This pressing desire for careers is enforced by the preference for careers which are thought respectable. "Even if his salary is small, his occupation will be that of a gentleman," thinks the father, who wants to get a Government-clerkship for his son. And this relative dignity of State-servants as compared with those occupied in business, increases as the administrative organization becomes a larger and more powerful element in society, and tends more and more to fix the standard of honour. The prevalent ambition with a young Frenchman is to get some small official post in his locality, to rise thence to a place in the local centre of government, and finally to reach some head office in Paris. And in Russia, where that universality of State-regulation which characterizes the militant type of society has been carried furthest, we see this ambition pushed to its extreme. Says Mr. Wallace, quoting a passage from a play:– "All men, even shopkeepers and cobblers, aim at becoming officers, and the man who has passed his whole life without official rank seems to be not a human being."[7]

---

[7] *Russia*, i. 422. [Sir D. M. Wallace, *Russia*, Vol. 1, London, 1877.]

These various influences working from above downwards meet with an increasing response of expectations and solicitations proceeding from below upwards. The hard-worked and over-burdened who form the great majority, and still more the incapables perpetually helped who are ever led to look for more help, are ready supporters of schemes which promise them this or the other benefit by State agency, and ready believers of those who tell them that such benefits can be given, and ought to be given. They listen with eager faith to all builders of political air-castles, from Oxford graduates down to Irish irreconcilables; and every additional tax-supported appliance for their welfare raises hopes of further ones. Indeed the more numerous public instrumentalities become, the more is there generated in citizens the notion that everything is to be done for them, and nothing by them. Each generation is made less familiar with the attainment of desired ends by individual actions or private combinations, and more familiar with the attainment of them by governmental agencies; until, eventually, governmental agencies come to be thought of as the only available agencies. This result was well shown in the recent Trades-Unions Congress at Paris. The English delegates, reporting to their constituents, said that between themselves and their foreign colleagues "the point of difference was the extent to which the State should be asked to protect labour:" reference being thus made to the fact, conspicuous in the reports of the proceedings, that the French delegates always invoked governmental power as the only means of satisfying their wishes.

The diffusion of education has worked, and will work still more, in the same direction. "We must educate our masters," is the well-known saying of a Liberal who opposed the last extension of the franchise. Yes, if the education were worthy to be so called, and were relevant to the political enlightenment needed, much might be hoped from it. But knowing rules of syntax, being able to add up correctly, having geographical information, and a memory stocked with the dates of kings' accessions and generals' victories, no more implies fitness to form political conclusions than acquirement of skill in drawing implies expertness in telegraphing, or than ability to play cricket implies proficiency on the violin. "Surely," rejoins some one, "facility in reading opens the way to political knowledge." Doubtless; but will the way be followed? Table-talk proves that nine out of ten people read what amuses them or interests them rather than what instructs them; and that the last thing they read is something which tells them disagreeable truths or dispels groundless hopes. That popular education results in an extensive reading of publications which foster pleasant illusions rather than of those which insist on hard realities, is beyond question. Says "A Mechanic," writing in the *Pall Mall Gazette* of December 3, 1883:–

"Improved education instils the desire for culture – culture instils the desire for many things as yet quite beyond working men's reach . . . in the furious competition to which the present age is given up they are utterly impossible to the poorer classes; hence they are discontented with things as they are, and the more educated the more discontented. Hence, too, Mr. Ruskin and Mr. Morris are regarded as true prophets by many of us."

And that the connexion of cause and effect here alleged is a real one, we may see clearly enough in the present state of Germany.

Being possessed of electoral power, as are now the mass of those who are thus led to nurture sanguine anticipations of benefits to be obtained by social reorganization, it results that whoever seeks their votes must at least refrain from exposing their mistaken beliefs; even if he does not yield to the temptation to express agreement with them. Every candidate for Parliament is prompted to propose or support some new piece of *ad captandum* legislation. Nay, even the chiefs of parties – these anxious to retain office and those to wrest it from them – severally aim to get adherents by outbidding one another. Each seeks popularity by promising more than his opponent has promised, as we have lately seen. And then, as divisions in Parliament show us, the traditional loyalty to leaders overrides questions concerning the intrinsic propriety of proposed measures. Representatives are unconscientious enough to vote for Bills which they believe to be wrong in principle, because party-needs and regard for the next election demand it. And thus a vicious policy is strengthened even by those who see its viciousness.

Meanwhile there goes on out-of-doors an active propaganda to which all these influences are ancillary. Communistic theories, partially indorsed by one Act of Parliament after another, and tacitly if not avowedly favoured by numerous public men seeking supporters, are being advocated more and more vociferously under one or other form by popular leaders, and urged on by organized societies. There is the movement for land-nationalization which, aiming at a system of land-tenure equitable in the abstract, is, as all the world knows, pressed by Mr. George and his friends with avowed disregard for the just claims of existing owners, and as the basis of a scheme going more than half-way to State-socialism. And then there is the thorough-going Democratic Federation of Mr. Hyndman and his adherents. We are told by them that "the handful of marauders who now hold possession [of the land] have and can have no right save brute force against the tens of millions whom they wrong." They exclaim against "the shareholders who have been allowed to lay hands upon (!) our great railway communications." They condemn "above all, the active capitalist class, the loan-mongers, the farmers, the mine exploiters, the contractors, the middle-men, the factory lords – these, the modern slave drivers" who exact "more and yet more surplus value out of the wage-slaves whom they employ." And they think it "high time" that trade should be "removed from the control of individual greed."[8]

It remains to point out that the tendencies thus variously displayed, are being strengthened by press-advocacy, daily more pronounced. Journalists, always chary of saying that which is distasteful to their readers, are some of them going with the stream and adding to its force. Legislative meddlings which they would once have condemned they now pass in silence, if they do not advocate them; and they speak of *laissez-faire* as an exploded doctrine. "People are no longer frightened at the thought of socialism," is the statement which meets us one day. On another day, a town which does not adopt the Free Libraries Act is sneered at as being alarmed by a measure so moderately communistic. And then, along with editorial assertions that this economic evolution is coming and must be accepted, there is prominence given to the contributions of its advocates. Meanwhile those who regard the recent course of legislation as disastrous, and see that its future course is likely to be still more disastrous, are being reduced to silence by the belief that it is useless to reason with people in a state of political intoxication.

See, then, the many concurrent causes which threaten continually to accelerate the transformation now going on. There is that spread of regulation caused by following precedents, which become the more

---

[8] *Socialism made Plain*, Reeves, 185, Fleet Street. [Democratic Federation, *Socialism made Plain: being the Social and Political Manifesto of the Democratic Federation*, London, 1884.]

authoritative the further the policy is carried. There is that increasing need for administrative compulsions and restraints, which results from the unforeseen evils and shortcomings of preceding compulsions and restraints. Moreover, every additional State-interference strengthens the tacit assumption that it is the duty of the State to deal with all evils and secure all benefits. Increasing power of a growing administrative organization is accompanied by decreasing power of the rest of the society to resist its further growth and control. The multiplication of careers opened by a developing bureaucracy, tempts members of the classes regulated by it to favour its extension, as adding to the chances of safe and respectable places for their relatives. The people at large, led to look on benefits received through public agencies as gratis benefits, have their hopes continually excited by the prospects of more. A spreading education, furthering the diffusion of pleasing errors rather than of stern truths, renders such hopes both stronger and more general. Worse still, such hopes are ministered to by candidates for public choice, to augment their chances of success; and leading statesmen, in pursuit of party ends, bid for popular favour by countenancing them. Getting repeated justifications from new laws harmonizing with their doctrines, political enthusiasts and unwise philanthropists push their agitations with growing confidence and success. Journalism, ever responsive to popular opinion, daily strengthens it by giving it voice; while counter-opinion, more and more discouraged, finds little utterance.

Thus influences of various kinds conspire to increase corporate action and decrease individual action. And the change is being on all sides aided by schemers, each of whom thinks only of his pet project and not at all of the general re-organization which his, joined with others such, are working out. It is said that the French Revolution devoured its own children. Here an analogous catastrophe seems not unlikely. The numerous socialistic changes made by Act of Parliament, joined with the numerous others presently to be made, will by-and-by be all merged in State-Socialism – swallowed in the vast wave which they have little by little raised.

"But why is this change described as 'the coming slavery'?" is a question which many will still ask. The reply is simple. All socialism involves slavery.

What is essential to the idea of a slave? We primarily think of him as one who is owned by another. To be more than nominal, however, the ownership must be shown by control of the slave's actions – a control which is habitually for the benefit of the controller. That which fundamentally distinguishes the slave is that he labours under coercion to satisfy another's desires. The relation admits of sundry gradations. Remembering that originally the slave is a prisoner whose life is at the mercy of his captor, it suffices here to note that there is a harsh form of slavery in which, treated as an animal, he has to expend his entire effort for his owner's advantage. Under a system less harsh, though occupied chiefly in working for his owner, he is allowed a short time in which to work for himself, and some ground on which to grow extra food. A further amelioration gives him power to sell the produce of his plot and keep the proceeds. Then we come to the still more moderated form which commonly arises where, having been a free man working on his own land, conquest turns him into what we distinguish as a serf; and he has to give to his owner each year a fixed amount of labour or produce, or both: retaining the rest himself. Finally, in some cases, as in Russia until recently, he is allowed to leave his owner's estate and work or trade for himself elsewhere, under the condition that he shall pay an annual sum. What is it which, in these cases, leads us to qualify our conception of the slavery as more or less severe? Evidently the greater or smaller extent to which effort is compulsorily expended for the benefit of another instead of for self-benefit. If all the slave's labour is for his owner the slavery is heavy, and if but little it is light. Take now a further step. Suppose an owner dies, and his estate with its slaves comes into the hands of trustees; or suppose the estate and everything on it to be bought by a company; is the condition of the slave any the better if the amount of his compulsory labour remains the same? Suppose that for a company we substitute the community; does it make any difference to the slave if the time he has to work for others is as great, and the time left for himself is as small, as before? The essential question is – How much is he compelled to labour for other benefit than his own, and how much can he labour for his own benefit? The degree of his slavery varies according to the ratio between that which he is forced to yield up and that which he is allowed to retain; and it matters not whether his master is a single person or a society. If, without option, he has to labour for the society, and receives from the general stock such portion as the society awards him, he becomes a slave to the society. Socialistic arrangements necessitate an enslavement of this kind; and towards such an enslavement many recent measures, and still more the measures advocated, are carrying us. Let us observe, first, their proximate effects, and then their ultimate effects.

The policy initiated by the Industrial Dwellings Acts admits of development, and will develop. Where municipal bodies turn house-builders, they inevitably lower the values of houses otherwise built, and check the supply of more. Every dictation respecting modes of building and conveniences to be provided, diminishes the builder's profit, and prompts him to use his capital where the profit is not thus diminished. So, too, the owner, already finding that small houses entail much labour and many losses – already subject to troubles of inspection and interference, and to consequent costs, and having his property daily rendered a more undesirable investment, is prompted to sell; and as buyers are for like reasons deterred, he has to sell at a loss. And now these still-multiplying regulations, ending, it may be, as Lord Grey proposes, in one requiring the owner to maintain the salubrity of his houses by evicting dirty tenants, and thus adding to his other responsibilities that of inspector of nuisances, must further prompt sales and further deter purchasers: so necessitating greater depreciation. What must happen? The multiplication of houses, and especially small houses, being increasingly checked, there must come an increasing demand upon the local authority to make up for the deficient supply. More and more the municipal or kindred body will have to build houses, or to purchase houses rendered unsaleable to private persons in the way shown – houses which, greatly lowered in value as they must become, it will, in many cases, pay to buy rather than to build new ones. Nay, this process must work in a double way; since every entailed increase of local taxation still further depreciates property.[9] And then, when in towns this process has gone so far as to make the local authority the chief owner of houses, there will be

[9] If any one thinks such fears are groundless, let him contemplate the fact that from 1867–8 to 1880–1, our annual local expenditure for the United Kingdom has grown from £36,132,834 to £63,276,283; and that during the same 13 years, the municipal expenditure in England and Wales alone, has grown from 13 millions to 30 millions a year! How the increase of public burdens will join with other causes in bringing about public ownership, is shown by a statement made by Mr. W. Rathbone, M.P., to which my attention has been drawn since the above paragraph was in type. He says, "within my own experience, local taxation in New York has risen from 12s. 6d. per cent. to £2 12s. 6d. per cent. on the capital of its citizens – a charge which would more than absorb the whole income of an average English landlord." *Nineteenth Century*, February, 1883. [W. Rathbone, 'Local Government in England and Wales (Part 1)', *Nineteenth Century*, Vol. 13, February, 1883, pp. 297–313.]

a good precedent for publicly providing houses for the rural population, as proposed in the Radical programme,[10] and as urged by the
Democratic Federation; which insists on "the compulsory construction of healthy artisans' and agricultural labourers' dwellings in proportion to the population." Manifestly, the tendency of that which
has been done, is being done, and is presently to be done, is to
approach the socialistic ideal in which the community is sole
house-proprietor.

Such, too, must be the effect of the daily-growing policy on the
tenure and utilization of the land. More numerous public benefits,
to be achieved by more numerous public agencies, at the cost of
augmented public burdens, must increasingly deduct from the
returns on land; until, as the depreciation in value becomes greater
and greater, the resistance to change of tenure becomes less and less.
Already, as every one knows, there is in many places difficulty in
obtaining tenants, even at greatly reduced rents; and land of inferior
fertility in some cases lies idle, or when farmed by the owner is often
farmed at a loss. Clearly the profit on capital invested in land is not
such that taxes, local and general, can be greatly raised to support
extended public administrations, without an absorption of it which
will prompt owners to sell, and make the best of what reduced price
they can get by emigrating and buying land not subject to heavy
burdens; as, indeed, some are now doing. This process, carried far,
must have the result of throwing inferior land out of cultivation; after
which there will be raised more generally the demand made by Mr.
Arch, who, addressing the Radical Association of Brighton lately, and
contending that existing landlords do not make their land adequately
productive for the public benefit, said "he should like the present
Government to pass a Compulsory Cultivation Bill:" an applauded
proposal which he justified by instancing compulsory vaccination
(thus illustrating the influence of precedent). And this demand will
be pressed, not only by the need for making the land productive,
but also by the need for employing the rural population. After the
Government has extended the practice of hiring the unemployed to
work on deserted lands, or lands acquired at nominal prices, there
will be reached a stage whence there is but a small further step

[10] *Fortnightly Review*, November, 1883, pp. 619–20. [J. Collings, 'The Radical Programme (No. iv): the Agricultural Labourer', *Fortnightly Review*, Vol. 40, November,
1883, pp. 609–25.]

to that arrangement which, in the programme of the Democratic Federation, is to follow nationalization of the land – the "organization of agricultural and industrial armies under State control on co-operative principles."

To one who doubts whether such a revolution may be so reached, facts may be cited showing its likelihood. In Gaul, during the decline of the Roman Empire, "so numerous were the receivers in comparison with the payers, and so enormous the weight of taxation, that the labourer broke down, the plains became deserts, and woods grew where the plough had been."[11] In like manner, when the French Revolution was approaching, the public burdens had become such, that many farms remained uncultivated and many were deserted: one-quarter of the soil was absolutely lying waste; and in some provinces one-half was in health.[12] Nor have we been without incidents of a kindred nature at home. Besides the facts that under the old Poor Law the rates had in some parishes risen to half the rental, and that in various places farms were lying idle, there is the fact that in one case the rates had absorbed the whole proceeds of the soil.

At Cholesbury, in Buckinghamshire, in 1832, the poor-rate "suddenly ceased in consequence of the impossibility to continue its collection, the landlords having given up their rents, the farmers their tenancies, and the clergyman his glebe and his tithes. The clergyman, Mr. Jeston, states that in October, 1832, the parish officers threw up their books, and the poor assembled in a body before his door while he was in bed, asking for advice and food. Partly from his own small means, partly from the charity of neighbours, and partly by rates in aid, imposed on the neighbouring parishes, they were for some time supported."[13]

And the Commissioners add that "the benevolent rector recommends that the whole of the land should be divided among the able-bodied paupers:" hoping that after help afforded for two years, they might be able to maintain themselves. These facts, giving colour to the prophecy made in Parliament that continuance of the old Poor Law for another thirty years would throw the land out of cultivation, clearly

[11] Lactant. *De M. Persecut.*, cc. 7, 23. [L. C. F. Lactantius, *De Mortibus Persecutorum*.]
[12] Taine, *L'Ancien Régime*, pp. 337–8 (in the English translation). [H. A. Taine, *L'Ancien Régime*, English translation by J. Durand, London, 1876.]
[13] *Report of Commissioners for Inquiry into the Administration and Practical Operation of the Poor Laws*, p. 37. February 20, 1834.

show that increase of public burdens may end in forced cultivation under public control.

Then, again, comes State-ownership of railways. Already this exists to a large extent on the Continent. Already we have had here a few years ago loud advocacy of it. And now the cry, which was raised by sundry politicians and publicists, is taken up afresh by the Democratic Federation; which proposes "State-appropriation of railways, with or without compensation." Evidently, pressure from above joined by pressure from below, is likely to effect this change dictated by the policy everywhere spreading; and with it must come many attendant changes. For railway-proprietors, at first owners and workers of railways only, have become masters of numerous businesses directly or indirectly connected with railways; and these will have to be purchased by Government when the railways are purchased. Already exclusive letter-carrier, exclusive transmitter of telegrams, and on the way to become exclusive carrier of parcels, the State will not only be exclusive carrier of passengers, goods, and minerals, but will add to its present various trades many other trades. Even now, besides erecting its naval and military establishments and building harbours, docks, breakwaters, &c., it does the work of shipbuilder, cannon-founder, small-arms maker, manufacturer of ammunition, army-clothier and bootmaker; and when the railways have been appropriated "with or without compensation," as the Democratic Federationists say, it will have to become locomotive-engine-builder, carriage-maker, tarpaulin and grease manufacturer, passenger-vessel owner, coal-miner, stone-quarrier, omnibus proprietor, &c. Meanwhile its local lieutenants, the municipal governments, already in many places suppliers of water, gas-makers, owners and workers of tramways, proprietors of baths, will doubtless have undertaken various other businesses. And when the State, directly or by proxy, has thus come into possession of, or has established, numerous concerns for wholesale production and for wholesale distribution, there will be good precedents for extending its function to retail distribution: following such an example, say, as is offered by the French Government, which has long been a retail tobacconist.

Evidently then, the changes made, the changes in progress, and the changes urged, will carry us not only towards State-ownership of land and dwellings and means of communication, all to be administered and worked by State-agents, but towards State-usurpation of all industries: the private forms of which, disadvantaged more and more in competition with the State, which can arrange everything for its own convenience, will more and more die away; just as many voluntary schools have, in presence of Board-schools. And so will be brought about the desired ideal of the Socialists.

And now when there has been compassed this desired ideal, which "practical" politicians are helping Socialists to reach, and which is so tempting on that bright side which Socialists contemplate, what must be the accompanying shady side which they do not contemplate? It is a matter of common remark, often made when a marriage is impending, that those possessed by strong hopes habitually dwell on the promised pleasures and think nothing of the accompanying pains. A further exemplification of this truth is supplied by these political enthusiasts and fanatical revolutionists. Impressed with the miseries existing under our present social arrangements, and not regarding these miseries as caused by the ill-working of a human nature but partially adapted to the social state, they imagine them to be forthwith curable by this or that re-arrangement. Yet, even did their plans succeed it could only be by substituting one kind of evil for another. A little deliberate thought would show that under their proposed arrangements, their liberties must be surrendered in proportion as their material welfares were cared for.

For no form of co-operation, small or great, can be carried on without regulation, and an implied submission to the regulating agencies. Even one of their own organizations for effecting social changes yields them proof. It is compelled to have its councils, its local and general officers, its authoritative leaders, who must be obeyed under penalty of confusion and failure. And the experience of those who are loudest in their advocacy of a new social order under the paternal control of a Government, shows that even in private voluntarily-formed societies, the power of the regulative organization becomes great, if not irresistible; often, indeed, causing grumbling and restiveness among those controlled. Trades Unions which carry on a kind of industrial war in defence of workers' interests *versus* employers' interests, find that subordination almost military in its strictness is needful to secure efficient action; for divided councils prove fatal to success. And even in bodies of co-operators, formed for carrying on manufacturing or distributing businesses, and not needing that obedience to leaders which is required where the aims are offensive or defensive, it is still found that the administrative agency gains such supremacy that there arise complaints about "the tyranny of organization." Judge then what must happen when, instead of relatively small combinations, to which men may belong or not as they please, we have a national combination in which each citizen finds himself incorporated, and from which he cannot separate himself without leaving the country. Judge what must under such conditions become the despotism of a graduated and centralized officialism, holding in its hands the resources of the community, and having behind it whatever amount of force it finds requisite to carry out its decrees and maintain what it calls order. Well may Prince Bismarck display leanings towards State-socialism.

And then after recognizing, as they must if they think out their scheme, the power possessed by the regulative agency in the new social system so temptingly pictured, let its advocates ask themselves to what end this power must be used. Not dwelling exclusively, as they habitually do, on the material well-being and the mental gratifications to be provided for them by a beneficent administration, let them dwell a little on the price to be paid. The officials cannot create the needful supplies: they can but distribute among individuals that which the individuals have joined to produce. If the public agency is required to provide for them, it must reciprocally require them to furnish the means. There cannot be, as under our existing system, agreement between employer and employed – this the scheme excludes. There must in place of it be command by local authorities over workers, and acceptance by the workers of that which the authorities assign to them. And this, indeed, is the arrangement distinctly, but as it would seem inadvertently, pointed to by the members of the Democratic Federation. For they propose that production should be carried on by "agricultural and industrial *armies* under State-control:" apparently not remembering that armies pre-suppose grades of officers, by whom obedience would have to be insisted upon; since otherwise neither order nor efficient work could be ensured. So that each would stand toward the governing agency in the relation of slave to master.

"But the governing agency would be a master which he and others made and kept constantly in check; and one which therefore would not control him or others more than was needful for the benefit of each and all."

To which reply the first rejoinder is that, even if so, each member of the community as an individual would be a slave to the community as a whole. Such a relation has habitually existed in militant communities, even under quasi-popular forms of government. In ancient Greece the accepted principle was that the citizen belonged neither to himself nor to his family, but belonged to his city – the city being with the Greek equivalent to the community. And this doctrine, proper to a state of constant warfare, is a doctrine which socialism unawares re-introduces into a state intended to be purely industrial. The services of each will belong to the aggregate of all; and for these services, such returns will be given as the authorities think proper. So that even if the administration is of the beneficent kind intended to be secured, slavery, however mild, must be the outcome of the arrangement.

A second rejoinder is that the administration will presently become not of the intended kind, and that the slavery will not be mild. The socialist speculation is vitiated by an assumption like that which vitiates the speculations of the "practical" politician. It is assumed that officialism will work as it is intended to work, which it never does. The machinery of Communism, like existing social machinery, has to be framed out of existing human nature; and the defects of existing human nature will generate in the one the same evils as in the other. The love of power, the selfishness, the injustice, the untruthfulness, which often in comparatively short times bring private organizations to disaster, will inevitably, where their effects accumulate from generation to generation, work evils far greater and less remediable; since, vast and complex and possessed of all the resources, the administrative organization once developed and consolidated, must become irresistible. And if there needs proof that the periodic exercise of electoral power would fail to prevent this, it suffices to instance the French Government, which, purely popular in origin, and subject at short intervals to popular judgment, nevertheless tramples on the freedom of citizens to an extent which the English delegates to the late Trades Unions Congress say "is a disgrace to, and an anomaly in, a Republican nation."

The final result would be a revival of despotism. A disciplined army of civil officials, like an army of military officials, gives supreme power to its head – a power which has often led to usurpation, as in mediæval Europe and still more in Japan – nay, has thus so led among our neighbours, within our own times. The recent confessions of M. de Maupas have shown how readily a constitutional head, elected and trusted by the whole people, may, with the aid of a few unscrupulous confederates, paralyse the representative body and make himself autocrat. That those who rose to power in a socialistic organization would not scruple to carry out their aims at all costs, we have good reason for concluding. When we find that shareholders who, sometimes gaining but often losing, have made that railway-system by which national prosperity has been so greatly increased, are spoken of by the council of the Democratic Federation as having "laid hands" on the means of communication, we may infer that those who directed a socialistic administration might interpret with extreme perversity the claims of individuals and classes under their control. And when, further, we find members of this same council urging that the State should take possession of the railways, "with or without compensation," we may suspect that the heads of the ideal society desired, would be but little deterred by considerations of equity from pursuing whatever policy they thought needful: a policy which would always be one identified with their own supremacy. It would need but a war with an adjacent society, or some internal discontent demanding forcible suppression, to at once transform a socialistic administration into a grinding tyranny like that of ancient Peru; under which the mass of the people, controlled by grades of officials, and leading lives that were inspected out-of-doors and in-doors, laboured for the support of the organization which regulated them, and were left with but a bare subsistence for themselves. And then would be completely revived, under a different form, that *régime* of status – that system of compulsory co-operation, the decaying tradition of which is represented by the old Toryism, and towards which the new Toryism is carrying us back.

"But we shall be on our guard against all that – we shall take precautions to ward off such disasters," will doubtless say the enthusiasts. Be they "practical" politicians with their new regulative measures, or communists with their schemes for re-organizing labour, their reply is ever the same:– "It is true that plans of kindred nature have, from unforeseen causes or adverse accidents, or the misdeeds of those concerned, been brought to failure; but this time we shall profit by past experiences and succeed." There seems no getting people to accept the truth, which nevertheless is conspicuous enough, that the welfare of a society and the justice of its arrangements are at bottom dependent on the characters of its members; and that improvement in neither can take place without that improvement in character which results from carrying on peaceful industry under the restraints imposed by an orderly social life. The belief, not only of the socialists but also of those so-called Liberals who are diligently preparing the way for them, is that by due skill an ill-working humanity may be framed into well-working institutions. It is a delusion. The defective natures of citizens will show themselves in the bad acting of whatever social structure they are arranged into. There is no political alchemy by which you can get golden conduct out of leaden instincts.

NOTE – Two replies by socialists to the foregoing article have appeared since its publication – *Socialism and Slavery* by H. M. Hyndman and *Herbert Spencer on Socialism* by Frank Fairman.[14] Notice of them here must be limited to saying that, as usual with antagonists, they ascribe to me opinions which I do not hold. Disapproval of Socialism does not, as Mr. Hyndman assumes, necessitate approval of existing arrangements. Many things he reprobates I reprobate quite as much; but I dissent from his remedy. The gentleman who writes under the pseudonym of "Frank Fairman," reproaches me with having receded from that sympathetic defence of the labouring-classes which he finds in *Social Statics*; but I am quite unconscious of any such change as he alleges. Looking with a lenient eye upon the irregularities of those whose lives are hard, by no means involves tolerance of good-for-nothings.

---

[14] [H. M. Hyndman, *Socialism and Slavery: Being an Answer to Mr. Herbert Spencer's Attack upon the Democratic Federation*, London, 1884; and F. Fairman, *Herbert Spencer on Socialism: A Reply to the Article Entitled 'The Coming Slavery'*, London, 1884.]

The Sins of Legislators

Be it or be it not true that Man is shapen in iniquity and conceived in sin, it is unquestionably true that Government is begotten of aggression and by aggression. In small undeveloped societies where for ages complete peace has continued, there exists nothing like what we call Government: no coercive agency, but mere honorary headship, if any headship at all. In these exceptional communities, unaggressive and from special causes unaggressed upon, there is so little deviation from the virtues of truthfulness, honesty, justice, and generosity, that nothing beyond an occasional expression of public opinion by informally-assembled elders is needful.[1] Conversely, we find proofs that, at first recognized but temporarily during leadership in war, the authority of a chief is permanently established by continuity of war; and grows strong where successful aggression ends in subjection of neighbouring tribes. And thence onwards, examples furnished by all races put beyond doubt the truth, that the coercive power of the chief, developing into king, and king of kings (a frequent title in the ancient East), becomes great in proportion as conquest becomes habitual and the union of subdued nations extensive.[2] Comparisons disclose a further truth which should be ever present to us – the truth that the aggressiveness of the ruling power inside a society increases with its aggressiveness outside the society. As, to make an efficient army, the soldiers in their several grades must be subordinate to the commander; so, to make an efficient fighting community, must the citizens be subordinate to the ruling power. They must furnish

[1] Political Institutions, §§437, 573 [in Vol. 2 of *The Principles of Sociology*].
[2] *Ibid.*, §471–3.

recruits to the extent demanded, and yield up whatever property is required.

An obvious implication is that the ethics of Government, originally identical with the ethics of war, must long remain akin to them; and can diverge from them only as warlike activities and preparations become less. Current evidence shows this. At present on the Continent, the citizen is free only when his services as a soldier are not demanded; and during the rest of his life he is largely enslaved in supporting the military organization. Even among ourselves, a serious war would, by the necessitated conscription, suspend the liberties of large numbers and trench on the liberties of the rest, by taking from them through taxes whatever supplies were needed – that is, forcing them to labour so many days more for the State. Inevitably the established code of conduct in the dealings of Governments with citizens, must be allied to their code of conduct in their dealings with one another.

I am not, under the title of this article, about to treat of the trespasses and the revenges for trespasses, accounts of which constitute the great mass of history; nor to trace the internal inequities which have ever accompanied the external inequities. I do not propose here to catalogue the crimes of irresponsible legislators; beginning with that of King Khufu, the stones of whose vast tomb were laid in the bloody sweat of tens of thousands of slaves toiling through long years under the lash; going on to those committed by conquerors, Egyptian, Assyrian, Persian, Macedonian, Roman, and the rest; and ending with those of Napoleon, whose ambition to set his foot on the neck of the civilized world, cost not less than two million lives.[3] Nor do I propose here to enumerate those sins of responsible legislators seen in the long list of laws made in the interests of dominant classes – a list coming down in our own country to those under which there were long maintained slavery and the slave-trade, torturing nearly 40,000 negroes annually by close packing during a tropical voyage, and killing a large percentage of them, and ending with that of the corn-laws, by which, says Sir Erskine May, "to ensure high rents, it had been decreed that multitudes should hunger."[4]

[3] Lanfrey. See also *Study of Sociology*, p. 42, and Appendix. [P. Lanfrey, *The History of Napoleon the First*, 4 vols., London and New York, 1871-9.]

[4] *Constitutional History of England*, ii. p. 617. [Sir T. E. May, *The Constitutional History of England since the Accession of George the Third, 1760-1860*, 2 vols., London, 1863.]

Not, indeed, that a presentation of the conspicuous misdeeds of legislators, responsible and irresponsible, would be useless. It would have several uses – one of them relevant to the truth above pointed out. Such a presentation would make clear how that identity of governmental ethics with military ethics which necessarily exists during primitive times, when the army is simply the mobilized society and the society is the quiescent army, continues through long stages, and even now affects in great degrees our law-proceedings and our daily lives. Having, for instance, shown that in numerous savage tribes the judicial function of the chief does not exist, or is nominal, and that very generally during early stages of European civilization, each man had to defend himself and rectify his private wrongs as best he might – having shown that in mediæval times the right of private war among members of the military order was brought to an end, not because the head ruler thought it his duty to arbitrate, but because private wars interfered with the efficiency of his army in public wars – having shown that the administration of justice displayed through subsequent ages a large amount of its primitive nature, in trial by battle carried on before the king or his deputy as umpire, and which, among ourselves, continued nominally to be an alternative form of trial down to 1819; it might then be pointed out that even now there survives trial by battle under another form: counsel being the champions and purses the weapons. In civil cases, the ruling agency cares scarcely more than of old about rectifying the wrongs of the injured; but, practically, its deputy does little else than to enforce the rules of the fight: the result being less a question of equity than a question of pecuniary ability and forensic skill. Nay, so little concern for the administration of justice is shown by the ruling agency, that when, by legal conflict carried on in the presence of its deputy, the combatants have been pecuniarily bled even to the extent of producing prostration, and when an appeal being made by one of them the decision is reversed, the beaten combatant is made to pay for the blunders of the deputy, or of a preceding deputy; and not unfrequently the wronged man, who sought protection or restitution, is taken out of court pecuniarily dead.

Adequately done, such a portrayal of governmental misdeeds of commission and omission, proving that the partially-surviving code of ethics arising in, and proper to, a state of war, still vitiates governmental action, might greatly moderate the hopes of those who are anxious to extend governmental control. After observing that along with the still-manifest traits of that primitive political structure which chronic militancy produces, there goes a still-manifest survival of its primitive principles; the reformer and the philanthropist might be less sanguine in their anticipations of good from its all-pervading agency, and might be more inclined to trust agencies of a non-governmental kind.

But leaving out the greater part of the large topic comprehended under the title of this article, I propose here to deal only with a comparatively small remaining part – those sins of legislators which are not generated by their personal ambitions or class interests, but result from a lack of the study by which they are morally bound to prepare themselves.

A druggist's assistant who, after listening to the description of pains which he mistakes for those of colic, but which are really caused by inflammation of the cæcum, prescribes a sharp purgative and kills the patient, is found guilty of manslaughter. He is not allowed to excuse himself on the ground that he did not intend harm but hoped for good. The plea that he simply made a mistake in his diagnosis is not entertained. He is told that he had no right to risk disastrous consequences by meddling in a matter concerning which his knowledge was so inadequate. The fact that he was ignorant how great was his ignorance is not accepted in bar of judgment. It is tacitly assumed that the experience common to all should have taught him that even the skilled, and much more the unskilled, make mistakes in the identification of disorders and in the appropriate treatment; and that having disregarded the warning derivable from common experience, he was answerable for the consequences.

We measure the responsibilities of legislators for mischiefs they may do, in a much more lenient fashion. In most cases, so far from thinking of them as deserving punishment for causing disasters by laws ignorantly enacted, we scarcely think of them as deserving reprobation. It is held that common experience should have taught the druggist's assistant, untrained as he is, not to interfere; but it is not held that common experience should have taught the legislator not to interfere till he has trained himself. Though multitudinous facts are before him in the recorded legislation of our own country and of other countries, which should impress on him the immense evils caused by wrong treatment, he is not condemned for disregarding these warnings against rash meddling. Contrariwise, it is thought meritorious in him when – perhaps lately from college, perhaps fresh from keeping a pack of hounds which made him popular in his county, perhaps emerging from a provincial town where he acquired a fortune, perhaps rising from the bar at which he has gained a name as an advocate – he enters Parliament; and forthwith, in quite a light-hearted way, begins to aid or hinder this or that means of operating on the body politic. In this case there is no occasion even to make for him the excuse that he does not know how little he knows; for the public at large agrees with him in thinking it needless that he should know anything more than what the debates on the proposed measures tell him.

And yet the mischiefs wrought by uninstructed law-making, enormous in their amount as compared with those caused by uninstructed medical treatment, are conspicuous to all who do but glance over its history. The reader must pardon me while I recall a few familiar instances. Century after century, statesmen went on enacting usury laws which made worse the condition of the debtor – raising the rate of interest "from five to six when intending to reduce it to four,"[5] as under Louis XV.; and indirectly producing undreamt of evils of many kinds, such as preventing the reproductive use of spare capital, and "burdening the small proprietors with a multitude of perpetual services."[6] So, too, the endeavours which in England continued through five hundred years to stop forestalling, and which in France, as Arthur Young witnessed, prevented any one from buying "more than two bushels of wheat at market,"[7] went on generation after generation increasing the miseries and mortality due to dearth; for, as everybody now knows, the wholesale dealer, who was in the statute "De Pistoribus" vituperated as "an open oppressor of poor people,"[8] is simply one whose function it is to equalize the supply of

---

[5] Lecky, *Rationalism*, ii. 293–4. [W. E. H. Lecky, *History of the Rise and Influence of the Spirit of Rationalism in Europe*, 2 vols., London 1865, p. 294.]
[6] De Tocqueville, *The State of Society in France before the Revolution*, p. 421. [A. De Tocqueville, *On the State of Society in France before the Revolution*, London, 1856.]
[7] Young's *Travels*, i. 128–9. [A. Young, *Travels during the Years 1787, 1788 and 1789. Undertaken more particularly with a View of Ascertaining the Cultivation, Wealth, Resources and National Prosperity of the Kingdom of France*, 2 vols., Bury St Edmunds, 1792.]
[8] Craik's *History of British Commerce*, i. 134. [G. L. Craik, *The History of British Commerce From the Earliest Times*, 3 vols., London, 1844.]

a commodity by checking unduly rapid consumption. Of kindred nature was the measure which, in 1315, to diminish the pressure of famine, prescribed the prices of foods, but which was hastily repealed after it had caused entire disappearance of various foods from the markets; and also such measures, more continuously operating, as those which settled by magisterial order "the reasonable gains" of victuallers.[9] Of like spirit and followed by allied mischiefs have been the many endeavours to fix wages, which began with the Statute of Labourers under Edward III., and ceased only sixty years ago; when, having long galvanized in Spitalfields a decaying industry, and fostered there a miserable population, Lords and Commons finally gave up fixing silk-weavers' earnings by the decisions of magistrates.

Here I imagine an impatient interruption. "We know all that; the story is stale. The mischiefs of interfering with trade have been dinned in our ears till we are weary; and no one needs to be taught the lesson afresh." My first reply is that by the great majority the lesson was never properly learnt at all, and that many of those who did learn it have forgotten it. For just the same pleas which of old were put in for these dictations, are again put in. In the statute 35 of Edward III., which aimed to keep down the price of herrings (but was soon repealed because it raised the price), it was complained that people "coming to the fair . . . do bargain for herring, and every of them, by malice and envy, increase upon other, and, if one proffer forty shillings, another will proffer ten shillings more, and the third sixty shillings, and so every one surmounteth other in the bargain."[10] And now the "higgling of the market," here condemned and ascribed to "malice and envy," is being again condemned. The evils of competition have all along been the stock cry of the Socialists; and the council of the Democratic Federation denounces the carrying on of exchange under "the control of individual greed and profit." My second reply is that interferences with the law of supply and demand, which a generation ago were admitted to be habitually mischievous, are now being daily made by Acts of Parliament in new fields; and that, as I shall presently show, they are in these fields increasing the evils to be cured and producing fresh ones, as of old they did in fields no longer intruded upon.

Returning from this parenthesis, I go on to explain that the above

[9] *Ibid.*, 136–7 [p. 136].
[10] *Ibid.*, 137.

Acts are named to remind the reader that uninstructed legislators have in past times continually increased human suffering in their endeavours to mitigate it; and I have now to add that if these evils, shown to be legislatively intensified or produced, be multiplied by ten or more, a conception will be formed of the aggregate evils caused by law-making unguided by social science. In a paper read to the Statistical Society in May, 1873, Mr. Janson, vice-president of the Law Society, stated that from the Statute of Merton (20 Henry III.) to the end of 1872, there had been passed 18,110 public Acts; of which he estimated that four-fifths had been wholly or partially repealed. He also stated that the number of public Acts repealed wholly or in part, or amended, during the three years 1870–71–72 had been 3,532, of which 2,759 had been totally repealed. To see whether this rate of repeal has continued, I have referred to the annually-issued volumes of "The Public General Statutes" for the last three sessions. Saying nothing of the numerous amended Acts, the result is that in the last three sessions there have been totally repealed, separately or in groups, 650 Acts, *belonging to the present reign*, besides many of preceding reigns. This, of course, is greatly above the average rate; for there has of late been an active purgation of the statute-book. But making every allowance, we must infer that within our own times, repeals have mounted some distance into the thousands. Doubtless a number of them have been of laws that were obsolete; others have been demanded by changes of circumstances (though seeing how many of them are of quite recent Acts, this has not been a large cause); others simply because they were inoperative; and others have been consequent on the consolidations of numerous Acts into single Acts. But unquestionably in multitudinous cases, repeals came because the Acts had proved injurious. We talk glibly of such changes – we think of cancelled legislation with indifference. We forget that before laws are abolished they have generally been inflicting evils more or less serious; some for a few years, some for tens of years, some for centuries. Change your vague idea of a bad law into a definite idea of it as an agency operating on people's lives, and you see that it means so much of pain, so much of illness, so much of mortality. A vicious form of legal procedure, for example, either enacted or tolerated, entails on suitors, costs, or delays, or defeats. What do these imply? Loss of money, often ill-spared; great and prolonged anxiety; frequently consequent illness; unhappiness of family and dependents; children stinted in food and clothing – all of them miseries which bring after them multiplied remoter miseries. Add to which there are the far more numerous cases of those who, lacking the means or the courage to enter on law-suits, and therefore submitting to frauds, are impoverished; and have similarly to bear the pains of body and mind which ensue. Even to say that a law has been simply a hindrance, is to say that it has caused needless loss of time, extra trouble, and additional worry; and among over-burdened people extra trouble and worry imply, here and there, break-downs in health with their entailed direct and indirect sufferings. Seeing, then, that bad legislation means injury to men's lives, judge what must be the total amount of mental distress, physical pain, and raised mortality, which these thousands of repealed Acts of Parliament represent! Fully to bring home the truth that law-making unguided by adequate knowledge brings immense evils, let me take a special case which a question of the day recalls.

Already I have hinted that interferences with the connexion between supply and demand, given up in certain fields after immense mischiefs had been done during many centuries, are now taking place in other fields. This connexion is supposed to hold only where it has been proved to hold by the evils of disregarding it: so feeble is men's belief in it. There seems no suspicion that in cases where it seems to fail, natural causation has been traversed by artificial hindrances. And yet in the case to which I now refer – that of the supply of houses for the poor – it needs but to ask what laws have been doing for a long time past, to see that the terrible evils complained of are mostly law-made.

A generation ago discussion was taking place concerning the inadequacy and badness of industrial dwellings, and I had occasion to deal with the question. Here is a passage then written:–

"An architect and surveyor describes it [the Building Act] as having worked after the following manner. In those districts of London consisting of inferior houses built in that unsubstantial fashion which the New Building Act was to mend, there obtains an average rent, sufficiently remunerative to landlords whose houses were run up economically before the New Building Act was passed. This existing average rent fixes the rent that must be charged in these districts for new houses of the same accommodation – that is the same number of rooms, for the people they are built for do not appreciate the extra safety of living within walls strengthened with hoop-iron bond. Now it turns out upon trial, that houses built in accordance with the present regulations, and let at this established rate, bring in nothing like a reasonable return. Builders have consequently confined themselves to erecting houses in better districts (where the possibility of a profitable competition with pre-existing houses shows that those pre-existing houses were tolerably substantial), and have ceased to erect dwellings for the masses, except in the suburbs where no pressing sanitary evils exist. Meanwhile, in the inferior districts above described, has resulted an increase of overcrowding – half-a-dozen families in a house, a score of lodgers to a room. Nay, more than this has resulted. That state of miserable dilapidation into which these abodes of the poor are allowed to fall, is due to the absence of competition from new houses. Landlords do not find their tenants tempted away by the offer of better accommodation. Repairs, being unnecessary for securing the largest amount of profit, are not made ... In fact for a large percentage of the very horrors which our sanitary agitators are trying to cure by law, we have to thank previous agitators of the same school!"

Social Statics, p. 384 (edition of 1851)

These were not the only law-made causes of such evils. As shown in the following further passage, sundry others were recognized:–

"Writing before the repeal of the brick-duty, the *Builder* says:– 'It is supposed that one-fourth of the cost of a dwelling which lets for 2s. 6d. or 3s. a week is caused by the expense of the title-deeds and the tax on wood and bricks used in its construction. Of course, the owner of such property must be remunerated, and he therefore charges 7½d. or 9d. a week to cover these burdens.' Mr. C. Gatliff, secretary to the Society for Improving the Dwellings of the Working Classes, describing the effect of the window-tax, says:– 'They are now paying upon their institution in St. Pancras the sum of £162 16s. in window-duties, or 1 per cent. per annum upon the original outlay. The average rental paid by the Society's tenants is 5s. 6d. per week, and the window-duty deducts from this 7¼d. per week.' " *Times*, January 31, 1850.

Social Statics, p. 385 (edition of 1851).

Neither is this all the evidence which the press of those days afforded. There was published in the *Times* of December 7, 1850 (too late to be used in the above-named work, which I issued in the last week of 1850), a letter dated from the Reform Club, and signed "Architect," which contained the following passages:–

"Lord Kinnaird recommends in your paper of yesterday the construction of model lodging-houses by throwing two or three houses into one.

"Allow me to suggest to his Lordship, and to his friend Lord Ashley to whom he refers, that if, –

1. The window-tax were repealed,
2. The Building Act repealed (excepting the clauses enacting that party and external walls shall be fireproof),
3. The timber duties either equalized or repealed, and,
4. An Act passed to facilitate the transfer of property,

"There would be no more necessity for model lodging-houses than there is for model ships, model cotton-mills, or model steam-engines.

"The first limits the poor man's house to seven windows,

"The second limits the size of the poor man's house to 25 feet by 18 (about the size of a gentleman's dining-room), into which space the builder has to cram a staircase, an entrance-passage, a parlour, and a kitchen (walls and partitions included).

"The third induces the builder to erect the poor man's house of timber unfit for building purposes, the duty on the good material (Baltic) being fifteen times more than the duty on the bad or injurious article (Canadian). The Government, even, exclude the latter from all their contractors.

"The fourth would have considerable influence upon the present miserable state of the dwellings of the poor. Small freeholds might then be transferred as easily as leaseholds. The effect of building leases has been a direct inducement to bad building."

To guard against mis-statement or over-statement, I have taken the precaution to consult a large East-end builder and contractor of forty years' experience, Mr. C. Forrest, Museum Works, 17, Victoria Park Square, Bethnal Green, who, being churchwarden, member of the vestry, and of the board of guardians, adds extensive knowledge of local public affairs to his extensive knowledge of the building business. Mr. Forrest, who authorizes me to give his name, verifies the foregoing statements with the exception of one which he strengthens. He says that "Architect" understates the evil entailed by the definition of a "fourth-rate house;" since the dimensions are much less than those he gives (perhaps in conformity with the provisions of a more recent Building Act). Mr. Forrest has done more than this. Besides illustrating the bad effects of great increase in ground-rents (in sixty years from £1 to £8 10s. for a fourth-rate house) which, joined with other causes, had obliged him to abandon plans for industrial dwellings he had intended to build – besides agreeing with "Architect" that this evil has been greatly increased by the difficulties of land-transfer due to the law-established system of trusts and entails; he pointed out that a further penalty on the building of small houses is inflicted by additions to local burdens ("prohibitory imposts" he called them): one of the instances he named being that to the cost of each new house has to be added the cost of pavement, roadway and sewerage, which is charged according to length of frontage, and which, consequently, bears a far larger ratio to the value of a small house than to the value of a large one.

From these law-produced mischiefs, which were great a generation ago and have since been increasing, let us pass to more recent law-produced mischiefs. The misery, the disease, the mortality in "rookeries," made continually worse by artificial impediments to the increase of fourth-rate houses, and by the necessitated greater crowding of those which existed, having become a scandal, Government was invoked to remove the evil. It responded by Artisans' Dwellings Acts; giving to local authorities powers to pull down bad houses and provide for the building of good ones. What have been the results? A summary of the operations of the Metropolitan Board of Works, dated December 21, 1883, shows that up to last September it had, at a cost of a million and a quarter to ratepayers, unhoused 21,000 persons and provided houses for 12,000 – the remaining 9,000 to be hereafter provided for, being, meanwhile, left houseless. This is not all. Another local lieutenant of the Government, the Commission of Sewers for the City, working on the same lines, has, under legislative compulsion, pulled down in Golden Lane and Petticoat Square, masses of condemned small houses, which, together, accommodated 1,734 poor people; and of the spaces thus cleared five years ago, one has, by State-authority, been sold for a railway station, and the other is only now being covered with industrial dwellings which will eventually accommodate one-half of the expelled population: the result up to the present time being that, added to those displaced by the Metropolitan Board of Works, these 1,734 displaced five years ago, form a total of nearly 11,000 artificially made homeless, who have had to find corners for themselves in miserable places that were already overflowing!

See then what legislation has done. By ill-imposed taxes, raising the prices of bricks and timber, it added to the costs of houses; and prompted, for economy's sake, the use of bad materials in scanty quantities. To check the consequent production of wretched dwellings, it established regulations which, in mediæval fashion, dictated the quality of the commodity produced: there being no perception that by insisting on a higher quality and therefore higher price, it would limit the demand and eventually diminish the supply. By additional local burdens, legislation has of late still further hindered the building of small houses. Finally, having, by successive measures, produced first bad houses and then a deficiency of better ones, it has at length provided for the artificially-increased overflow of poor people by diminishing the house-capacity which already could not contain them!

Where then lies the blame for the miseries of the East-end? Against whom should be raised "the bitter cry of outcast London?"

The German anthropologist Bastian, tells us that a sick native of Guinea who causes the fetish to lie by not recovering, is strangled;[11] and we may reasonably suppose that among the Guinea people, any one audacious enough to call in question the power of the fetish would be promptly sacrificed. In days when governmental authority was enforced by strong measures, there was a kindred danger in saying anything disrespectful of the political fetish. Nowadays, however, the worst punishment to be looked for by one who questions its omnipotence, is that he will be reviled as a reactionary who talks *laissez-faire*. That any facts he may bring forward will appreciably decrease the established faith is not to be expected; for we are daily shown that this faith is proof against all adverse evidence. Let us contemplate a small part of that vast mass of it which passes unheeded.

"A Government-office is like an inverted filter: you send in accounts clear and they come out muddy." Such was the comparison I heard made many years ago by the late Sir Charles Fox, who, in the conduct of his business, had considerable experience of public departments. That his opinion was not a singular one, though his comparison was, all men know. Exposures by the press and criticisms in Parliament, leave no one in ignorance of the vices of red-tape routine. Its delays, perpetually complained of, and which in the time

---

[11] *Mensch*, iii., p. 225. [A. Bastian, *Der Mensch in d. Geschicte*, 3 vols., Leipzig, 1860.]

of Mr. Fox Maule went to the extent that "the commissions of officers in the army" were generally "about two years in arrear," is afresh illustrated by the issue of the first volume of the detailed census of 1881, more than two years after the information was collected. If we seek explanations of such delays, we find one origin to be a scarcely credible confusion. In the case of the census returns, the Registrar-General tells us that "the difficulty consists not merely in the vast multitude of different areas that have to be taken into account, but still more in the bewildering complexity of their boundaries:" there being 39,000 administrative areas of twenty-two different kinds which overlap one another – hundreds, parishes, boroughs, wards, petty sessional divisions, lieutenancy divisions, urban and rural sanitary districts, dioceses, registration districts, &c. And then, as Mr. Rathbone, M.P., points out,[12] these many superposed sets of areas with intersecting boundaries, have their respective governing bodies with authorities running into one another's districts. Does any one ask why for each additional administration Parliament has established a fresh set of divisions? The reply which suggests itself is – To preserve consistency of method. For this organized confusion corresponds completely with that organized confusion which Parliament each year increases by throwing on to the heap of its old Acts a hundred new Acts, the provisions of which traverse and qualify in all kinds of ways the provisions of multitudinous Acts on to which they are thrown: the onus of settling what is the law being left to private persons, who lose their property in getting judges' interpretations. And again, this system of putting networks of districts over other networks, with their conflicting authorities, is quite consistent with the method under which the reader of the Public Health Act of 1872, who wishes to know what are the powers exercised over him, is referred to 26 preceding Acts of several classes and numerous dates.[13] So, too, with administrative inertia. Continually there occur cases showing the resistance of officialism to improvements; as by the Admiralty when use of the electric telegraph was proposed, and the reply was – "We have a very good semaphore system;" or as by the Post Office, which the late Sir Charles Siemens years ago said had obstructed the employment of improved methods of telegraphing,

[12] *The Nineteenth Century*, February, 1883. [Rathbone, 'Local Government'.]
[13] "The Statistics of Legislation." By F. H. Janson, Esq., F.L.S., Vice-president of the Incorporated Law Society. [Read before the Statistical Society, May, 1873.]

and which since then has impeded the use of the telephone. Other cases akin to the case of industrial dwellings, now and then show how the State with one hand increases evils which with the other hand it tries to diminish; as when it puts a duty on fire-insurances and then makes regulations for the better putting out of fires: dictating, too, certain modes of construction, which, as Captain Shaw shows, entail additional dangers.[14] Again, the absurdities of official routine, rigid where it need not be and lax where it should be rigid, occasionally become glaring enough to cause scandals; as when a secret State-document of importance, put into the hands of an ill-paid copying clerk who was not even in permanent Government employ, was made public by him; or as when the mode of making the Moorsom fuse, which was kept secret even from our highest artillery officers, was taught to them by the Russians, who had been allowed to learn it; or as when a diagram showing the "distances at which British and foreign iron-clads could be perforated by our large guns," communicated by an enterprising *attaché* to his own Government, then became known "to all the Governments of Europe," while English officers remained ignorant of the facts.[15] So, too, with State-supervision. Guaranteeing of quality by inspection has been shown, in the hall-marking of silver, to be superfluous, while the silver trade has been decreased by it;[16] and in other cases it has lowered the quality by establishing a standard which it is useless to exceed: instance the case of the Cork butter-market, where the higher kinds are disadvantaged in not adequately profiting by their better repute;[17] or, instance the case of herring-branding (now optional) the effect of which is to put the many inferior curers who just reach the level of official approval, on a par with the few better ones who rise above it, and so to discourage these. But such lessons pass unlearned. Even where the failure of inspection is most glaring, no notice is taken of it; as instance the terrible catastrophe by which a train full of people was destroyed along with the Tay bridge. Countless denunciations, loud and unsparing, were vented against engineer and contractor;

[14] *Fire Surveys; or, a Summary of the Principles to be observed in Estimating the Risk of Buildings.* [Sir E. M. Shaw, *Fire Surveys: Principles to be Observed in Estimating the Risk of Buildings*, London, 1872.]
[15] See *Times*, October 6, 1874, where other instances are given.
[16] *The State in its Relation to Trade*, by Sir Thomas Farrer, p. 147 [London, 1883].
[17] *Ibid.*, p. 149.

but little, if anything, was said about the Government officer from whom the bridge received State-approval. So, too, with prevention of disease. It matters not that under the management or dictation of State-agents some of the worst evils occur; as when the lives of 87 wives and children of soldiers are sacrificed in the ship *Accrington*,[18] or as when typhoid fever and diphtheria are diffused by a State-ordered drainage system, as in Edinburgh;[19] or as when officially-enforced sanitary appliances, ever getting out of order, increase the evils they were to decrease.[20] Masses of such evidence leave unabated the confidence with which sanitary inspection is invoked – invoked, indeed, more than ever; as is shown in the recent suggestion that all public schools should be under the supervision of health-officers. Nay, even when the State has manifestly caused the mischief complained of, faith in its beneficent agency is not at all diminished; as we see in the fact that, having a generation ago authorized, or rather required, towns to establish drainage systems which delivered sewage into the rivers, and having thus polluted the sources of water-supply, an outcry was raised against the water-companies for the impurities of their water – an outcry which continued after these towns had been compelled, at vast extra cost, to revolutionize their drainage systems. And now, as the only remedy, there follows the demand that the State, by its local proxies, shall undertake the whole business. The State's misdoings become, as in the case of industrial dwellings, reasons for praying it to do more.

This worship of the legislature is, in one respect, indeed, less excusable than the fetish-worship to which I have tacitly compared it. The savage has the defence that his fetish is silent – does not confess its inability. But the civilized man persists in ascribing to this idol made with his own hands, powers which in one way or other it confesses it has not got. I do not mean merely that the debates daily

---

[18]   Hansard, vol. clvi., p. 718, and vol. clvii., p. 4464.
[19]   Letter of an Edinburgh M.D. in *Times* of 17th January, 1876, verifying other testimonies; one of which I had previously cited concerning Windsor, where, as in Edinburgh, there was absolutely no typhoid in the undrained parts, while it was very fatal in the drained parts. *Study of Sociology*, chap. i., notes.
[20]   I say this partly from personal knowledge; having now before me memoranda made 25 years ago, concerning such results produced under my own observation. Verifying facts have recently been given by Sir Richard Cross in the *Nineteenth Century* for January, 1884, p. 155. [Sir R. Cross, 'Homes of the Poor', *Nineteenth Century*, vol. 15, January 1884, pp. 150–66.]

tell us of legislative measures which have done evil instead of good; nor do I mean merely that the thousands of Acts of Parliament which repeal preceding Acts, are so many tacit admissions of failure. Neither do I refer only to such quasi-governmental confessions as that contained in the report of the Poor Law Commissioners, who said that – "We find, on the one hand, that there is scarcely one statute connected with the administration of public relief which has produced the effect designed by the legislature, and that the majority of them have created new evils, and aggravated those which they were intended to prevent."[21] I refer rather to confessions made by statesmen, and by State-departments. Here, for example, in a memorial addressed to Mr. Gladstone, and adopted by a highly influential meeting held under the chairmanship of the late Lord Lyttelton, I read:–

"We, the undersigned, Peers, Members of the House of Commons, Ratepayers, and Inhabitants of the Metropolis, feeling strongly the truth and force of your statement made in the House of Commons, in 1866, that, 'there is still a lamentable and deplorable state of our whole arrangements, with regard to public works – vacillation, uncertainty, costliness, extravagance, meanness, and all the conflicting vices that could be enumerated, are united in our present system,' " &c., &c.[22]

Here, again, is an example furnished by a recent minute of the Board of Trade (November, 1883), in which it is said that since "the Shipwreck Committee of 1836 scarcely a session has passed without some Act being passed or some step being taken by the legislature or the Government with this object" [prevention of ship-wrecks]; and that "the multiplicity of statutes, which were all consolidated into one Act in 1854, has again become a scandal and a reproach:" each measure being passed because previous ones had failed. And then comes presently the confession that "the loss of life and of ships has been greater since 1876 than it ever was before." Meanwhile, the cost of administration has been raised from £17,000 a year to £73,000 a year.[23]

<hr>

[21] Nicholl's *History of English Poor Law*, ii., p. 252. [Sir G. Nicholls, *History of the English Poor Law*, 2 vols., London, 1854, p. 259.]

[22] See *Times*, March 31, 1863.

[23] In these paragraphs are contained just a few additional examples. Numbers which I have before given in books and essays, will be found in *Social Statics* (1851); "Over-

It is surprising how, spite of better knowledge, the imagination is excited by artificial appliances used in particular ways. We see it all through human history, from the war-paint with which the savage frightens his adversary, down through religious ceremonies and regal processions, to the robes of a Speaker and the wand of an officially-dressed usher. I remember a child who, able to look with tolerable composure on a horrible cadaverous mask while it was held in the hand, ran away shrieking when his father put it on. A kindred change of feeling comes over constituencies when, from boroughs and counties, their members pass to the Legislative Chamber. While before them as candidates, they are, by one or other party, jeered at, lampooned, "heckled," and in all ways treated with utter disrespect. But as soon as they assemble at Westminster, those against whom taunts and invectives, charges of incompetence and folly, had been showered from press and platform, excite unlimited faith. Judging from the prayers made to them, there is nothing which their wisdom and their power cannot compass.

The reply to all this will doubtless be that nothing better than guidance by "collective wisdom" can be had – that the select men of the nation, led by a re-selected few, bring their best powers, enlightened by all the knowledge of the time, to bear on the matters before them. "What more would you have?" will be the question asked by most.

My answer is that this best knowledge of the time with which legislators are said to come prepared for their duties, is a knowledge of which the greater part is obviously irrelevant, and that they are blameworthy for not seeing what is the relevant knowledge. No amount of the linguistic acquirements by which many of them are distinguished will help their judgments in the least; nor will they be appreciably helped by the literatures these acquirements open to them. Political experiences and speculations coming from small ancient societies, through philosophers who assume that war is the normal state, that slavery is alike needful and just, and that women must remain in perpetual tutelage, can yield them but small aid in

Legislation" (1853); "Representative Government" (1857); "Specialized Administration" (1871); *Study of Sociology* (1873), and Postscript to ditto (1880); besides cases in smaller essays. [The articles are to be found in *Essays: Scientific, Political and Speculative*, vol. 3.]

judging how Acts of Parliament will work in great nations of modern types. They may ponder on the doings of all the great men by whom, according to the Carlylean theory, society is framed, and they may spend years over those accounts of international conflicts, and treacheries, and intrigues, and treaties, which fill historical works, without being much nearer understanding the how and the why of social structures and actions, and the ways in which laws affect them. Nor does such information as is picked up at the factory, on 'Change, or in the justice room, go far towards the required preparation.

That which is really needed is a systematic study of natural causation as displayed among human beings socially aggregated. Though a distinct consciousness of causation is the last trait which intellectual progress brings – though with the savage a simple mechanical cause is not conceived as such – though even among the Greeks the flight of a spear was thought of as guided by a god – though from their times down almost to our own, epidemics have been habitually regarded as of supernatural origin – and though among social phenomena, the most complex of all, causal relations may be expected to continue longest unrecognized; yet in our days, the existence of such causal relations has become clear enough to force on all who think, the inference that before meddling with them they should be diligently studied. The mere facts, now familiar, that there is a connexion between the numbers of births, deaths, and marriages, and the price of corn, and that in the same society during the same generation, the ratio of crime to population varies within narrow limits, should be sufficient to make all see that human desires, using as guide such intellect as is joined with them, act with approximate uniformity. It should be inferred that among social causes, those initiated by legislation, similarly operating with an average regularity, must not only change men's actions, but, by consequence, change their natures – probably in ways not intended. There should be recognition of the fact that social causation, more than all other causation, is a fructifying causation; and it should be seen that indirect and remote effects are no less inevitable than proximate effects. I do not mean that there is denial of these statements and inferences. But there are beliefs and beliefs – some which are held nominally, some which influence conduct in small degrees, some which sway it irresistibly under all circumstances; and unhappily the beliefs of lawmakers respecting causation in social affairs, are of the superficial sort. Let us look at some of the truths which all tacitly admit, but which scarcely any take deliberate account of in legislation.

There is the indisputable fact that each human being is in a certain degree modifiable both physically and mentally. Every theory of education, every discipline, from that of the arithmetician to that of the prize-fighter, every proposed reward for virtue or punishment for vice, implies the belief, embodied in sundry proverbs, that the use or disuse of each faculty, bodily or mental, is followed by an adaptive change in it – loss of power or gain of power, according to demand.

There is the fact, also in its broader manifestations universally recognized, that modifications of Nature in one way or other produced, are inheritable. No one denies that by the accumulation of small changes, generation after generation, constitution fits itself to conditions; so that a climate which is fatal to other races is innocuous to the adapted race. No one denies that peoples who belong to the same original stock but have spread into different habitats where they have led different lives, have acquired in course of time different aptitudes and different tendencies. No one denies that under new conditions new national characters are even now being moulded; as witness the Americans. And if no one denies a process of adaptation everywhere and always going on, it is a manifest implication that adaptive modifications must be set up by every change of social conditions.

To which there comes the undeniable corollary that every law which serves to alter men's modes of action – compelling, or restraining, or aiding, in new ways – so affects them as to cause in course of time adjustments of their natures. Beyond any immediate effect wrought, there is the remote effect, wholly ignored by most – a re-moulding of the average character: a re-moulding which may be of a desirable kind or of an undesirable kind, but which in any case is the most important of the results to be considered.

Other general truths which the citizen, and still more the legislator, ought to contemplate until they become wrought into his intellectual fabric, are disclosed when we ask how social activities are produced; and when we recognize the obvious answer that they are the aggregate results of the desires of individuals who are severally seeking satisfactions, and ordinarily pursuing the ways which, with their pre-existing habits and thoughts, seem the easiest – following the lines of least resistance: the truths of political economy being so many sequences.

It needs no proving that social structures and social actions must in some way or other be the outcome of human emotions guided by ideas – either those of ancestors or those of living men. And that the right interpretation of social phenomena is to be found in the co-operation of these factors from generation to generation, follows inevitably.

Such an interpretation soon brings us to the inference that of the aggregate results of men's desires seeking their gratifications, those which have prompted their private activities and their spontaneous co-operations, have done much more towards social development than those which have worked through governmental agencies. That abundant crops now grow where once only wild berries could be gathered, is due to the pursuit of individual satisfactions through many centuries. The progress from wigwams to good houses has resulted from wishes to increase personal welfare; and towns have arisen under the like promptings. Beginning with traffic at gatherings on occasions of religious festivals, the trading organization, now so extensive and complex, has been produced entirely by men's efforts to achieve their private ends. Perpetually Governments have thwarted and deranged the growth, but have in no way furthered it; save by partially discharging their proper function and maintaining social order. So, too, with those advances of knowledge and those improvements of appliances, by which these structural changes and these increasing activities have been made possible. It is not to the State that we owe the multitudinous useful inventions from the spade to the telephone; it was not the State which made possible extended navigation by a developed astronomy; it was not the State which made the discoveries in physics, chemistry, and the rest, which guide modern manufacturers; it was not the State which devised the machinery for producing fabrics of every kind, for transferring men and things from place to place, and for ministering in a thousand ways to our comforts. The world-wide transactions conducted in merchants' offices, the rush of traffic filling our streets, the retail distributing system which brings everything within easy reach and delivers the necessaries of life daily at our doors, are not of governmental origin. All these are results of the spontaneous activities of citizens, separate or grouped. Nay, to these spontaneous activities Governments owe the very means of performing their duties. Divest the political machinery of all those aids which Science and Art have yielded it – leave it with those only which State-officials have invented; and its functions would cease. The very language in which its laws are registered and the orders of its agents daily given, is an instrument not in the remotest degree due to the legislator; but is one which has unawares grown up during men's intercourse while pursuing their personal satisfactions.

And then a truth to which the foregoing one introduces us, is that this spontaneously-formed social organization is so bound together that you cannot act on one part without acting more or less on all parts. We see this unmistakably when a cotton-famine, first paralysing certain manufacturing districts and then affecting the doings of wholesale and retail distributors throughout the kingdom, as well as the people they supply, goes on to affect the makers and distributors, as well as the wearers, of other fabrics – woollen, linen, &c. Or we see it when a rise in the price of coal, besides influencing domestic life everywhere, hinders the greater part of our industries, raises the prices of the commodities produced, alters the consumption of them, and changes the habits of consumers. What we see clearly in these marked cases happens in every case, in sensible or in insensible ways. And manifestly, Acts of Parliament are among those factors which, beyond the effects directly produced, have countless other effects of multitudinous kinds. As I heard remarked by a distinguished professor, whose studies give ample means of judging – "When once you begin to interfere with the order of Nature there is no knowing where the results will end." And if this is true of that sub-human order of Nature to which he referred, still more is it true of that order of Nature existing in the social arrangements produced by aggregated human beings.

And now to carry home the conclusion that the legislator should bring to his business a vivid consciousness of these and other such broad truths concerning the human society with which he proposes to deal, let me present somewhat more fully one of them not yet mentioned.

The continuance of every higher species of creature depends on conformity, now to one, now to the other, of two radically-opposed principles. The early lives of its members, and the adult lives of its members, have to be dealt with in contrary ways. We will contemplate them in their natural order.

One of the most familiar facts is that animals of superior types, comparatively slow in reaching maturity, are enabled when they have reached it, to give more aid to their offspring than animals of inferior types. The adults foster their young during periods more or less prolonged, while yet the young are unable to provide for themselves; and it is obvious that maintenance of the species can be secured only by a parental care adjusted to the need consequent on imperfection. It requires no proving that the blind unfledged hedge-bird, or the young puppy even after it has acquired sight, would forthwith die if it had to keep itself warm and obtain its own food. The gratuitous parental aid must be great in proportion as the young one is of little worth, either to itself or to others; and it may diminish as fast as, by increasing development, the young one acquires worth, at first for self-sustentation, and by-and-by for sustentation of others. That is to say, during immaturity, benefits received must be inversely as the power or ability of the receiver. Clearly if during this first part of life benefits were proportioned to merits, or rewards to deserts, the species would disappear in a generation.

From this *régime* of the family-group, let us turn to the *régime* of that larger group formed by the adult members of the species. Ask what happens when the new individual, acquiring complete use of its powers and ceasing to have parental aid, is left to itself. Now there comes into play a principle just the reverse of that above described. Throughout the rest of its life, each adult gets benefit in proportion to merit – reward in proportion to desert: merit and desert in each case being understood as ability to fulfil all the requirements of life – to get food, to secure shelter, to escape enemies. Placed in competition with members of its own species and in antagonism with members of other species, it dwindles and gets killed off, or thrives and propagates, according as it is ill-endowed or well-endowed. Manifestly an opposite *régime*, could it be maintained, would, in course of time, be fatal to the species. If the benefits received by each individual were proportionate to its inferiority – if, as a consequence, multiplication of the inferior was furthered and multiplication of the superior hindered, progressive degradation would result; and eventually the degenerate species would fail to hold its ground in presence of antagonistic species and competing species.

The broad fact then, here to be noted, is that Nature's modes of treatment inside the family-group and outside the family-group, are diametrically opposed to one another; and that the intrusion of either mode into the sphere of the other, would be fatal to the species either immediately or remotely.

Does any one think that the like does not hold of the human species? He cannot deny that within the human family, as within any inferior family, it would be fatal to proportion benefits to merits. Can he assert that outside the family, among adults, there should not be a proportioning of benefits to merits? Will he contend that no mischief will result if the lowly endowed are enabled to thrive and multiply as much as, or more than, the highly endowed? A society of men, standing towards other societies in relations of either antagonism or competition, may be considered as a species, or, more literally, as a variety of a species; and it must be true of it as of other species or varieties, that it will be unable to hold its own in the struggle with other societies, if it disadvantages its superior units that it may advantage its inferior units. Surely none can fail to see that were the principle of family life to be adopted and fully carried out in social life – were reward always great in proportion as desert was small, fatal results to the society would quickly follow; and if so, then even a partial intrusion of the family *régime* into the *régime* of the State, will be slowly followed by fatal results. Society in its corporate capacity, cannot without immediate or remoter disaster interfere with the play of these opposed principles under which every species has reached such fitness for its mode of life as it possesses, and under which it maintains that fitness.

I say advisedly – society in its corporate capacity: not intending to exclude or condemn aid given to the inferior by the superior in their individual capacities. Though when given so indiscriminately as to enable the inferior to multiply, such aid entails mischief; yet in the absence of aid given by society, individual aid, more generally demanded than now, and associated with a greater sense of responsibility, would, on the average, be given with the effect of fostering the unfortunate worthy rather than the innately unworthy: there being always, too, the concomitant social benefit arising from culture of the sympathies. But all this may be admitted while asserting that the radical distinction between family-ethics and State-ethics must be maintained; and that while generosity must be the essential principle of the one, justice must be the essential principle of the other – a rigorous maintenance of those normal relations among citizens under which each gets in return for his labour, skilled or unskilled, bodily or mental, as much as is proved to be its value by the demand for it: such return, therefore, as will enable him to thrive and rear offspring in proportion to the superiorities which make him valuable to himself and others.

And yet, notwithstanding the conspicuousness of these truths, which should strike every one who leaves his lexicons, and his law-deeds, and his ledgers, and looks abroad into that natural order of things under which we exist, and to which we must conform, there is continual advocacy of paternal government. The intrusion of family-ethics into the ethics of the State, instead of being regarded as socially injurious, is more and more demanded as the only efficient means to social benefit. So far has this delusion now gone, that it vitiates the beliefs of those who might, more than all others, be thought safe from it. In the essay to which the Cobden Club awarded its prize in 1880, there occurs the assertion that "the truth of Free Trade is clouded over by the *laissez-faire* fallacy;" and we are told that "we need a great deal more of paternal government – that bugbear of the old economists."[24]

Vitally important as is the truth above insisted upon, since acceptance or rejection of it affects the entire fabric of political conclusions formed, I may be excused if I emphasize it by here quoting certain passages contained in a work I published in 1851: premising, only, that the reader must not hold me committed to such teleological implications as they contain. After describing "that state of universal warfare maintained throughout the lower creation," and showing that an average of benefit results from it, I have continued thus:–

"Note further, that their carnivorous enemies not only remove from herbivorous herds individuals past their prime, but also weed out the sickly, the malformed, and the least fleet or powerful. By the aid of which purifying process, as well as by the fighting so universal in the pairing season, all vitiation of the race through the multiplication of its inferior samples is prevented; and the maintenance of a constitution completely adapted to surrounding conditions, and therefore most productive of happiness, is ensured.

"The development of the higher creation is a progress towards a form

[24] *On the Value of Political Economy to Mankind.* By A. N. Cumming; pp. 47, 48 [Glasgow, 1881].

of being capable of a happiness undiminished by these drawbacks. It is in the human race that the consummation is to be accomplished. Civilization is the last stage of its accomplishment. And the ideal man is the man in whom all the conditions of that accomplishment are fulfilled. Meanwhile, the well-being of existing humanity, and the unfolding of it into this ultimate perfection, are both secured by that same beneficent, though severe discipline, to which the animate creation at large is subject: a discipline which is pitiless in the working out of good: a felicity-pursuing law which never swerves for the avoidance of partial and temporary suffering. The poverty of the incapable, the distresses that came upon the imprudent, the starvation of the idle, and those shoulderings aside of the weak by the strong, which leave so many 'in shallows and in miseries,' are the decrees of a large, far-seeing benevolence."

* * * * * *

"To become fit for the social state, man has not only to lose his savageness, but he has to acquire the capacities needful for civilized life. Power of application must be developed; such modification of the intellect as shall qualify it for its new tasks must take place; and, above all, there must be gained the ability to sacrifice a small immediate gratification for a future great one. The state of transition will of course be an unhappy state. Misery inevitably results from incongruity between constitutions and conditions. All these evils which afflict us, and seem to the uninitiated the obvious consequences of this or that removable cause, are unavoidable attendants on the adaptation now in progress. Humanity is being pressed against the inexorable necessities of its new position – is being moulded into harmony with them, and has to bear the resulting unhappiness as best it can. The process *must* be undergone, and the sufferings *must* be endured. No power on earth, no cunningly-devised laws of statesmen, no world-rectifying schemes of the humane, no communist panaceas, no reforms that men ever did broach or ever will broach, can diminish them one jot. Intensified they may be, and are; and in preventing their intensification, the philanthropic will find ample scope for exertion. But there is bound up with the changes a *normal* amount of suffering, which cannot be lessened without altering the very laws of life."

* * * * * *

"Of course, in so far as the severity of this process is mitigated by the spontaneous sympathy of men for each other, it is proper that it should be mitigated: albeit there is unquestionably harm done when sympathy is shown, without any regard to ultimate results. But the drawbacks hence arising are nothing like commensurate with the benefits otherwise conferred. Only when this sympathy prompts to a breach of equity – only when it originates an interference forbidden by the law of equal freedom – only when, by so doing, it suspends in some particular department of life the relationship between constitution and conditions, does it work pure evil. Then, however, it defeats its own end. Instead of diminishing suffering, it eventually increases it. It favours the multiplication of those worst fitted for existence, and, by consequence, hinders the multiplication of those best fitted for existence – leaving, as it does, less room for them. It tends to fill the world with those to whom life will bring most pain, and tends to keep out of it those to whom life will bring most pleasure. It inflicts positive misery, and prevents positive happiness."

Social Statics, pp. 322–5 and pp. 380–1 (edition of 1851).

The lapse of a third of a century since these passages were published, has brought me no reasons for retreating from the position taken up in them. Contrariwise, it has brought a vast amount of evidence strengthening that position. The beneficial results of the survival of the fittest, prove to be immeasurably greater than those above indicated. The process of "natural selection," as Mr. Darwin called it, co-operating with a tendency to variation and to inheritance of variations, he has shown to be a chief cause (though not, I believe, the sole cause) of that evolution through which all living things, beginning with the lowest and diverging and re-diverging as they evolved, have reached their present degrees of organization and adaptation to their modes of life. So familiar has this truth become that some apology seems needed for naming it. And yet, strange to say, now that this truth is recognized by most cultivated people – now that the beneficent working of the survival of the fittest has been so impressed on them that, much more than people in past times, they might be expected to hesitate before neutralizing its action – now more than ever before in the history of the world, are they doing all they can to further survival of the unfittest!

But the postulate that men are rational beings, continually leads one to draw inferences which prove to be extremely wide of the mark.[25]

[25] The saying of Emerson that most people can understand a principle only when its light falls on a fact, induces me here to cite a fact which may carry home the above principle to those on whom, in its abstract form, it will produce no effect. It rarely happens that the amount of evil caused by fostering the vicious and good-for-nothing

"Yes truly; your principle is derived from the lives of brutes, and is a brutal principle. You will not persuade me that men are to be under the discipline which animals are under. I care nothing for your natural-history arguments. My conscience shows me that the feeble and the suffering must be helped; and if selfish people won't help them, they must be forced by law to help them. Don't tell me that the milk of human kindness is to be reserved for the relations between individuals, and that Governments must be the administrators of nothing but hard justice. Every man with sympathy in him must feel that hunger and pain and squalor must be prevented; and that if private agencies do not suffice, then public agencies must be established."

Such is the kind of response which I expect to be made by nine out of ten. In some of them it will doubtless result from a fellow-feeling so acute that they cannot contemplate human misery without an impatience which excludes all thoughts of remote results. Concerning the susceptibilities of the rest, we may, however, be somewhat sceptical. Persons who, now in this case and now in that, are angry if, to maintain our supposed national "interests" or national "*prestige*," those in authority do not promptly send out some thousands of men to be partially destroyed while destroying other thousands of men whose intentions we suspect, or whose institutions we think dangerous to us, or whose territory our colonists want, cannot after all be so tender in feeling that contemplating the hardships of the poor is intolerable to them. Little admiration need be felt for the professed sympathies of people who urge on a policy which breaks up progressing societies; and who then look on with cynical indifference at the weltering confusion left behind, with all its entailed suffering and death. Those who, when Boers asserting their independence successfully resisted us, were angry because British "honour" was

can be estimated. But in America, at a meeting of the States Charities Aid Association, held on December 18, 1874, a startling instance was given in detail by Dr. Harris. It was furnished by a county on the Upper Hudson, remarkable for the ratio of crime and poverty to population. Generations ago there had existed a certain "gutter-child," as she would be here called, known as "Margaret," who proved to be the prolific mother of a prolific race. Besides great numbers of idiots, imbeciles, drunkards, lunatics, paupers, and prostitutes, "the county records show two hundred of her descendants who have been criminals." Was it kindness or cruelty which, generation after generation, enabled these to multiply and become an increasing curse to the society around them? (For particulars see *The Jukes: a Study in Crime, Pauperism, Disease and Heredity*. By R. L. Dugdale. New York, [1884]: Putnams.)

not maintained by fighting to avenge a defeat, at the cost of more mortality and misery to our own soldiers and their antagonists, cannot have so much "enthusiasm of humanity" as protests like that indicated above would lead one to expect. Indeed, along with this sensitiveness which they profess will not let them look with patience on the pains of "the battle of life" as it quietly goes on around, they appear to have a callousness which not only tolerates but enjoys contemplating the pains of battles of the literal kind; as one sees in the demand for illustrated papers containing scenes of carnage, and in the greediness with which detailed accounts of bloody engagements are read. We may reasonably have our doubts about men whose feelings are such that they cannot bear the thought of hardships borne, mostly by the idle and the improvident, and who, nevertheless, have demanded thirty-one editions of *The Fifteen Decisive Battles of the World*,[26] in which they may revel in accounts of slaughter. Nay, even still more remarkable is the contrast between the professed tender-heartedness and the actual hard-heartedness of those who would reverse the normal course of things that immediate miseries may be prevented, even at the cost of greater miseries hereafter produced. For on other occasions you may hear them, with utter disregard of bloodshed and death, contend that in the interests of humanity at large it is well that the inferior races should be exterminated and their places occupied by the superior races. So that, marvellous to relate, though they cannot think with calmness of the evils accompanying the struggle for existence as it is carried on without violence among individuals in their own society, they contemplate with contented equanimity such evils in their intense and wholesale forms, when inflicted by fire and sword on entire communities. Not worthy of much respect then, as it seems to me, is this generous consideration of the inferior at home which is accompanied by unscrupulous sacrifice of the inferior abroad.

Still less respectable appears this extreme concern for those of our own blood which goes along with utter unconcern for those of other blood, when we observe its methods. Did it prompt personal effort to relieve the suffering, it would rightly receive approving recognition. Were the many who express this cheap pity like the few who patiently, week after week and year after year, devote large parts of their time

---

[26] [Sir Edward Creasey, *The Fifteen Decisive Battles of the World*, London, 1883.]

to helping and encouraging, and occasionally amusing, those who, in some cases by ill-fortune and in other cases by incapacity or misconduct, are brought to lives of hardship, they would be worthy of unqualified admiration. The more there are of men and women who help the poor to help themselves – the more there are of those whose sympathy is exhibited directly and not by proxy, the more we may rejoice. But the immense majority of the persons who wish to mitigate by law the miseries of the unsuccessful and the reckless, propose to do this in small measure at their own cost and mainly at the cost of others – sometimes with their assent but mostly without. More than this is true; for those who are to be forced to do so much for the distressed, often equally or more require something doing for them. The deserving poor are among those who are burdened to pay the costs of caring for the undeserving poor. As, under the old Poor Law, the diligent and provident labourer had to pay that the good-for-nothings might not suffer, until frequently under this extra burden he broke down and himself took refuge in the workhouse – as, at present, it is admitted that the total rates levied in large towns for all public purposes, have now reached such a height that they "cannot be exceeded without inflicting great hardship on the small shop-keepers and artisans, who already find it difficult enough to keep themselves free from the pauper taint;"[24] so in all cases, the policy is one which intensifies the pains of those most deserving of pity, that the pains of those least deserving of pity may be mitigated. In short, men who are so sympathetic that they cannot allow the struggle for existence to bring on the unworthy the sufferings consequent on their incapacity or misconduct, are so unsympathetic that they can, without hesitation, make the struggle for existence harder for the worthy, and inflict on them and their children artificial evils in addition to the natural evils they have to bear!

And here we are brought round to our original topic – the sins of legislators. Here there comes clearly before us the commonest of the transgressions which rulers commit – a transgression so common, and so sanctified by custom, that no one imagines it to be a transgression. Here we see that, as indicated at the outset, Government, begot-

[27]   Mr. Chamberlain in *Fortnightly Review*, December, 1883, p. 772. [J. Chamberlain, 'Labourers' and Artisans' Dwellings', *Fortnightly Review*, vol. 40, December 1883, pp. 761–76.]

ten of aggression and by aggression, ever continues to betray its original nature by its aggressiveness; and that even what on its nearer face seems beneficence only, shows, on its remoter face, not a little maleficence – kindness at the cost of cruelty. For is it not cruel to increase the sufferings of the better that the sufferings of the worse may be decreased?

It is, indeed, marvellous how readily we let ourselves be deceived by words and phrases which suggest one aspect of the facts while leaving the opposite aspect unsuggested. A good illustration of this, and one germane to the immediate question, is seen in the use of the words "protection" and "protectionist" by the antagonists of free-trade, and in the tacit admission of its propriety by free-traders. While the one party has habitually ignored, the other party has habitually failed to emphasize, the truth that this so-called protection always involves aggression; and that the name aggressionist ought to be substituted for the name protectionist. For nothing can be more certain than that if, to maintain A's profit, B is forbidden to buy of C, or is fined to the extent of the duty if he buys of C, B is aggressed upon that A may be "protected." Nay, "aggressionists" is a title doubly more applicable to the anti-free-traders than is the euphemistic title "protectionists;" since, that one producer may gain, ten consumers are fleeced.

Now just the like confusion of ideas, caused by looking at one face only of the transaction, may be traced throughout all the legislation which forcibly takes the property of this man for the purpose of giving gratis benefits to that man. Habitually when one of the numerous measures thus characterized is discussed, the dominant thought is concerning the pitiable Jones who is to be protected against some evil; while no thought is given to the hard-working Brown who is aggressed upon, often much more to be pitied. Money is exacted (either directly or through raised rent) from the huckster who only by extreme pinching can pay her way, from the mason thrown out of work by a strike, from the mechanic whose savings are melting away during an illness, from the widow who washes or sews from dawn to dark to feed her fatherless little ones; and all that the dissolute may be saved from hunger, that the children of less impoverished neighbours may have cheap lessons, and that various people, mostly better off, may read newspapers and novels for nothing! The error of nomenclature is, in one respect, more misleading than that which allows aggressionists to be called protectionists; for, as just shown, protection of the vicious poor involves aggression on the virtuous poor. Doubtless it is true that the greater part of the money exacted comes from those who are relatively well-off. But this is no consolation to the ill-off from whom the rest is exacted. Nay, if the comparison be made between the pressures borne by the two classes respectively, it becomes manifest that the case is even worse than at first appears; for while to the well-off the exaction means loss of luxuries, to the ill-off it means loss of necessaries.

And now see the Nemesis which is threatening to follow this chronic sin of legislators. They and their class, in common with all owners of property, are in danger of suffering from a sweeping application of that general principle practically asserted by each of these confiscating Acts of Parliament. For what is the tacit assumption on which such Acts proceed? It is the assumption that no man has any claim to his property, not even to that which he has earned by the sweat of his brow, save by permission of the community; and that the community may cancel the claim to any extent it thinks fit. No defence can be made for this appropriation of A's possessions for the benefit of B, save one which sets out with the postulate that society as a whole has an absolute right over the possessions of each member. And now this doctrine, which has been tacitly assumed, is being openly proclaimed. Mr. George and his friends, Mr. Hyndman and his supporters, are pushing the theory to its logical issue. They have been instructed by examples, yearly increasing in number, that the individual has no rights but what the community may equitably over-ride; and they are now saying – "It shall go hard but we will better the instruction," and over-ride individual rights altogether.

Legislative misdeeds of the classes above indicated are in large measure explained, and reprobation of them mitigated, when we look at the matter from afar off. They have their root in the error that society is a manufacture; whereas it is a growth. Neither the culture of past times nor the culture of the present time, has given to any considerable number of people a scientific conception of a society – a conception of it as having a natural structure in which all its institutions, governmental, religious, industrial, commercial, &c., &c., are interdependently bound – a structure which is in a sense organic. Or if such a conception is nominally entertained, it is not entertained in such way as to be operative on conduct. Contrariwise, incorporated humanity is very commonly thought of as though it were like so much dough which the cook can mould as she pleases into pie-crust, or puff, or tartlet. The communist shows us unmistakably that he thinks of the body politic as admitting of being shaped thus or thus at will; and the tacit implication of many Acts of Parliament is that aggregated men, twisted into this or that arrangement, will remain as intended.

It may indeed be said that even irrespective of this erroneous conception of a society as a plastic mass instead of as an organized body, facts forced on his attention hour by hour should make every one sceptical as to the success of this or that proposed way of changing a people's actions. Alike to the citizen and to the legislator, home-experiences daily supply proofs that the conduct of human beings baulks calculation. He has given up the thought of managing his wife and lets her manage him. Children on whom he has tried now reprimand, now punishment, now suasion, now reward, do not respond satisfactorily to any method; and no expostulation prevents their mother from treating them in ways he thinks mischievous. So, too, his dealings with his servants, whether by reasoning or by scolding, rarely succeed for long: the falling short of attention, or punctuality, or cleanliness, or sobriety, leads to constant changes. Yet, difficult as he finds it to deal with humanity in detail, he is confident of his ability to deal with embodied humanity. Citizens, not one-thousandth of whom he knows, not one-hundredth of whom he ever saw, and the great mass of whom belong to classes having habits and modes of thought of which he has but dim notions, he feels sure will act in certain ways he foresees, and fulfil ends he wishes. Is there not a marvellous incongruity between premises and conclusion?

One might have expected that whether they observed the implications of these domestic failures, or whether they contemplated in every newspaper the indications of a social life too vast, too varied, too involved, to be even vaguely pictured in thought, men would have entered on the business of law-making with the greatest hesitation. Yet in this more than in anything else do they show a confident readiness. Nowhere is there so astounding a contrast between the difficulty of the task and the unpreparedness of those who undertake it. Unquestionably among monstrous beliefs one of the most monstrous is that while for a simple handicraft, such as shoe-making, a long apprenticeship is needful, the sole thing which needs no apprenticeship is making a nation's laws!

Summing up the results of the discussion, may we not reasonably say that there lie before the legislator several open secrets, which yet are so open that they ought not to remain secrets to one who undertakes the vast and terrible responsibility of dealing with millions upon millions of human beings by measures which, if they do not conduce to their happiness, will increase their miseries and accelerate their deaths?

There is first of all the undeniable truth, conspicuous and yet absolutely ignored, that there are no phenomena which a society presents but what have their origins in the phenomena of individual human life, which again have their roots in vital phenomena at large. And there is the inevitable implication that unless these vital phenomena, bodily and mental, are chaotic in their relations (a supposition excluded by the very maintenance of life) the resulting phenomena cannot be wholly chaotic: there must be some kind of order in the phenomena which grow out of them when associated human beings have to co-operate. Evidently, then, when one who has not studied such resulting phenomena of social order, undertakes to regulate society, he is pretty certain to work mischiefs.

In the second place, apart from *à priori* reasoning, this conclusion should be forced on the legislator by comparisons of societies. It ought to be sufficiently manifest that before meddling with the details of social organization, inquiry should be made whether social organization has a natural history; and that to answer this inquiry, it would be well, setting out with the simplest societies, to see in what respects social structures agree. Such comparative sociology, pursued to a very small extent, shows a substantial uniformity of genesis. The habitual existence of chieftainship, and the establishment of chiefly authority by war; the rise everywhere of the medicine man and priest; the presence of a cult having in all places the same fundamental traits; the traces of division of labour, early displayed, which gradually become more marked; and the various complications, political, ecclesiastical, industrial, which arise as groups are compounded and recompounded by war; quickly prove to any who compares them that, apart from all their special differences, societies have general resemblances in their modes of origin and development. They present traits of structure showing that social organization has laws which over-ride individual wills; and laws the disregard of which must be fraught with disaster.

And then, in the third place, there is that mass of guiding information yielded by the records of legislation in our own country and in other countries, which still more obviously demands attention. Here and elsewhere, attempts of multitudinous kinds, made by kings and statesmen, have failed to do the good intended and have worked unexpected evils. Century after century new measures like the old ones, and other measures akin in principle, have again disappointed hopes and again brought disaster. And yet it is thought neither by electors nor by those they elect, that there is any need for systematic study of that law-making which in bygone ages went on working the ill-being of the people when it tried to achieve their well-being. Surely there can be no fitness for legislative functions without the wide knowledge of those legislative experiences which the past has bequeathed.

Reverting, then, to the analogy drawn at the outset, we must say that the legislator is morally blameless or morally blameworthy, according as he has or has not acquainted himself with these several classes of facts. A physician who, after years of study, has gained a competent knowledge of physiology, pathology and therapeutics, is not held criminally responsible if a man dies under his treatment: he has prepared himself as well as he can, and has acted to the best of his judgment. Similarly the legislator whose measures produce evil instead of good, notwithstanding the extensive and methodic inquiries which helped him to decide, cannot be held to have committed more than an error of reasoning. Contrariwise, the legislator who is wholly or in great part uninformed concerning these masses of facts which he must examine before his opinion on a proposed law can be of any value, and who nevertheless helps to pass that law, can no more be absolved if misery and mortality result, than the journeyman druggist can be absolved when death is caused by the medicine he ignorantly prescribes.

The Great Political Superstition

The great political superstition of the past was the divine right of kings. The great political superstition of the present is the divine right of parliaments. The oil of anointing seems unawares to have dripped from the head of the one on to the heads of the many, and given sacredness to them also and to their decrees.

However irrational we may think the earlier of these beliefs, we must admit that it was more consistent than is the latter. Whether we go back to times when the king was a god, or to times when he was a descendant of a god, or to times when he was god-appointed, we see good reason for passive obedience to his will. When, as under Louis XIV., theologians like Bossuet taught that kings "are gods, and share in a manner the Divine independence," or when it was thought, as by our own Tory party in old days, that "the monarch was the delegate of heaven;" it is clear that, given the premise, the inevitable conclusion was that no bounds could be set to governmental commands. But for the modern belief such a warrant does not exist. Making no pretension to divine descent or divine appointment, a legislative body can show no supernatural justification for its claim to unlimited authority; and no natural justification has ever been attempted. Hence, belief in its unlimited authority is without that consistency which of old characterized belief in a king's unlimited authority.

It is curious how commonly men continue to hold in fact, doctrines which they have rejected in name – retaining the substance after they have abandoned the form. In Theology an illustration is supplied by

Carlyle, who, in his student days, giving up, as he thought, the creed of his fathers, rejected its shell only, keeping the contents; and was proved by his conceptions of the world, and man, and conduct, to be still among the sternest of Scotch Calvinists. Similarly, Science furnishes an instance in one who united naturalism in Geology with supernaturalism in Biology – Sir Charles Lyell. While, as the leading expositor of the uniformitarian theory in Geology, he ignored wholly the Mosaic cosmogony, he long defended that belief in special creations of organic types, for which no other source than the Mosaic cosmogony could be assigned; and only in the latter part of his life surrendered to the arguments of Mr. Darwin. In Politics, as above implied, we have an analogous case. The tacitly-asserted doctrine, common to Tories, Whigs, and Radicals, that governmental authority is unlimited, dates back to times when the law-giver was supposed to have a warrant from God; and it survives still, though the belief that the law-giver has God's warrant has died out. "Oh, an Act of Parliament can do anything," is the reply made to a citizen who questions the legitimacy of some arbitrary State-interference; and the citizen stands paralysed. It does not occur to him to ask the how, and the when, and the whence, of this asserted omnipotence bounded only by physical impossibilities.

Here we will take leave to question it. In default of the justification, once logically valid, that the ruler on Earth being a deputy of the ruler in Heaven, submission to him in all things is a duty, let us ask what reason there is for asserting the duty of submission in all things to a ruling power, constitutional or republican, which has no Heaven-derived supremacy. Evidently this inquiry commits us to a criticism of past and present theories concerning political authority. To revive questions supposed to be long since settled, may be thought to need some apology; but there is a sufficient apology in the implication above made clear, that the theory commonly accepted is ill-based or unbased.

The notion of sovereignty is that which first presents itself; and a critical examination of this notion, as entertained by those who do not postulate the supernatural origin of sovereignty, carries us back to the arguments of Hobbes.

Let us grant Hobbes's postulate that, "during the time men live without a common power to keep them all in awe, they are in that condition which is called war . . . of every man against every man;"[1] though this is not true, since there are some small uncivilized societies in which, without any "common power to keep them all in awe," men maintain peace and harmony better than it is maintained in societies where such a power exists. Let us suppose him to be right, too, in assuming that the rise of a ruling power over associated men, results from their desires to preserve order among themselves; though, in fact, it habitually arises from the need for subordination to a leader in war, defensive or offensive, and has originally no necessary, and often no actual, relation to the preservation of order among the combined individuals. Once more, let us admit the indefensible assumption that to escape the evils of chronic conflicts, which must otherwise continue among them, the members of a community enter into a "pact or covenant," by which they all bind themselves to surrender their primitive freedom of action, and subordinate themselves to the will of a ruling power agreed upon:[2] accepting, also, the implication that their descendants for ever are bound by the covenant which remote ancestors made for them. Let us, I say, not object to these data, but pass to the conclusions Hobbes draws. He says:—

"For where no covenant hath preceded, there hath no right been transferred, and every man has right to every thing; and consequently, no action can be unjust. But when a covenant is made, then to break it is *unjust*: and the definition of INJUSTICE, is no other than the *not performance of covenant* . . . Therefore before the names of just and unjust can have place, there must be some coercive power, to compel men equally to the performance of their covenants, by the terror of some punishment, greater than the benefit they expect by the breach of their covenant."[3]

Were people's characters in Hobbes's day really so bad as to warrant his assumption that none would perform their covenants in the absence of a coercive power and threatened penalties? In our day "the names of just and unjust can have place" quite apart from recognition of any coercive power. Among my friends I could name half a dozen whom I would implicitly trust to perform their covenants without any "terror of some punishment" and over whom the require-

[1] Hobbes, *Collected Works*, Vol. iii. pp. 112–13. [T. Hobbes, *The English Works of Thomas Hobbes of Malmesbury*, ed. Sir W. Molesworth, 11 vols., London, 1839.]
[2] *Ibid.*, p. 159.
[3] *Ibid.*, pp. 130–1.

ments of justice would be as imperative in the absence of a coercive power as in its presence. Merely noting, however, that this unwarranted assumption vitiates Hobbes's argument for State-authority, and accepting both his premises and conclusion, we have to observe two significant implications. One is that State-authority as thus derived, is a means to an end, and has no validity save as subserving that end: if the end is not subserved, the authority, by the hypothesis, does not exist. The other is that the end for which the authority exists, as thus specified, is the enforcement of justice – the maintenance of equitable relations. The reasoning yields no warrant for other coercion over citizens than that which is required for preventing direct aggressions, and those indirect aggressions constituted by breaches of contract; to which, if we add protection against external enemies, the entire function implied by Hobbes's derivation of sovereign authority is comprehended.

Hobbes argued in the interests of absolute monarchy. His modern admirer, Austin, had for his aim to derive the authority of law from the unlimited sovereignty of one man, or of a number of men, small or large compared with the whole community. Austin was originally in the army; and it has been truly remarked that "the permanent traces left" may be seen in his *Province of Jurisprudence*. When, undeterred by the exasperating pedantries – the endless distinctions and definitions and repetitions – which serve but to hide his essential doctrines, we ascertain what these are, it becomes manifest that he assimilates civil authority to military authority: taking for granted that the one, as the other, is above question in respect of both origin and range. To get justification for positive law, he takes us back to the absolute sovereignty of the power imposing it – a monarch, an aristocracy, or that larger body of men who have votes in a democracy; for such a body also, he styles the sovereign, in contrast with the remaining portion of the community which, from incapacity or other cause, remains subject. And having affirmed, or, rather, taken for granted, the unlimited authority of the body, simple or compound, small or large, which he styles sovereign, he, of course, has no difficulty in deducing the legal validity of its edicts, which he calls positive law. But the problem is simply moved a step further back and there left unsolved. The true question is – Whence the sovereignty? What is the assignable warrant for this unqualified supremacy assumed by one, or by a small number, or by a large number, over the rest? A critic might fitly say – "We will dispense with your process of deriving positive law from unlimited sovereignty: the sequence is obvious enough. But first prove your unlimited sovereignty."

To this demand there is no response. Analyse his assumption, and the doctrine of Austin proves to have no better basis than that of Hobbes. In the absence of admitted divine descent or appointment, neither single-headed ruler nor many-headed ruler can produce such credentials as the claim to unlimited sovereignty implies.

"But surely," will come in deafening chorus the reply, "there is the unquestionable right of the majority, which gives unquestionable rights to the parliament it elects."

Yes, now we are coming down to the root of the matter. The divine right of parliaments means the divine right of majorities. The fundamental assumption made by legislators and people alike, is that a majority has powers to which no limits can be put. This is the current theory which all accept without proof as a self-evident truth. Nevertheless, criticism will, I think, show that this current theory requires a radical modification.

In an essay on "Railway Morals and Railway Policy," published in the *Edinburgh Review* for October, 1854,[4] I had occasion to deal with the question of a majority's powers as exemplified in the conduct of public companies; and I cannot better prepare the way for conclusions presently to be drawn, than by quoting a passage from it:–

"Under whatever circumstances, or for whatever ends, a number of men co-operate, it is held that if difference of opinion arises among them, justice requires that the will of the greater number shall be executed rather than that of the smaller number; and this rule is supposed to be uniformly applicable, be the question at issue what it may. So confirmed is this conviction and so little have the ethics of the matter been considered, that to most this mere suggestion of a doubt will cause some astonishment. Yet it needs but a brief analysis to show that the opinion is little better than a political superstition. Instances may readily be selected which prove, by *reductio ad absurdum*, that the right of a majority is a purely conditional right, valid only within specific limits. Let us take a few. Suppose that at the general meeting of some philanthropic association, it was resolved that in addition to relieving distress the association should employ home-missionaries to preach down popery. Might the

4   [Also in *Essays*, Vol. 3.]

subscriptions of Catholics, who had joined the body with charitable views, be rightfully used for this end? Suppose that of the members of a book-club, the greater number, thinking that under existing circumstances rifle-practice was more important than reading, should decide to change the purpose of their union, and to apply the funds in hand for the purchase of powder, ball, and targets. Would the rest be bound by this decision? Suppose that under the excitement of news from Australia, the majority of a Freehold Land Society should determine, not simply to start in a body for the gold-diggings, but to use their accumulated capital to provide outfits. Would this appropriation of property be just to the minority? and must these join the expedition? Scarcely anyone would venture an affirmative answer even to the first of these questions; much less to the others. And why? Because everyone must perceive that by uniting himself with others, no man can equitably be betrayed into acts utterly foreign to the purpose for which he joined them. Each of these supposed minorities would properly reply to those seeking to coerce them:– 'We combined with you for a defined object; we gave money and time for the furtherance of that object; on all questions thence arising we tacitly agreed to conform to the will of the greater number; but we did not agree to conform on any other questions. If you induce us to join you by professing a certain end, and then undertake some other end of which we were not apprised, you obtain our support under false pretences; you exceed the expressed or understood compact to which we committed ourselves; and we are no longer bound by your decisions.' Clearly this is the only rational interpretation of the matter. The general principle underlying the right government of every incorporated body, is, that its members contract with each other severally to submit to the will of the majority in all matters concerning the fulfilment of the objects for which they are incorporated; but in no others. To this extent only can the contract hold. For as it is implied in the very nature of a contract, that those entering into it must know what they contract to do; and as those who unite with others for a specified object, cannot contemplate all the unspecified objects which it is hypothetically possible for the union to undertake; it follows that the contract entered into cannot extend to such unspecified objects. And if there exists no expressed or understood contract between the union and its members respecting unspecified objects, then for the majority to coerce the minority into undertaking them, is nothing less than gross tyranny."

Naturally, if such a confusion of ideas exists in respect of the powers of a majority where the deed of incorporation tacitly limits these powers, still more must there exist such a confusion where there has been no deed of incorporation. Nevertheless the same principle holds. I again emphasize the proposition that the members of an incorporated body are bound "severally to submit to the will of the majority *in all matters concerning the fulfilment of the objects for which they are incorporated; but in no others.*" And I contend that this holds of an incorporated nation as much as of an incorporated company.

"Yes, but," comes the obvious rejoinder, "as there is no deed by which the members of a nation are incorporated – as there neither is, nor ever was, a specification of purposes for which the union was formed, there exist no limits; and, consequently, the power of the majority is unlimited."

Evidently it must be admitted that the hypothesis of a social contract, either under the shape assumed by Hobbes or under the shape assumed by Rousseau, is baseless. Nay more, it must be admitted that even had such a contract once been formed, it could not be binding on the posterity of those who formed it. Moreover, if any say that in the absence of those limitations to its powers which a deed of incorporation might imply, there is nothing to prevent a majority from imposing its will on a minority by force, assent must be given – an assent, however, joined with the comment that if the superior force of the majority is its justification, then the superior force of a despot backed by an adequate army, is also justified: the problem lapses. What we here seek is some higher warrant for the subordination of minority to majority than that arising from inability to resist physical coercion. Even Austin, anxious as he is to establish the unquestionable authority of positive law, and assuming, as he does, an absolute sovereignty of some kind, monarchic, aristocratic, constitutional, or popular, as the source of its unquestionable authority, is obliged, in the last resort, to admit a moral limit to its action over the community. While insisting, in pursuance of his rigid theory of sovereignty, that a sovereign body originating from the people "is *legally* free to abridge their political liberty, at its own pleasure or discretion," he allows that "a government may be hindered by *positive morality* from abridging the political liberty which it leaves or grants to its subjects."[5] Hence, we have to find, not a physical justification, but a moral justification, for the supposed absolute power of the majority.

[5] *The Province of Jurisprudence Determined* (second edition), p. 241. [J. Austin, London, 1861.]

This will at once draw forth the rejoinder – "Of course, in the absence of any agreement, with its implied limitations, the rule of the majority is unlimited; because it is more just that the majority should have its way than that the minority should have its way." A very reasonable rejoinder this seems until there comes the re-rejoinder. We may oppose to it the equally tenable proposition that, in the absence of an agreement, the supremacy of a majority over a minority does not exist at all. It is co-operation of some kind, from which there arise these powers and obligations of majority and minority; and in the absence of any agreement to co-operate, such powers and obligations are also absent.

Here the argument apparently ends in a dead lock. Under the existing condition of things, no moral origin seems assignable either for the sovereignty of the majority or for the limitation of its sovereignty. But further consideration reveals a solution of the difficulty. For if, dismissing all thought of any hypothetical agreement to co-operate heretofore made, we ask what would be the agreement into which citizens would now enter with practical unanimity, we get a sufficiently clear answer; and with it a sufficiently clear justification for the rule of the majority inside a certain sphere, but not outside that sphere. Let us first observe a few of the limitations which at once become apparent.

Were all Englishmen now asked if they would agree to co-operate for the teaching of religion, and would give the majority power to fix the creed and the forms of worship, there would come a very emphatic "No" from a large part of them. If, in pursuance of a proposal to revive sumptuary laws, the inquiry were made whether they would bind themselves to abide by the will of the majority in respect of the fashions and qualities of their clothes, nearly all of them would refuse. In like manner if (to take an actual question of the day) people were polled to ascertain whether, in respect of the beverages they drank, they would accept the decision of the greater number, certainly half, and probably more than half, would be unwilling. Similarly with respect to many other actions which most men now-a-days regard as of purely private concern. Whatever desire there might be to co-operate for carrying on, or regulating, such actions, would be far from a unanimous desire. Manifestly, then, had social co-operation to be commenced by ourselves, and had its purposes to be specified before consent to co-operate could be obtained, there would be large parts of human conduct in respect of which co-operation would be declined; and in respect of which, consequently, no authority by the majority over the minority could be rightfully exercised.

Turn now to the converse question – For what ends would all men agree to co-operate? None will deny that for resisting invasion the agreement would be practically unanimous. Excepting only the Quakers, who, having done highly useful work in their time, are now dying out, all would unite for defensive war (not, however, for offensive war); and they would, by so doing, tacitly bind themselves to conform to the will of the majority in respect of measures directed to that end. There would be practical unanimity, also, in the agreement to co-operate for defence against internal enemies as against external enemies. Omitting criminals, all must wish to have person and property adequately protected. In short, each citizen desires to preserve his life, to preserve those things which conduce to maintenance of his life and enjoyment of it, and to preserve intact his liberties both of using these things and getting further such. It is obvious to him that he cannot do all this if he acts alone. Against foreign invaders he is powerless unless he combines with his fellows; and the business of protecting himself against domestic invaders, if he did not similarly combine, would be alike onerous, dangerous, and inefficient. In one other co-operation all are interested – use of the territory they inhabit. Did the primitive communal ownership survive, there would survive the primitive communal control of the uses to be made of land by individuals or by groups of them; and decisions of the majority would rightly prevail respecting the terms on which portions of it might be employed for raising food, for making means of communication, and for other purposes. Even at present, though the matter has been complicated by the growth of private landownership, yet, since the State is still supreme owner (every landowner being in law a tenant of the Crown) able to resume possession, or authorize compulsory purchase, at a fair price; the implication is that the will of the majority is valid respecting the modes in which, and conditions under which, parts of the surface or sub-surface, may be utilized: involving certain agreements made on behalf of the public with private persons and companies.

Details are not needful here; nor is it needful to discuss that border region lying between these classes of cases, and to say how much is included in the last and how much is excluded with the first. For present purposes, it is sufficient to recognize the undeniable truth that there are numerous kinds of actions in respect of which men would not, if they were asked, agree with anything like unanimity to be bound by the will of the majority; while there are some kinds of actions in respect of which they would almost unanimously agree to be thus bound. Here, then, we find a definite warrant for enforcing the will of the majority within certain limits, and a definite warrant for denying the authority of its will beyond those limits.

But evidently, when analysed, the question resolves itself into the further question – What are the relative claims of the aggregate and of its units? Are the rights of the community universally valid against the individual? or has the individual some rights which are valid against the community? The judgment given on this point underlies the entire fabric of political convictions formed, and more especially those convictions which concern the proper sphere of government. Here, then, I propose to revive a dormant controversy, with the expectation of reaching a different conclusion from that which is fashionable.

Says Professor Jevons,[6] in his work, *The State in Relation to Labour* – "The first step must be to rid our minds of the idea that there are any such things in social matters as abstract rights." Of like character is the belief expressed by Mr. Matthew Arnold, in his article on copyright:– "An author has no natural right to a property in his production. But then neither has he a natural right to anything whatever which he may produce or acquire."[7] So, too, I recently read in a weekly journal of high repute, that "to explain once more that there is no such thing as 'natural right' would be a waste of philosophy." And the view expressed in these extracts is commonly uttered by statesmen and lawyers in a way implying that only the unthinking masses hold any other.

One might have expected that utterances to this effect would have been rendered less dogmatic by the knowledge that a whole school of legists on the Continent, maintains a belief diametrically opposed to that maintained by the English school. The idea of *Natur-recht* is

⁶ [W. S. Jevons, *The State in Relation to Labour*, London, 1882.]
⁷ *Fortnightly Review* in 1880, vol. xxvii, p. 322. [M. Arnold, 'Copyright', *Fortnightly Review*, Vol. 27, March, 1880, pp. 319–34.]

the root-idea of German jurisprudence. Now whatever may be the
opinion held respecting German philosophy at large, it cannot be
characterized as shallow. A doctrine current among a people distinguished above all others as laborious inquirers, and certainly not to be
classed with superficial thinkers, should not be dismissed as though it
were nothing more than a popular delusion. This, however, by the
way. Along with the proposition denied in the above quotations, there
goes a counter-proposition affirmed. Let us see what it is; and what
results when we go behind it and seek its warrant.

On reverting to Bentham, we find this counter-proposition overtly
expressed. He tells us that government fulfils its office "by creating
rights which it confers upon individuals: rights of personal security;
rights of protection for honour; rights of property;" &c.[8] Were this
doctrine asserted as following from the divine right of kings, there
would be nothing in it manifestly incongruous. Did it come to us
from ancient Peru, where the Ynca "was the source from which
everything flowed";[9] or from Shoa (Abyssinia), where "of their persons and worldly substance he [the king] is absolute master";[10] or
from Dahome, where "all men are slaves to the king";[11] it would be
consistent enough. But Bentham, far from being an absolutist like
Hobbes, wrote in the interests of popular rule. In his *Constitutional
Code*[12] he fixes the sovereignty in the whole people; arguing that it is
best "to give the sovereign power to the largest possible portion of
those whose greatest happiness is the proper and chosen object,"
because "this proportion is more apt than any other that can be
proposed" for achievement of that object.

Mark, now, what happens when we put these two doctrines
together. The sovereign people jointly appoint representatives, and
so create a government; the government thus created, creates rights;
and then, having created rights, it confers them on the separate members of the sovereign people by which it was itself created. Here is
a marvellous piece of political legerdemain! Mr. Matthew Arnold,
contending, in the article above quoted, that "property is the creation
of law," tells us to beware of the "metaphysical phantom of property

[8] Bentham's Works (Bowring's edition), vol. 1, p. 301. [J. Bentham, *The Works of
Jeremy Bentham*, ed. J. Bowring, 11 vols., Edinburgh, 1843.]
[9] Prescott, [W.H.] *Conquest of Peru*, bk. i., ch. i [2 vols., London, 1847].
[10] Harris, [Sir W.C.] *Highland of Aethiopia*, ii. 94 [3 vols., London, 1844.]
[11] Burton, [Sir R.F.] *Mission to Gelele, King of Dahome*, i. p. 226 [2 vols., London,
1864].
[12] Bentham's Work, vol. ix., p. 97.

in itself." Surely, among metaphysical phantoms the most shadowy is this which supposes a thing to be obtained by creating an agent, which creates the thing, and then confers the thing on its own creator!

From whatever point of view we consider it, Bentham's proposition proves to be unthinkable. Government, he says, fulfils its office "by creating rights." Two meanings may be given to the word "creating." It may be supposed to mean the production of something out of nothing; or it may be supposed to mean the giving form and structure to something which already exists. There are many who think that the production of something out of nothing cannot be conceived as effected even by omnipotence; and probably none will assert that the production of something out of nothing is within the competence of a human government. The alternative conception is that a human government creates only in the sense that it shapes something pre-existing. In that case, the question arises – "What is the something pre-existing which it shapes?" Clearly the word "creating" begs the whole question – passes off an illusion on the unwary reader. Bentham was a stickler for definiteness of expression, and in his *Book of Fallacies* has a chapter on "Impostor-terms." It is curious that he should have furnished so striking an illustration of the perverted belief which an impostor-term may generate.

But now let us overlook these various impossibilities of thought, and seek the most defensible interpretation of Bentham's view.

It may be said that the totality of all powers and rights, originally existed as an undivided whole in the sovereign people; and that this undivided whole is given in trust (as Austin would say) to a ruling power, appointed by the sovereign people, for the purpose of distribution. If, as we have seen, the proposition that rights are created is simply a figure of speech; then the only intelligible construction of Bentham's view is that a multitude of individuals, who severally wish to satisfy their desires, and have, as an aggregate, possession of all the sources of satisfaction, as well as power over all individual actions, appoint a government, which declares the ways in which, and the conditions under which, individual actions may be carried on and the satisfactions obtained. Let us observe the implications. Each man exists in two capacities. In his private capacity he is subject to the government. In his public capacity he is one of the sovereign people who appoint the government. That is to say, in his private capacity he is one of those to whom rights are given; and in his public capacity he is one of those who, through the government they appoint, give the rights. Turn this abstract statement into a concrete statement, and see what it means. Let the community consist of a million men, who, by the hypothesis, are not only joint possessors of the inhabited region, but joint possessors of all liberties of action and appropriation: the only right recognized being that of the aggregate to everything. What follows? Each person, while not owning any product of his own labour, has, as a unit in the sovereign body, a millionth part of the ownership of the products of all others' labour. This is an unavoidable implication. As the government, in Bentham's view, is but an agent; the rights it confers are rights given to it in trust by the sovereign people. If so, such rights must be possessed *en bloc* by the sovereign people before the government, in fulfilment of its trust, confers them on individuals; and, if so, each individual has a millionth portion of these rights in his public capacity, while he has no rights in his private capacity. These he gets only when all the rest of the million join to endow him with them; while he joins to endow with them every other member of the million!

Thus, in whatever way we interpret it, Bentham's proposition leaves us in a plexus of absurdities.

Even though ignoring the opposite opinion of German writers on jurisprudence, and even without an analysis which proves their own opinion to be untenable, Bentham's disciples might have been led to treat less cavalierly the doctrine of natural rights. For sundry groups of social phenomena unite to prove that this doctrine is well warranted, and the doctrine they set against it unwarranted.

Tribes in various parts of the world show us that before definite government arises, conduct is regulated by customs. The Bechuanas are controlled by "long-acknowledged customs."[13] Among the Koranna Hottentots, who only "tolerate their chiefs rather than obey them,"[14] "when ancient usages are not in the way, every man seems to act as is right in his own eyes."[15] The Araucanians are guided by

---

[13] Burchell, W. J., *Travels in the Interior of Southern Africa*, vol. i, p. 544 [2 vols., London, 1824, vol. ii, p. 545].

[14] Arbousset and Daumas, *Voyage of Exploration*, p. 27. [T. Arbousset and F. Daumas, *Narrative of an Exploratory Tour to the North-east of the Colony of the Cape of Good Hope*, translated by J. C. Brown, Cape Town, 1846.]

[15] Thompson, G., *Travels and Adventures in Southern Africa*, vol. ii, p. 30 [2 vols., London, 1827].

"nothing more than primordial usages or tacit conventions."[16] Among
the Kirghizes the judgments of the elders are based on "universally-
recognized customs."[17] So, too, of the Dyaks, Rajah Brooke tells us
that "custom seems simply to have become the law; and breaking
custom leads to a fine."[18] So sacred are immemorial customs with
the primitive man, that he never dreams of questioning their authority; and when government arises, its power is limited by them. In
Madagascar the king's word suffices only "where there is no law,
custom, or precedent."[19] Raffles tells us that in Java "the customs of
the country"[20] restrain the will of the ruler. In Sumatra, too, the
people do not allow their chiefs to "alter their ancient usages."[21] Nay,
occasionally, as in Ashantee, "the attempt to change some customs"
has caused a king's dethronement."[22] Now, among the customs which
we thus find to be pre-governmental, and which subordinate governmental power when it is established, are those which recognize certain individual rights – rights to act in certain ways and possess certain
things. Even where the recognition of property is least developed,
there is proprietorship of weapons, tools, and personal ornaments;
and, generally, the recognition goes far beyond this. Among such
North-American Indians as the Snakes, who are without government,
there is private ownership of horses. By the Chippewayans, "who
have no regular government," game taken in private traps "is considered as private property."[23] Kindred facts concerning huts, utensils,
and other personal belongings, might be brought in evidence from
accounts of the Ahts, the Comanches, the Esquimaux, and the Brazilian Indians. Among various uncivilized peoples, custom has established the claim to the crop grown on a cleared plot of ground, though
not to the ground itself; and the Todas, who are wholly without

[16] Thompson, G. A., *Alcedo's Geographical and Historical Dictionary of America*, vol. i,
p. 405. [A. de Alcedo, *Geographical and Historical Dictionary of America and West Indies*,
translated by G. A. Thompson, 5 vols. London, 1812.]
[17] Mitchell, Alex., *Siberian Overland Route*, p. 248. [A. Michie, *The Siberian Overland
Route from Peking to Petersburg*, London, 1864, seems to be the source meant, but the
page reference is wrong.]
[18] Brooke, C., *Ten Years in Saráwak*, vol. i, p. 129 [2 vols., London, 1866. Again, the
page reference is wrong. C. Brooke was Rajah Brooke's uncle.]
[19] Ellis, *History of Madagascar*, vol. i, p. 377 [2 vols., London, 1838].
[20] Raffles, Sir T. S., *History of Java*, vol. i, 274 [2 vols., London, 1816].
[21] Marsden, W., *History of Sumatra*, p. 217 [London, 1811].
[22] Beecham, J., *Ashantee and the Gold Coast*, p. 90 [London, 1841, p. 91].
[23] Schoolcraft, H. R., *Expedition to the Sources of the Mississippi River*, v., 177. [The
title is incorrect. The correct entry is *Information Respecting the History, Condition and
Prospects of the Indian Tribes of the United States*, Philadelphia, 1856, Part V, p. 177.]

political organization, make a like distinction between ownership of cattle and of land. Kolff's statement respecting "the peaceful Arafuras" well sums up the evidence. They "recognize the right of property, in the fullest sense of the word, without there being any [other] authority among them than the decisions of their elders, according to the customs of their forefathers."[24] But even without seeking proofs among the uncivilized, sufficient proofs are furnished by early stages of the civilized. Bentham and his followers seem to have forgotten that our own common law is mainly an embodiment of "the customs of the realm." It did but give definite shape to that which it found existing. Thus, the fact and the fiction are exactly opposite to what they allege. The fact is that property was well recognized before law existed; the fiction is that "property is the creation of law."

Considerations of another class might alone have led them to pause had they duly considered their meanings. Were it true, as alleged by Bentham, that Government fulfils its office "by creating rights which it confers on individuals;" then, the implication would be, that there should be nothing approaching to uniformity in the rights conferred by different governments. In the absence of a determining cause over-ruling their decisions, the probabilities would be many to one against considerable correspondence among their decisions. But there is very great correspondence. Look where we may, we find that governments interdict the same kinds of aggressions; and, by implication, recognize the same kinds of claims. They habitually forbid homicide, theft, adultery: thus asserting that citizens may not be trespassed against in certain ways. And as society advances, minor individual claims are protected by giving remedies for breach of contract, libel, false witness, &c. In a word, comparisons show that though codes of law differ in their details as they become elaborated, they agree in their fundamentals. What does this prove? It cannot be by chance that they thus agree. They agree because the alleged creating of rights was nothing else than giving formal sanction and better definition to those assertions of claims and recognitions of claims which naturally originate from the individual desires of men who have to live in presence of one another.

Comparative Sociology discloses another group of facts having the

---

[24] Earl's *Kolff's Voyage of the Domga*, p. 161. [D. H. Kolff, *Voyages of the Dutch Brig of War Dourga*, translated by G. W. Earl, London, 1840.]

same implication. Along with social progress it becomes in an increasing degree the business of the State, not only to give formal sanction to men's rights, but also to defend them against aggressors. Before permanent government exists, and in many cases after it is considerably developed, the rights of each individual are asserted and maintained by himself, or by his family. Alike among savage tribes at present, among civilized peoples in the past, and even now in unsettled parts of Europe, the punishment for murder is a matter of private concern: "the sacred duty of blood revenge" devolves on some one of a cluster of relatives. Similarly, compensations for aggressions on property and for injuries of other kinds, are in early states of society independently sought by each man or family. But as social organization advances, the central ruling power undertakes more and more to secure to individuals their personal safety, the safety of their possessions, and, to some extent, the enforcement of their claims established by contract. Originally concerned almost exclusively with defence of the society as a whole against other societies, or with conducting its attacks on other societies, Government has come more and more to discharge the function of defending individuals against one another. It needs but to recall the days when men habitually carried weapons, or to bear in mind the greater safety to person and property achieved by improved police-administration during our own time, or to note the increased facilities now given for recovering small debts, to see that the insuring to each individual the unhindered pursuit of the objects of life, within limits set by others' like pursuits, is more and more recognized as a duty of the State. In other words, along with social progress, there goes not only a fuller recognition of these which we call natural rights, but also a better enforcement of them by Government: Government becomes more and more the servant to these essential pre-requisites for individual welfare.

An allied and still more significant change has accompanied this. In early stages, at the same time that the State failed to protect the individual against aggression, it was itself an aggressor in multitudinous ways. Those ancient societies which progressed enough to leave records, having all been conquering societies, show us everywhere the traits of the militant *régime*. As, for the effectual organization of fighting bodies, the soldiers, absolutely obedient, must act independently only when commanded to do it; so, for the effectual organization of fighting societies, citizens must have their individualities subordinated. Private claims are over-ridden by public claims; and the subject loses much of his freedom of action. One result is that the system of regimentation, pervading the society as well as the army, causes detailed regulation of conduct. The dictates of the ruler, sanctified by ascription of them to his divine ancestor, are unrestrained by any conception of individual liberty; and they specify men's actions to an unlimited extent – down to kinds of food eaten, modes of preparing them, shaping of beards, fringing of dresses, sowing of grain, &c. This omnipresent control, which the ancient Eastern nations in general exhibited, was exhibited also in large measure by the Greeks; and was carried to its greatest pitch in the most militant city, Sparta. Similarly during mediæval days throughout Europe, characterized by chronic warfare with its appropriate political forms and ideas, there were scarcely any bounds to Governmental interference: agriculture, manufactures, trade, were regulated in detail; religious beliefs and observances were imposed; and rulers said by whom alone furs might be worn, silver used, books issued, pigeons kept, &c. &c. But along with increase of industrial activities, and implied substitution of the *régime* of contract for the *régime* of status, and growth of associated sentiments, there went (until the recent reaction accompanying reversion to militant activity) a decrease of meddling with people's doings. Legislation gradually ceased to regulate the cropping of fields, or dictate the ratio of cattle to acreage, or specify modes of manufacture and materials to be used, or fix wages and prices, or interfere with dresses and games (except where there was gambling), or put bounties and penalties on imports or exports, or prescribe men's beliefs, religious or political, or prevent them from combining as they pleased, or travelling where they liked. That is to say, throughout a large range of conduct, the right of the citizen to uncontrolled action has been made good against the pretensions of the State to control him. While the ruling agency has increasingly helped him to exclude intruders from that private sphere in which he pursues the objects of life, it has itself retreated from that sphere; or, in other words – decreased its intrusions.

Not even yet have we noted all the classes of facts which tell the same story. It is told afresh in the improvements and reforms of law itself; as well as in the admissions and assertions of those who have effected them. "So early as the fifteenth century," says Professor Pollock, "we find a common-law judge declaring that, as in a case unprovided for by known rules the civilians and canonists devise a new rule according to 'the law of nature which is the ground of all laws,' the Courts of Westminster can and will do the like.''[25] Again, our system of Equity, introduced and developed as it was to make up for the shortcomings of Common-law, or rectify its inequities, proceeded throughout on a recognition of men's claims considered as existing apart from legal warrant. And the changes of law now from time to time made after resistance, are similarly made in pursuance of current ideas concerning the requirements of justice: ideas which, instead of being derived from the law, are opposed to the law. For example, that recent Act which gives to a married woman a right of property in her own earnings, evidently originated in the consciousness that the natural connexion between labour expended and benefit enjoyed, is one which should be maintained in all cases. The reformed law did not create the right, but recognition of the right created the reformed law.

Thus, historical evidences of five different kinds unite in teaching that, confused as are the popular notions concerning rights, and including, as they do, a great deal which should be excluded, yet they shadow forth a truth.

It remains now to consider the original source of this truth. In a previous paper I have spoken of the open secret, that there can be no social phenomena but what, if we analyse them to the bottom, bring us down to the laws of life; and that there can be no true understanding of them without reference to the laws of life. Let us, then, transfer this question of natural rights from the court of politics to the court of science – the science of life. The reader need feel no alarm: its simplest and most obvious facts will suffice. We will contemplate first the general conditions to individual life; and then the general conditions to social life. We shall find that both yield the same verdict.

Animal life involves waste; waste must be met by repair; repair implies nutrition. Again, nutrition presupposes obtainment of food; food cannot be got without powers of prehension, and, usually, of locomotion; and that these powers may achieve their ends, there must be freedom to move about. If you shut up a mammal in a small space,

[25] "The Methods of Jurisprudence: an Introductory Lecture at University College, London," October 31, 1882.

or tie its limbs together, or take from it the food it has procured, you eventually, by persistence in one or other of these courses, cause its death. Passing a certain point, hindrance to the fulfilment of these requirements is fatal. And all this, which holds of the higher animals at large, of course holds of man.

If we adopt pessimism as a creed, and with it accept the implication that life in general being an evil should be put an end to, then there is no ethical warrant for these actions by which life is maintained: the whole question drops. But if we adopt either the optimist view or the meliorist view – if we say that life on the whole brings more pleasure than pain; or that it is on the way to become such that it will yield more pleasure than pain; then these actions by which life is maintained are justified, and there results a warrant for the freedom to perform them. Those who hold that life is valuable, hold, by implication, that men ought not to be prevented from carrying on life-sustaining activities. In other words, if it is said to be "right" that they should carry them on, then, by permutation, we get the assertion that they "have a right" to carry them on. Clearly the conception of "natural rights" originates in recognition of the truth that if life is justifiable, there must be a justification for the performance of acts essential to its preservation; and, therefore, a justification for those liberties and claims which make such acts possible.

But being true of other creatures as of man, this is a proposition lacking ethical character. Ethical character arises only with the distinction between what the individual *may* do in carrying on his life-sustaining activities, and what he *may not* do. This distinction obviously results from the presence of his fellows. Among those who are in close proximity, or even at some distance apart, the doings of each are apt to interfere with the doings of others; and in the absence of proof that some may do what they will without limit, while others may not, mutual limitation is necessitated. The non-ethical form of the right to pursue ends, passes into the ethical form, when there is recognized the difference between acts which can be performed without transgressing the limits, and others which cannot be so performed.

This, which is the *a priori* conclusion, is the conclusion yielded *a posteriori*, when we study the doings of the uncivilized. In its vaguest form, mutual limitation of spheres of action, and the ideas and sentiments associated with it, are seen in the relations of groups to one another. Habitually there come to be established, certain bounds to the territories within which each tribe obtains its livelihood; and these bounds, when not respected, are defended. Among the Wood-Veddahs, who have no political organization, the small clans have their respective portions of forest; and "these conventional allotments are always honourably recognized."[26] Of the ungoverned tribes of Tasmania, we are told that "their hunting grounds were all determined, and trespassers were liable to attack."[27] And, manifestly, the quarrels caused among tribes by intrusions on one another's territories, tend, in the long run, to fix bounds and to give a certain sanction to them. As with each inhabited area, so with each inhabiting group. A death in one, rightly or wrongly ascribed to somebody in another, prompts "the sacred duty of blood-revenge;" and though retaliations are thus made chronic, some restraint is put on new aggressions. Like causes worked like effects in those early stages of civilized societies, during which families or clans, rather than individuals, were the political units; and during which each family or clan had to maintain itself and its possessions against others such. This mutual restraint, which in the nature of things arises between small communities, similarly arises between individuals in each community; and the ideas and usages appropriate to the one are more or less appropriate to the other. Though within each group there is ever a tendency for the stronger to aggress on the weaker; yet, in most cases, consciousness of the evils resulting from aggressive conduct serves to restrain. Everywhere among primitive peoples, trespasses are followed by counter-trespasses. Says Turner of the Tannese, "adultery and some other crimes are kept in check by the fear of club-law."[28] Fitzroy tells us that the Patagonian, "if he does not injure or offend his neighbour, is not interfered with by others:"[29] personal vengeance being the penalty for injury. We read of the Uaupés that "they have very little law of any kind; but what they have is of strict retaliation, – an eye for an eye and a tooth for a tooth."[30] And that the *lex talionis* tends to establish a distinction between what each member of the

---

[26] Tennant, *Ceylon: an Account of the Island, &c.*, ii. 440. [Sir J. E. Tennent, *Ceylon: An Account of the Island, Physical, Historical and Topographical*, 2 vols., London, 1860. The quotation in fact refers to the Rock Veddahs.]

[27] Bonwick, J., *Daily Life and Origin of the Tasmanians*, 83 [London, 1870].

[28] *Polynesia*, p. 86. [G. Turner, *Nineteenth Years in Polynesia: Missionary Life, Travels and Researches in the Islands of the Pacific*, London 1861.]

[29] *Voyages of the Adventure and Beagle*, ii. 167. [R. Fitzroy, *Narrative of the Surveying Voyages of His Majesty's Ships Adventure and Beagle*, 3 vols., London, 1839.]

[30] Wallace, A. R., *Travels on Amazon and Rio Negro*, p. 499. [London, 1853. Wallace is writing of the Cobeas tribe, and the Uaupés river.].

community may safely do and what he may not safely do, and consequently to give sanctions to actions within a certain range but not beyond that range, is obvious. Though, says Schoolcraft of the Chippewayans, they "have no regular government, as every man is lord in his own family, they are influenced more or less by certain principles which conduce to their general benefit:"[31] one of the principles named being recognition of private property.

How mutual limitation of activities originates the ideas and sentiments implied by the phrase "natural rights," we are shown most distinctly by the few peaceful tribes which have either nominal governments or none at all. Beyond those facts which illustrate scrupulous regard for one another's claims among the Todas, Santals, Lepchas, Bodo, Chakmas, Jakuns, Arafuras, &c., we have the fact that the utterly uncivilized Wood-Veddahs, without any social organization at all, "think it perfectly inconceivable that any person should ever take that which does not belong to him, or strike his fellow, or say anything that is untrue."[32] Thus it becomes clear, alike from analysis of causes and observation of facts, that while the positive element in the right to carry on life-sustaining activities, originates from the laws of life, that negative element which gives ethical character to it, originates from the conditions produced by social aggregation.

So alien to the truth, indeed, is the alleged creation of rights by government, that, contrariwise, rights having been established more or less clearly before government arises, become obscured as government develops along with that militant activity which, both by the taking of slaves and the establishment of ranks, produces *status*; and the recognition of rights begins again to get definiteness only as fast as militancy ceases to be chronic and governmental power declines.

When we turn from the life of the individual to the life of the society, the same lesson is taught us.

Though mere love of companionship prompts primitive men to live in groups, yet the chief prompter is experience of the advantages to be derived from co-operation. On what condition only can co-

---

[31] Schoolcraft, *Expedition to the Sources of the Mississippi*, v., 177. [Again, Spencer gives the wrong title. See footnote 23.]

[32] B. F. Hartshorne, *Fortnightly Review*, March, 1876. See also H. C. Sirr, *Ceylon and the Ceylonese*, ii. 219. [B. F. Hartshorne, 'The Wessas', *Fortnightly Review*, Vol. 25, March, 1876, pp. 406–17. See also H. C. Sirr, *Ceylon and the Cingalese*, 2 vols., London, 1850.]

operation arise? Evidently on condition that those who join their efforts severally gain by doing so. If, as in the simplest cases, they unite to achieve something which each by himself cannot achieve, or can achieve less readily, it must be on the tacit understanding, either that they shall share the benefit (as when game is caught by a party of them) or that if one reaps all the benefit now (as in building a hut or clearing a plot) the others shall severally reap equivalent benefits in their turns. When, instead of efforts joined in doing the same thing, different things are effected by them – when division of labour arises, with accompanying barter of products, the arrangement implies that each, in return for something which he has in superfluous quantity, gets an approximate equivalent of something which he wants. If he hands over the one and does not get the other, future proposals to exchange will meet with no response. There will be a reversion to that rudest condition in which each makes everything for himself. Hence the possibility of co-operation depends on fulfilment of contract, tacit or overt.

Now this which we see must hold of the very first step towards that industrial organization by which the life of a society is maintained, must hold more or less fully throughout its development. Though the militant type of organization, with its system of *status* produced by chronic war, greatly obscures these relations of contract, yet they remain partially in force. They still hold between freemen, and between the heads of those small groups which form the units of early societies; and, in a measure, they still hold within these small groups themselves; since survival of them as groups, implies such recognition of the claims of their members, even when slaves, that in return for their labours they get sufficiencies of food, clothing, and protection. And when, with diminution of warfare and growth of trade, voluntary co-operation more and more replaces compulsory co-operation, and the carrying on of social life by exchange under agreement, partially suspended for a time, gradually re-establishes itself; its re-establishment makes possible that vast elaborate industrial organization by which a great nation is sustained.

For in proportion as contracts are unhindered and the performance of them certain, the growth is great and the social life active. It is not now by one or other of two individuals who contract, that the evil effects of breach of contract are experienced. In an advanced society, they are experienced by entire classes of producers and distributors, which have arisen through division of labour; and, eventually, they are experienced by everybody. Ask on what condition it is that Birmingham devotes itself to manufacturing hardware, or part of Staffordshire to making pottery, or Lancashire to weaving cotton. Ask how the rural people who here grow wheat and there pasture cattle, find it possible to occupy themselves in their special businesses. These groups can severally thus act only if each gets from the others in exchange for its own surplus product, due shares of their surplus products. No longer directly effected by barter, this obtainment of their respective shares of one another's products is indirectly effected by money; and if we ask how each division of producers gets its due amount of the required money, the answer is – by fulfilment of contract. If Leeds makes woollens and does not, by fulfilment of contract, receive the means of obtaining from agricultural districts the needful quantity of food, it must starve, and stop producing woollens. If South Wales smelts iron and there comes no equivalent agreed upon, enabling it to get fabrics for clothing, its industry must cease. And so throughout, in general and in detail. That mutual dependence of parts which we see in social organization, as in individual organization, is possible only on condition that while each part does the particular kind of work it has become adjusted to, it receives its proportion of those materials required for repair and growth, which all the other parts have joined to produce: such proportion being settled by bargaining. Moreover, it is by fulfilment of contract that there is effected a balancing of all the various products to the various needs – the large manufacture of knives and the small manufacture of lancets; the great growth of wheat and the little growth of mustard-seed. The check on undue production of each commodity, results from finding that after a certain quantity, no one will agree to take any further quantity on terms that yield an adequate money equivalent. And so there is prevented a useless expenditure of labour in producing that which society does not want.

Lastly, we have to note the still more significant fact that the condition under which only any specialized group of workers can grow when the community needs more of its particular kind of work, is that contracts shall be free and fulfilment of them enforced. If when, from lack of material, Lancashire failed to supply the usual quantity of cotton-goods, there had been such interference with contracts as prevented Yorkshire from asking a greater price for its woollens, which it was enabled to do by the greater demand for them, there would have been no temptation to put more capital into the woollen manufacture, no increase in the amount of machinery and number of artizans employed, and no increase of woollens: the consequence being that the whole community would have suffered from not having deficient cottons replaced by extra woollens. What serious injury may result to a nation if its members are hindered from contracting with one another, was well shown in the contrast between England and France in respect of railways. Here, though obstacles were at first raised by classes predominant in the legislature, the obstacles were not such as prevented capitalists from investing, engineers from furnishing directive skill, or contractors from undertaking works; and the high interest originally obtained on investments, the great profits made by contractors, and the large payments received by engineers, led to that drafting of money, energy, and ability, into railway-making, which rapidly developed our railway-system, to the enormous increase of our national prosperity. But when M. Thiers, then Minister of Public Works, came over to inspect, and having been taken about by Mr. Vignoles, said to him when leaving: "I do not think railways are suited to France,"[33] there resulted, from the consequent policy of hindering free contract, a delay of "eight or ten years" in that material progress which France experienced when railways were made.

What do all these facts mean? They mean that for the healthful activity and due proportioning of those industries, occupations, professions, which maintain and aid the life of a society, there must, in the first place, be few restrictions on men's liberties to make agreements with one another, and there must, in the second place, be an enforcement of the agreements which they do make. As we have seen, the checks naturally arising to each man's actions when men become associated, are those only which result from mutual limitation; and there consequently can be no resulting check to the contracts they voluntarily make: interference with these is interference with those rights to free action which remain to each when the rights of others are fully recognized. And then, as we have seen, enforcement of their rights implies enforcement of contracts made; since breach of contract is indirect aggression. If, when a customer on one

[33] Address of C. B. Vignoles, Esq., F.R.S., on his Election as President of the Institution of Civil Engineers, Session 1869–70, p. 53.

side of the counter asks a shopkeeper on the other for a shilling's worth of his goods, and, while the shopkeeper's back is turned, walks off with the goods without leaving the shilling he tacitly contracted to give, his act differs in no essential way from robbery. In each such case the individual injured is deprived of something he possessed, without receiving the equivalent something bargained for; and is in the state of having expended his labour without getting benefit – has had an essential condition to the maintenance of life infringed.

Thus, then, it results that to recognize and enforce the rights of individuals, is at the same time to recognize and enforce the conditions to a normal social life. There is one vital requirement for both.

Before turning to those corollaries which have practical applications, let us observe how the special conclusions drawn converge to the one general conclusion originally foreshadowed – glancing at them in reversed order.

We have just found that the pre-requisite to individual life is in a double sense the pre-requisite to social life. The life of a society, in whichever of two senses conceived, depends on maintenance of individual rights. If it is nothing more than the sum of the lives of citizens, this implication is obvious. If it consists of those many unlike activities which citizens carry on in mutual dependence, still this aggregate impersonal life rises or falls according as the rights of individuals are enforced or denied.

Study of men's politico-ethical ideas and sentiments, leads to allied conclusions. Primitive peoples of various types show us that before governments exist, immemorial customs recognize private claims and justify maintenance of them. Codes of law independently evolved by different nations, agree in forbidding certain trespasses on the persons, properties, and liberties of citizens; and their correspondences imply, not an artificial source for individual rights, but a natural source. Along with social development, the formulating in law of the rights pre-established by custom, becomes more definite and elaborate. At the same time, Government undertakes to an increasing extent the business of enforcing them. While it has been becoming a better protector, Government has been becoming less aggressive – has more and more diminished its intrusions on men's spheres of private action. And, lastly, as in past times laws were avowedly modified to fit better with current ideas of equity; so now, law-reformers are guided by ideas of equity which are not derived from law but to which law has to conform.

Here, then, we have a politico-ethical theory justified alike by analysis and by history. What have we against it? A fashionable counter-theory which proves to be unjustifiable. On the one hand, while we find that individual life and social life both imply maintenance of the natural relation between efforts and benefits; we also find that this natural relation, recognized before Government existed, has been all along asserting and re-asserting itself, and obtaining better recognition in codes of law and systems of ethics. On the other hand, those who, denying natural rights, commit themselves to the assertion that rights are artificially created by law, are not only flatly contradicted by facts, but their assertion is self-destructive: the endeavour to substantiate it, when challenged, involves them in manifold absurdities.

Nor is this all. The re-institution of a vague popular conception in a definite form on a scientific basis, leads us to a rational view of the relation between the wills of majorities and minorities. It turns out that those co-operations in which all can voluntarily unite, and in the carrying on of which the will of the majority is rightly supreme, are co-operations for maintaining the conditions requisite to individual and social life. Defence of the society as a whole against external invaders, has for its remote end to preserve each citizen in possession of such means as he has for satisfying his desires, and in possession of such liberty as he has for getting further means. And defence of each citizen against internal invaders, from murderers down to those who inflict nuisances on their neighbours, has obviously the like end – an end desired by every one save the criminal and disorderly. Hence it follows that for maintenance of this vital principle, alike of individual life and social life, subordination of minority to majority is legitimate; as implying only such a trenching on the freedom and property of each, as is requisite for the better protecting of his freedom and property. At the same time it follows that such subordination is not legitimate beyond this; since, implying as it does a greater aggression upon the individual than is requisite for protecting him, it involves a breach of the vital principle which is to be maintained.

Thus we come round again to the proposition that the assumed divine right of parliaments, and the implied divine right of majorities, are superstitions. While men have abandoned the old theory respecting the source of State-authority, they have retained a belief in that unlimited extent of State-authority which rightly accompanied the old theory, but does not rightly accompany the new one. Unrestricted power over subjects, rationally ascribed to the ruling man when he was held to be a deputy-god, is now ascribed to the ruling body, the deputy-godhood of which nobody asserts.

Opponents will, possibly, contend that discussions about the origin and limits of governmental authority are mere pedantries. "Government," they may perhaps say, "is bound to use all the means it has, or can get, for furthering the general happiness. Its aim must be utility; and it is warranted in employing whatever measures are needful for achieving useful ends. The welfare of the people is the supreme law; and legislators are not to be deterred from obeying that law by questions concerning the source and range of their power." Is there really an escape here? or may this opening be effectually closed?

The essential question raised is the truth of the utilitarian theory as commonly held; and the answer here to be given is that, as commonly held, it is not true. Alike by the statements of utilitarian moralists, and by the acts of politicians knowingly or unknowingly following their lead, it is implied that utility is to be directly determined by simple inspection of the immediate facts and estimation of probable results. Whereas, utilitarianism as rightly understood, implies guidance by the general conclusions which analysis of experience yields. "Good and bad results cannot be accidental, but must be necessary consequences of the constitution of things;" and it is "the business of Moral Science to deduce, from the laws of life and the conditions of existence, what kinds of action necessarily tend to produce happiness, and what kinds to produce unhappiness."[34] Current utilitarian speculation, like current practical politics, shows inadequate consciousness of natural causation. The habitual thought is that, in the absence of some obvious impediment, things can be done this way or that way; and no question is put whether there is either agreement or conflict with the normal working of things.

The foregoing discussions have, I think, shown that the dictates of utility, and, consequently, the proper actions of governments, are

[34] *Data of Ethics*, §21. See also §§56–62. [The *Data* became the first part of *The Principles of Ethics*, Vol. 1.]

not to be settled by inspection of facts on the surface, and acceptance of their *prima facie* meanings; but are to be settled by reference to, and deduction from, fundamental facts. The fundamental facts to which all rational judgments of utility must go back, are the facts that life consists in, and is maintained by, certain activities; and that among men in a society, these activities, necessarily becoming mutually limited, are to be carried on by each within the limits thence arising, and not carried on beyond those limits: the maintenance of the limits becoming, by consequence, the function of the agency which regulates society. If each, having freedom to use his powers up to the bounds fixed by the like freedom of others, obtains from his fellow-men as much for his services as they find them worth in comparison with the services of others – if contracts uniformly fulfilled bring to each the share thus determined, and he is left secure in person and possessions to satisfy his wants with the proceeds; then there is maintained the vital principle alike of individual life and of social life. Further, there is maintained the vital principle of social progress; inasmuch as, under such conditions, the individuals of most worth will prosper and multiply more than those of less worth. So that utility, not as empirically estimated but as rationally determined, enjoins this maintenance of individual rights; and, by implication, negatives any course which traverses them.

Here, then, we reach the ultimate interdict against meddling legislation. Reduced to its lowest terms, every proposal to interfere with citizens' activities further than by enforcing their mutual limitations, is a proposal to improve life by breaking through the fundamental conditions to life. When some are prevented from buying beer that others may be prevented from getting drunk, those who make the law assume that more good than evil will result from interference with the normal relation between conduct and consequences, alike in the few ill-regulated and the many well-regulated. A government which takes fractions of the incomes of multitudinous people, for the purpose of sending to the colonies some who have not prospered here, or for building better industrial dwellings, or for making public libraries and public museums, &c., takes for granted that, not only proximately but ultimately, increased general happiness will result from transgressing the essential requirement to general happiness – the requirement that each shall enjoy all those means to happiness which his actions, carried on without aggression, have brought him.

In other cases we do not thus let the immediate blind us to the remote. When asserting the sacredness of property against private transgressors, we do not ask whether the benefit to a hungry man who takes bread from a baker's shop, is or is not greater than the injury inflicted on the baker: we consider, not the special effects, but the general effects which arise if property is insecure. But when the State exacts further amounts from citizens, or further restrains their liberties, we consider only the direct and proximate effects, and ignore the indirect and distant effects which are caused when these invasions of individual rights are continually multiplied. We do not see that by accumulated small infractions of them, the vital conditions of life, individual and social, come to be so imperfectly fulfilled that the life decays.

Yet the decay thus caused becomes manifest where the policy is pushed to an extreme. Any one who studies, in the writings of MM. Taine and de Tocqueville, the state of things which preceded the French Revolution, will see that the tremendous catastrophe came about from so excessive a regulation of men's actions in all their details, and such an enormous drafting away of the products of their actions to maintain the regulating organization, that life was fast becoming impracticable. The empirical utilitarianism of that day, like the empirical utilitarianism of our day, differed from rational utilitarianism in this, that in each successive case it contemplated only the effects of particular interferences on the actions of particular classes of men, and ignored the effects produced by a multiplicity of such interferences on the lives of men at large. And if we ask what then made, and what now makes, this error possible, we find it to be the political superstition that governmental power is subject to no restraints.

When that "divinity" which "doth hedge a king," and which has left a glamour around the body inheriting his power, has quite died away – when it begins to be seen clearly that, in a popularly-governed nation, the government is simply a committee of management; it will also be seen that this committee of management has no intrinsic authority. The inevitable conclusion will be that its authority is given by those appointing it; and has just such bounds as they choose to impose. Along with this will go the further conclusion that the laws it passes are not in themselves sacred; but that whatever sacredness they have, it is entirely due to the ethical sanction – an ethical sanction which, as we find, is derivable from the laws of human life as carried on under social conditions. And there will come the corollary that when they have not this ethical sanction they have no sacredness, and may rightly be challenged.

The function of Liberalism in the past was that of putting a limit to the powers of kings. The function of true Liberalism in the future will be that of putting a limit to the powers of Parliaments.

Postscript

"Do I expect this doctrine to meet with any considerable acceptance?" I wish I could say, yes; but unhappily various reasons oblige
me to conclude that only here and there a solitary citizen may have
his political creed modified. Of these reasons there is one from which
all the others originate.

This essential reason is that the restriction of governmental power
within the limits assigned, is appropriate to the industrial type of
society only; and, while wholly incongruous with the militant type of
society, is partially incongruous with that semi-militant semi-
industrial type, which now characterizes advanced nations. At every
stage of social evolution there must exist substantial agreement
between practices and beliefs – real beliefs I mean, not nominal ones.
Life can be carried on only by the harmonizing of thoughts and acts.
Either the conduct required by circumstances must modify the beliefs
to fit it; or else the changed beliefs must eventually modify the
conduct.

Hence if the maintenance of social life under one set of conditions,
necessitates extreme subordination to a ruler and entire faith in him,
there will be established a theory that the subordination and the faith
are proper – nay imperative. Conversely if, under other conditions,
great subjection of citizens to government is no longer needful for
preservation of the national life – if, contrariwise, the national life
becomes larger in amount and higher in quality as fast as citizens
gain increased freedom of action; there comes a progressive modification of their political theory, having the result of diminishing their
faith in governmental action, increasing their tendency to question

governmental authority, and leading them in more numerous cases to resist governmental power: involving, eventually, an established doctrine of limitation.

Thus it is not to be expected that current opinion respecting governmental authority, can at present be modified to any great extent. But let us look at the necessities of the case more closely.

Manifestly the success of an army depends very much on the faith of the soldiers in their general: disbelief in his ability will go far towards paralysing them in battle; while absolute confidence in him will make them fulfil their respective parts with courage and energy. If, as in the normally-developed militant type of society, the ruler in peace and the leader in war are one and the same, this confidence in him extends from military action to civil action; and the society, in large measure identical with the army, willingly accepts his judgments as law-giver. Even where the civil head, ceasing to be the military head, does his generalship by deputy, there still clings to him the traditional faith.

Similarly with the willingness to obey. Other things equal an army of insubordinate soldiers fails before an army of subordinate soldiers. Those whose obedience to their leader is perfect and prompt, are obviously more likely to succeed in battle than are those who disregard the commands issued to them. And as with the army so with the society as a whole; success in war must largely depend on that conformity to the ruler's will which brings men and money when wanted, and adjusts all conduct to his needs.

Thus by survival of the fittest, the militant type of society becomes characterized by profound faith in the governing power, joined with a loyalty causing submission to it in all matters whatever. And there must tend to be established among those who speculate about political affairs in a militant society, a theory giving form to the needful ideas and feelings; accompanied by assertions that the law-giver if not divine in nature is divinely directed, and that unlimited obedience to him is divinely ordered.

Change in the ideas and feelings which thus become characteristic of the militant form of organization, can take place only where circumstances favour development of the industrial form of organization. Being carried on by voluntary co-operation instead of by compulsory co-operation, industrial life as we now know it, habituates men to independent activities, leads them to enforce their own claims while respecting the claims of others, strengthens the consciousness of personal rights, and prompts them to resist excesses of governmental control. But since the circumstances which render war less frequent arise but slowly, and since the modifications of nature caused by the transition from a life predominantly militant to a life predominantly industrial can therefore go on only little by little, it happens that the old sentiments and ideas give place to new ones, by small degrees only. And there are several reasons why the transition not only is, but ought to be, gradual. Here are some of them.

In the primitive man and in man but little civilized, there does not exist the nature required for extensive voluntary co-operations. Efforts willingly united with those of others for a common advantage, imply, if the undertaking is large, a perseverance he does not possess. Moreover, where the benefits to be achieved are distant and unfamiliar, as are many for which men now-a-days combine, there needs a strength of constructive imagination not to be found in the minds of the uncivilized. And yet again, great combinations of a private kind for wholesale production, for large enterprises, and for other purposes, require a graduated subordination of the united workers – a graduated subordination such as that which militancy produces. In other words, the way to the developed industrial type as we now know it, is through the militant type; which, by discipline generates in long ages the power of continuous application, the willingness to act under direction (now no longer coercive but agreed to under contract) and the habit of achieving large results by organizations.

Consequently, during long stages of social evolution there needs, for the management of all matters but the simplest, a governmental power great in degree and wide in range, with a correlative faith in it and obedience to it. Hence the fact that, as the records of early civilizations show us, and as we are shown in the East at present, large undertakings can be achieved only by State-action. And hence the fact that only little by little can voluntary co-operation replace compulsory co-operation, and rightly bring about a correlative decrease of faith in governmental ability and authority.

Chiefly, however, the maintenance of this faith is necessitated by the maintenance of fitness for war. This involves continuance of such confidence in the ruling agency, and such subordination to it, as may enable it to wield all the forces of the society on occasions of attack or defence; and there must survive a political theory justifying the faith and the obedience. While their sentiments and ideas are of kinds which perpetually endanger peace, it is requisite that men should have such belief in the authority of government as shall give it adequate coercive power over them for war purposes – a belief in its authority which inevitably, at the same time, gives it coercive power over them for other purposes.

Thus, as said at first, the fundamental reason for not expecting much acceptance of the doctrine set forth, is that we have at present but partially emerged from the militant *régime* and have but partially entered on that industrial *régime* to which this doctrine is proper.

So long as the religion of enmity predominates over the religion of amity, the current political superstition must hold its ground. While throughout Europe, the early culture of the ruling classes is one which every day of the week holds up for admiration those who in ancient times achieved the greatest feats in battle, and only on Sunday repeats the injunction to put up the sword – while these ruling classes are subject to a moral discipline consisting of six-sevenths pagan example and one-seventh Christian precept; there is no likelihood that there will arise such international relations as may make a decline in governmental power practicable, and a corresponding modification of political theory acceptable. While among ourselves the administration of colonial affairs is such that native tribes who retaliate on Englishmen by whom they have been injured, are punished, not on their own savage principle of life for life, but on the improved civilized principle of wholesale massacre in return for single murder, there is little chance that a political doctrine consistent only with unaggressive conduct will gain currency. While the creed men profess is so interpreted that one of them who at home addresses missionary meetings, seeks, when abroad, to foment a quarrel with an adjacent people whom he wishes to subjugate, and then receives public honours after his death, it is not likely that the relations of our society to other societies will become such that there can spread to any extent that doctrine of limited governmental functions accompanying the diminished governmental authority proper to a peaceful state. A nation which, interested in ecclesiastical squabbles about the ceremonies of its humane cult, cares so little about the essence of that cult that fillibustering in its colonies receives applause rather than reprobation, and is not denounced even by the priests of its religion of love, is a nation which must continue to suffer from internal aggressions, alike of individuals on one another and of the State on individuals. It is impossible to unite the blessings of equity at home with the commission of inequities abroad.

Of course, there will arise the question – Why, then, enunciate and emphasize a theory at variance with the theory adapted to our present state?

Beyond the general reply that it is the duty of every one who regards a doctrine as true and important, to do what he can towards diffusing it, leaving the result to be what it may be, there are several more special replies, each of which is sufficient.

In the first place an ideal, far in advance of practicability though it may be, is always needful for rightful guidance. If, amid all those compromises which the circumstances of the times necessitate, or are thought to necessitate, there exist no true conceptions of better and worse in social organization – if nothing beyond the exigencies of the moment are attended to, and the proximately best is habitually identified with the ultimately best; there cannot be any true progress. However distant may be the goal, and however often intervening obstacles may necessitate deviation in our course towards it, it is obviously requisite to know whereabouts it lies.

Again, while something like the present degree of subjection of the individual to the State, and something like the current political theory adapted to it, may remain needful in presence of existing international relations; it is by no means needful that this subjection should be made greater and the adapted theory strengthened. In our days of active philanthropy, hosts of people eager to achieve benefits for their less fortunate fellows by the shortest methods, are busily occupied in developing administrative arrangements of a kind proper to a lower type of society – are bringing about retrogression while aiming at progression. The normal difficulties in the way of advance are sufficiently great, and it is lamentable that they should be made greater. Hence, something well worth doing may be done, if philanthropists can be shown that they are in many cases insuring the future ill-being of men while eagerly pursuing their present well-being.

Chiefly, however, it is important to impress on all the great truth, at present but little recognized, that a society's internal and external policies are so bound together, that there cannot be an essential improvement of the one without an essential improvement of the other. A higher standard of international justice must be habitually acted upon, before there can be conformity to a higher standard of justice in our national arrangements. The conviction that a dependence of this kind exists, could it be diffused among civilized peoples, would greatly check aggressive behaviour towards one another; and, by doing this, would diminish the coerciveness of their governmental systems while appropriately changing their political theories.

APPENDIX
Spencer's article of 1836 on the Poor Law
Poor Laws – Reply to "T.W.S."

SIR – In the last number of the Bath Magazine, I see an article from you, advocating the late system of Poor Laws. Being one of those who think that the "Poor Laws are bad in principle, and that they have in their effects operated most injuriously," I am desirous of making a few observations on your letter. – You say that the poor have a *right* to a maintenance out of the land. Who gave them that right? and where does nature declare, that "the earth was made productive for the support of all its inhabitants," without those inhabitants using the proper means for obtaining the produce? But, waiving the question of right, there is that natural tendency in human nature to lean upon any support that may be afforded, and that tendency in such support to corrupt and unhinge the mind, that even on this account alone, the Poor Laws ought to be considered as injurious. Your supposition that one person might "amass in his own possession all the means of subsistence that the earth has produced in that part of the country where he dwells," to the starvation of the rest, is an impossibility, since every person who has accumulated much property, must employ and pay labourers and shop-keepers, who therefore cannot starve. The whole tenor of your argument implies, also, that a person is not to be allowed to raise himself by his own exertions. What! is not a man to be benefitted by his superior industry? – is he always to be kept down in the ranks of pauperism? – is there no reward to be held out to perseverance, and no punishment to idleness? Again, you say that relief ought to be given to "the infirm, and those in want of work, but unable to procure it." What say you to the fact, that many who received parochial relief on account of old age, have, since the passing of the New Poor Law, returned to work again, rather than accept the offer of the workhouse? As to the complaint of want of work, every one knows, who has inquired into the subject, that it is generally a mere pretence, and that it has been used by labourers as a plea for relief, when there was abundance of employment. You maintain the necessity of Poor Laws, on account of the prevalence of mendicancy in the time of Queen Elizabeth. I reply, 1st., this was the fault of the monasteries, which, under mistaken notions of charity, brought up such a host of beggars; 2nd., it was the fault of those who destroyed the monasteries, without providing for these mendicants; and, 3rd., the Poor Laws were not calculated to remedy the evil, but rather to increase it, inasmuch as they still maintained thousands of persons in idleness, and, therefore, gave them leisure to meditate evil, for idleness is the parent of mischief. That the Poor Laws have increased the evil is proved by the fact, that where there was one pauper in the time of Queen Elizabeth there are now hundreds.

You say that "mendicancy had become so prevalent and oppressive to the people at large, that it was found necessary, in order to check it, to punish beggars with the infliction of slavery, and even death itself." What relief did the Poor Laws afford to the oppressed people? They still had to maintain these mendicants, and what did it matter whether they did it by forced subscription, or by voluntary contribution? Indeed, the preference is rather to be given to the latter method. Again, you assert that the Poor Laws have "been the means of tranquillizing the country, and advancing civilization." A dearly bought tranquillity, indeed! a peace which has been procured by maintaining, in idleness, a set of villains, who, if they had not been so well provided for, would soon have shewn themselves in their natural characters – of thieves and assassins. But have the Poor Laws tranquillised the country? What were the incendiarisms a few years back? They did not augur tranquillity. And have the Poor Laws advanced civilization? If ignorance, drunkenness, and crime, are the fruits of cultivated minds, then, indeed, we have arrived at perfection. It is not the Poor Laws that have caused "that vast difference between the labouring population of this country and that of Ireland." No! it is that gross ignorance and superstition – it is that ruinous system of subletting – it is whiskey, that has brought Ireland to its present state. You seem to have a low opinion of political economy. Is that science to be despised, upon which are founded all the principles of good government? which teaches the philanthropist, and the statesman the best methods of following their several pursuits? On the contrary, political economy is a subject which ought to be more admired, and more studied, than it has hitherto been.

And now let us examine a little into the New Poor Law, which you say was as "villainous in its conception, as it has been horrible in its practice." Who passed this law? Was it not supported by the leading men of every party, whether Tory, Whig, or Radical? And are the opinions of these men to be despised? Are laws passed by them to be called "villainous?" The grand feature in the New Law is the workhouse system: this is the great safeguard against imposition – this is the only true test of distress:– if a man is starving, he will gladly accept the offer of the workhouse: if he is not starving, he is not a proper object of relief. And what is the "villainous" in this? Perhaps you will allude to the cruelty of separating a man from his family: I would recommend you to read the recent report of the Poor Law Commissioners on that point.

In your Article, there are many assertions without a proof; these I pass over; but there are also assertions directly opposed to the truth of Scripture; and to these I shall briefly allude. You ask, "Are people only to live to labour?" and you advocate the right of the people to live ultimately without "toil and exertion, whilst at the same time they should receive from the national stock, comparatively sufficient means to render them comfortable." Do you, then, deny, or, have you forgotten, those declarations: "In the sweat of thy face shalt thou eat bread;" "Six days shalt thou labour;" "If any will not work neither let him eat?" The whole system of man's responsibility, and of his future reward or punishment, depending upon his being "diligent in business, fervent in spirit, serving the Lord," seems completely set aside by your reasoning.

Index

Abyssinia, 150
adaptation, xi, xv, xviii, 124, 129–30
Afghanistan, 25, 31–2
aggression and government, 106, 134–
  5, 154–7, 159, 164
Ahts, 153
America, xxi, xxv, 25, 27, 30, 31, 63,
  89, 124
anthropology, xix, 117
Arafuras, 154, 160
Araucanians, 152–3
Arch, J., 98
'Architect', 114–16
Ardtornish, Scotland, xvi
Arnold, M., 149, 150
Artisans' Dwellings Acts, 116
Ashantee, 153
Ashley, Lord, 115
Athenaeum Club, xxii
Athenians, 88
Austin, J., 143–4, 146, 151
Australia, 30–1, 145

Bain, A., xx
Balfour, A. J., xviii
Bastian, A., 117
Bath poor law union, ix, 82–3
Bechuanas, 152
Bennett, A., vii, xix
Bentham, J., xxv, 150–2, 154
biology, 141
Birmingham, industry in, 162
Bismarck, Prince, xxiii, 102
Blackley, W. L., xxiii

Bodo, 160
Bolingbroke, Viscount, 64–5
Brazilian Indians, 153
Brewster, Sir D., 75
Brooke, C., 153
bureaucracy, 90–1

Canada, 27, 30
Carlyle, T., xii, 123, 141
causation, 123–4, 166
census, 118
Chadwick, E., xiii
Chakmas, 160
Chamberlain, J., 134
character, 36, 49, 124
charity, (see also philanthropy), 5–6,
  13–16, 55
Charity Organisation Society, xxvi–
  xxvii
Charles II, 64
Chartists, xiv
China, 25
Chippewayans, 153, 160
Cholesbury, poor law in, 99
church, established, 6, 8–9, 13–14,
  39–40, 42, 43, 49, 55
class, xiv, 52, 78, 91, 94, 107, 136,
  173
classification, 67–9
Cobden Club, 129
Collings, J., 98
colonisation, xiii, 27–32, 56, 167,
  173–4
Comanches, 153

Index

rights, natural, xxv–xxvi, 7–8, 18, 149–58, 165
Ritchie, D., xvi
Roman Catholicism, 38, 66, 145
Roman Republic, 68
Rousseau, J.-J., 146
Ruskin, J., 93
Russell, Lord John, 72
Russia, militant type of society in, 91; slavery in, 96

Salisbury, Lord, xxii
Santals, 160
Schoolcraft, H., 153, 160
shipping, 72–3, 87, 121
Siemens, Sir C., 118
slavery, 95–6, 102, 107
Smith, O., xvi
Snakes, 153
social action, 123–5
social contract, xii, 6, 146
social Darwinism, xviii
Social Democratic Federation, xxv, 94, 98–100, 102, 104–5, 111
social organism, xvii, 136
social policy, xxvii (see also education, health, housing, insurance, philanthropy, poor law)
social reorganisation, 93, 101, 125–6
social structure, 88, 105, 123, 125, 136
socialism, xxiv, xxv, xxviii, xxix, 79, 94–105, 111
society, nature of, xii, xix, xxiv, 5, 17, 88, 104–5, 128–9, 136–8, 162, 164–5, 167, 173–4; as growth not manufacture, 136–7; industrial type, xix–xx, 63–5, 123–6, 161, 170–3; militant type, xix–xx, xxiii, 63–5, 91, 103, 108, 155–6, 161, 170–3
sociology, xix, 138, 154
sovereignty, 140–7, 150–2
Spain, 85
Sparta/Spartans, 88, 156
Spencer, H., boyhood and education, vii–x; health, xv–xvi, xxi; last years, xxviii–xxix; reputation, vii, xviii–xix, xxviii–xxix; theory of evolution, xvi–xxii, xxviii; Facts and Comments, xxviii; Essays, xv, xvi; Man versus the State, vii, xvii, xxii–xxviii; Principles of Psychology, xi, xiv; Proper Sphere of

Government, vii, xi–xiv; Social Statics, xi, xiv, xv, xix, xxv, xxviii, 105, 113–14, 129–31; Study of Sociology, vii, xxii; 'System of Synthetic Philosophy', xi, xvii; Various Fragments, xxviii
Spencer, Revd. T., viii, ix, x, xi, xv, 82–3
Staffordshire, industry in, 162
state-ethics, xxv, 128–9
status, régime of, 63, 79, 104, 156, 160–1
Sumatra, 153
supply and demand, law of, 111, 113
survival of the fittest, xvii, xviii, xxiv, xxvi, xxvii, 131, 171
Switzerland, xxi
sympathy, 130–2, 134

Taine, H. A., 168
Tannese, 159
Tasmania, 159
taxation, 50–1, 54, 75, 83–5, 92, 107
Tay Bridge, collapse of, 119–20
teachers, 36, 86–7
Tocqueville, A. de, 168
Todas, 153, 160
Tönnies, F., xix
Tories, 63–4, 66, 70, 78–9, 104, 140–1, 181
Trade, Board of, 72, 73
trades unions, xxvi, 66, 76, 101
Trades Unions Congress, 92
Turner, G., 159
typhoid, 120

Uaupés, 159
utilitarianism, vii, xii, 7–8, 166–7, 168

vaccination, 71, 73
Vignoles, C. B., 163
Von Baer, K. E., xvii

Wales, North, xvi, xxi
Wales, South, industry in, 162
Wallace, Sir D. M., 91
war, xiii, 22–6, 55–6, 104, 106–7, 138, 148, 171–2
Webb, Beatrice (née Potter), xviii, xxvii, xxviii
Wells, H. G., xxviii–xxix
Wemyss, Earl of, xxvi

Whigs, and Whiggism, 64–6, 141, 181
women, xv
Wood-Veddahs, 159, 160
workhouse system, xii, 82–3, 180–1

'X' Club, xxii

Yorkshire, industry in, 162
Youmans, E. L., xviii, xxi, xxii, xxiv
Young, A., 110

Cambridge Texts in the History of Political Thought

Titles published in the series thus far

Aristotle *The Politics and The Constitution of Athens* (edited by Stephen Everson)
0 521 48400 6 paperback
Arnold *Culture and Anarchy and other writings* (edited by Stefan Collini)
0 521 37796 x paperback
Astell *Political Writings* (edited by Patricia Springborg)
0 521 42845 9 paperback
Augustine *The City of God against the Pagans* (edited by R.W. Dyson)
0 521 46843 4 paperback
Austin *The Province of Jurisprudence Determined* (edited by Wilfrid E. Rumble)
0 521 44756 9 paperback
Bacon *The History of the Reign of King Henry VII* (edited by Brian Vickers)
0 521 58663 1 paperback
Bakunin *Statism and Anarchy* (edited by Marshall Shatz)
0 521 36973 8 paperback
Baxter *Holy Commonwealth* (edited by William Lamont)
0 521 40580 7 paperback
Bayle *Political Writings* (edited by Sally L. Jenkinson)
0 521 47677 1 paperback
Beccaria *On Crimes and Punishments and other writings* (edited by Richard Bellamy)
0 521 47982 7 paperback
Bentham *Fragment on Government* (introduction by Ross Harrison)
0 521 35929 5 paperback
Bernstein *The Preconditions of Socialism* (edited by Henry Tudor)
0 521 39808 8 paperback
Bodin *On Sovereignty* (edited by Julian H. Franklin)
0 521 34992 3 paperback
Bolingbroke *Political Writings* (edited by David Armitage)
0 521 58697 6 paperback
Bossuet *Politics Drawn from the Very Words of Holy Scripture* (edited by Patrick Riley)
0 521 36807 3 paperback
The British Idealists (edited by David Boucher)
0 521 45951 6 paperback
Burke *Pre-Revolutionary Writings* (edited by Ian Harris)
0 521 36800 6 paperback
Christine De Pizan *The Book of the Body Politic* (edited by Kate Langdon Forhan)
0 521 42259 0 paperback
Cicero *On Duties* (edited by M. T. Griffin and E. M. Atkins)
0 521 34835 8 paperback
Cicero *On the Commonwealth and On the Laws* (edited by James E. G. Zetzel)
0 521 45959 1 paperback
Comte *Early Political Writings* (edited by H. S. Jones)
0 521 46923 6 paperback
Conciliarism and Papalism (edited by J. H. Burns and Thomas M. Izbicki)
0 521 47674 7 paperback
Constant *Political Writings* (edited by Biancamaria Fontana)
0 521 31632 4 paperback
Dante *Monarchy* (edited by Prue Shaw)
0 521 56781 5 paperback
Diderot *Political Writings* (edited by John Hope Mason and Robert Wokler)
0 521 36911 8 paperback
The Dutch Revolt (edited by Martin van Gelderen)
0 521 39809 6 paperback
Early Greek Political Thought from Homer to the Sophists (edited by Michael Gagarin and Paul Woodruff)
0 521 43768 7 paperback
The Early Political Writings of the German Romantics (edited by Frederick C. Beiser)
0 521 44951 0 paperback
The English Levellers (edited by Andrew Sharp)
0 521 62511 4 paperback
Erasmus *The Education of a Christian Prince* (edited by Lisa Jardine)
0 521 58811 1 paperback
Fenelon *Telemachus* (edited by Patrick Riley)
0 521 45662 2 paperback

Ferguson *An Essay on the History of Civil Society* (edited by Fania Oz-Salzberger)
  0 521 44736 4 paperback
Filmer *Patriarcha and Other Writings* (edited by Johann P. Sommerville)
  0 521 39903 3 paperback
Fletcher *Political Works* (edited by John Robertson)
  0 521 43994 9 paperback
Sir John Fortescue *On the Laws and Governance of England* (edited by Shelley Lockwood)
  0 521 58996 7 paperback
Fourier *The Theory of the Four Movements* (edited by Gareth Stedman Jones and Ian Patterson)
  0 521 35693 8 paperback
Gramsci *Pre-Prison Writings* (edited by Richard Bellamy)
  0 521 42307 4 paperback
Guicciardini *Dialogue on the Government of Florence* (edited by Alison Brown)
  0 521 45623 1 paperback
Harrington *The Commonwealth of Oceana* and *A System of Politics* (edited by J. G. A. Pocock)
  0 521 42329 5 paperback
Hegel *Elements of the Philosophy of Right* (edited by Allen W. Wood and H. B. Nisbet)
  0 521 34888 9 paperback
Hegel *Political Writings* (edited by Laurence Dickey and H. B. Nisbet)
  0 521 45979 3 paperback
Hobbes *On the Citizen* (edited by Michael Silverthorne and Richard Tuck)
  0 521 43780 6 paperback
Hobbes *Leviathan* (edited by Richard Tuck)
  0 521 56797 1 paperback
Hobhouse *Liberalism and Other Writings* (edited by James Meadowcroft)
  0 521 43726 1 paperback
Hooker *Of the Laws of Ecclesiastical Polity* (edited by A. S. McGrade)
  0 521 37908 3 paperback
Hume *Political Essays* (edited by Knud Haakonssen)
  0 521 46639 3 paperback
King James VI and I *Political Writings* (edited by Johann P. Sommerville)
  0 521 44729 1 paperback
Jefferson *Political Writings* (edited by Joyce Appleby and Terence Ball)
  0 521 64841 6 paperback
John of Salisbury *Policraticus* (edited by Cary Nederman)
  0 521 36701 8 paperback
Kant *Political Writings* (edited by H. S. Reiss and H. B. Nisbet)
  0 521 39837 1 paperback
Knox *On Rebellion* (edited by Roger A. Mason)
  0 521 39988 2 paperback
Kropotkin *The Conquest of Bread and other writings* (edited by Marshall Shatz)
  0 521 45990 7 paperback
Lawson *Politica sacra et civilis* (edited by Conal Condren)
  0 521 39248 9 paperback
Leibniz *Political Writings* (edited by Patrick Riley)
  0 521 35899 X paperback
The Levellers (edited by Andrew Sharp)
  0 521 62511 4 paperback
Locke *Political Essays* (edited by Mark Goldie)
  0 521 47861 8 paperback
Locke *Two Treatises of Government* (edited by Peter Laslett)
  0 521 35730 6 paperback
Loyseau *A Treatise of Orders and Plain Dignities* (edited by Howell A. Lloyd)
  0 521 45624 X paperback
Luther and Calvin on Secular Authority (edited by Harro Höpfl)
  0 521 34986 9 paperback
Machiavelli *The Prince* (edited by Quentin Skinner and Russell Price)
  0 521 34993 1 paperback
de Maistre *Considerations on France* (edited by Isaiah Berlin and Richard Lebrun)
  0 521 46628 8 paperback
Malthus *An Essay on the Principle of Population* (edited by Donald Winch)
  0 521 42972 2 paperback
Marsiglio of Padua *Defensor minor* and *De translatione Imperii* (edited by Cary Nederman)
  0 521 40846 6 paperback
Marx *Early Political Writings* (edited by Joseph O'Malley)
  0 521 34994 X paperback
Marx *Later Political Writings* (edited by Terrell Carver)
  0 521 36739 5 paperback

James Mill *Political Writings* (edited by Terence Ball)
    0 521 38748 5 paperback
J. S. Mill *On Liberty*, with *The Subjection of Women* and *Chapters on Socialism*
(edited by Stefan Collini)
    0 521 37917 2 paperback
Milton *Political Writings* (edited by Martin Dzelzainis)
    0 521 34866 8 paperback
Montesquieu *The Spirit of the Laws* (edited by Anne M. Cohler, Basia Carolyn Miller and
Harold Samuel Stone)
    0 521 36974 6 paperback
More *Utopia* (edited by George M. Logan and Robert M. Adams)
    0 521 40318 9 paperback
Morris *News from Nowhere* (edited by Krishan Kumar)
    0 521 42233 7 paperback
Nicholas of Cusa *The Catholic Concordance* (edited by Paul E. Sigmund)
    0 521 56773 4 paperback
Nietzsche *On the Genealogy of Morality* (edited by Keith Ansell-Pearson)
    0 521 40610 2 paperback
Paine *Political Writings* (edited by Bruce Kuklick)
    0 521 66799 2 paperback
Plato *The Republic* (edited by G. R. F. Ferrari and Tom Griffith)
    0 521 48443 X paperback
Plato *Statesman* (edited by Julia Annas and Robin Waterfield)
    0 521 44778 X paperback
Price *Political Writings* (edited by D. O. Thomas)
    0 521 40969 1 paperback
Priestley *Political Writings* (edited by Peter Miller)
    0 521 42561 1 paperback
Proudhon *What is Property?* (edited by Donald R. Kelley and Bonnie G. Smith)
    0 521 40556 4 paperback
Pufendorf *On the Duty of Man and Citizen according to Natural Law* (edited by James Tully)
    0 521 35980 5 paperback
The Radical Reformation (edited by Michael G. Baylor)
    0 521 37948 2 paperback
Rousseau *The Discourses and other early political writings* (edited by Victor Gourevitch)
    0 521 42445 3 paperback
Rousseau *The Social Contract and other later political writings* (edited by Victor Gourevitch)
    0 521 42446 1 paperback
Seneca *Moral and Political Essays* (edited by John Cooper and John Procope)
    0 521 34818 8 paperback
Sidney *Court Maxims* (edited by Hans W. Blom, Eco Haitsma Mulier and Ronald Janse)
    0 521 46736 5 paperback
Sorel *Reflections on Violence* (edited by Jeremy Jennings)
    0 521 55910 3 paperback
Spencer *The Man versus the State* and *The Proper Sphere of Government* (edited by John Offer)
    0 521 43740 7 paperback
Stirner *The Ego and Its Own* (edited by David Leopold)
    0 521 45647 9 paperback
Thoreau *Political Writings* (edited by Nancy Rosenblum)
    0 521 47675 5 paperback
Utopias of the British Enlightenment (edited by Gregory Claeys)
    0 521 45590 1 paperback
Vitoria *Political Writings* (edited by Anthony Pagden and Jeremy Lawrance)
    0 521 36714 X paperback
Voltaire *Political Writings* (edited by David Williams)
    0 521 43727 X paperback
Weber *Political Writings* (edited by Peter Lassman and Ronald Speirs)
    0 521 39719 7 paperback
William of Ockham *A Short Discourse on Tyrannical Government* (edited by A. S. McGrade and
John Kilcullen)
    0 521 35803 5 paperback
William of Ockham *A Letter to the Friars Minor and other writings* (edited by A. S. McGrade and
John Kilcullen)
    0 521 35804 3 paperback
Wollstonecraft *A Vindication of the Rights of Men* and *A Vindication of the Rights of Woman*
(edited by Sylvana Tomaselli)
    0 521 43633 8 paperback

Printed by Printforce, United Kingdom